Untie the Lines

Untie the Lines

Setting sail and breaking free

Emma Bamford

ADLARD COLES NAUTICAL

BLOOMSBURY

LONDON · OXFORD · NEW YORK · NEW DELHI · SYDNEY

Adlard Coles Nautical
An imprint of Bloomsbury Publishing Plc

50 Bedford Square
London
WC1B 3DP
UK

1385 Broadway
New York
NY 10018
USA

www.bloomsbury.com

ADLARD COLES, ADLARD COLES NAUTICAL and the Buoy logo are trademarks of
Bloomsbury Publishing Plc

First published 2016

British Library Cataloguing-in-Publication Data
A catalogue record for this book is available from the British Library.

Library of Congress Cataloguing-in-Publication data has been applied for.

ISBN: PB: 978-1-4729-2832-0
ePDF: 978-1-4729-2834-4
ePub: 978-1-4729-2833-7

2 4 6 8 10 9 7 5 3 1

Typeset in ITC Slimbach by Deanta Global Publishing Services, Chennai, India
Printed and bound in Great Britain by CPI Group (UK) Ltd, Croydon CR0 4YY

To find out more about our authors and books visit www.bloomsbury.com.
Here you will find extracts, author interviews, details of forthcoming events
and the option to sign up for our newsletters.

Acknowledgements

Many thanks to my first beta readers, Karen Nicholson and Becki Hanford, and to Niki Valentine and the rest of the Nottingham Peacock writing group, who gave honest feedback. Thanks also to the Bloomsbury team, especially Liz Multon for giving me a second stab, and Jenny Clark, and my agents, Bell Lomax Moreton.

A special mention to Mike McCarthy for the push to write a book, Jane Davey and Katie Millan for helping me to see the light, my crewmates along the way, not least Tyrone Currie, Ben Thompson, Vicky Page, Moe Kafer and Aaron Duffy, and a final thumbs up to Jon van der Horst Bruyn, whose shots of idyllic Caribbean beaches, yachts and stunning blue waters set me off down this path in the first place and who is living proof that you can chase your dreams.

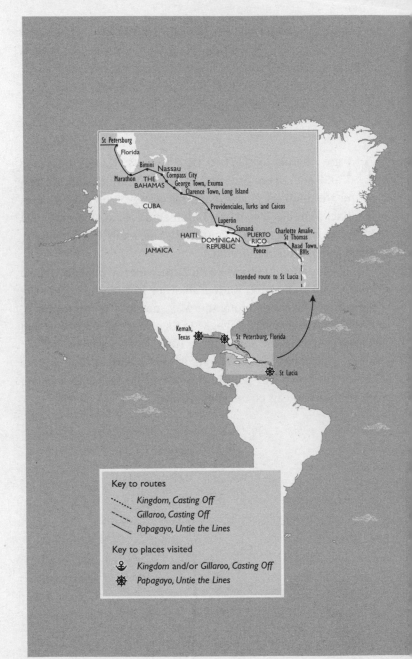

St Petersburg
Florida
Bimini
Nassau
Marathon
THE
BAHAMAS
Compass City
George Town, Exuma
Clarence Town, Long Island
CUBA
Providenciales, Turks and Caicos
Luperón
Samaná
HAITI
DOMINICAN
REPUBLIC
PUERTO
RICO
Charlotte Amalie,
St Thomas
Road Town,
BVIs
Ponce
JAMAICA
Intended route to St Lucia

Kemah,
Texas
St Petersburg, Florida
St Lucia

Key to routes

.... *Kingdom, Casting Off*

- - - - - *Gillaroo, Casting Off*

————— *Papagayo, Untie the Lines*

Key to places visited

⚓ *Kingdom and/or Gillaroo, Casting Off*

☸ *Papagayo, Untie the Lines*

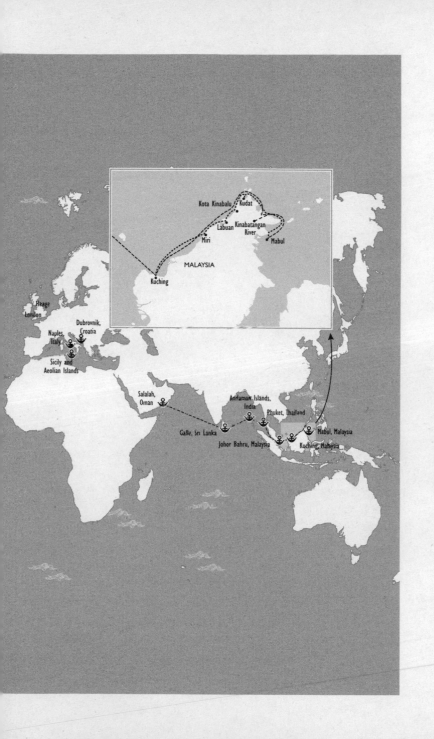

Contents

1

New beginnings

Malaysia, December 2011

The little waves in the harbour made for a slightly bumpy ride as we weaved our way back across the bay towards Guy's yacht. I held on to the top of my backpack with one hand, steadying it against my shin, as the grey rubber dinghy zipped towards the sunset. With every little crest, butterflies fluttered in my stomach, caused partly by the bucking action of the boat and partly by excitement about where I was and who I was with. I was spilling over with a thousand questions to ask him – how he was, what he'd been doing, what he was hoping was going to happen with this trip, what he was hoping was going to happen with us – but the engine was too loud for conversation and I knew I had to wait until we got to *Incognito*. I sat at the front of the dingy, facing forwards towards the setting sun, enjoying the feel of the wind drying the dampness that had collected along my hairline during the hot Malaysian evening. Every minute or so I glanced back at Guy. He was looking ahead, concentrating on navigating the dinghy safely, in the failing light, through the Bass Harbour car park of a hundred anchored yachts and their hazardous chains. The sunset was reflected on his sunglasses' lenses and I couldn't see his eyes.

Eventually I couldn't keep quiet any more. I turned to the rear, shifting my weight from my left buttock to my right, so I was angled towards the engine and Guy. I raised my voice to shout over the roar of the outboard. 'Which one is *Incognito*?'

He gestured loosely with his free hand to the far side of the crowd of yachts but I couldn't tell it apart from the others. Despite having spent a fair amount of time on boats by this point, they still all looked alike to me. Unless they had a bright-yellow hull or three masts or a *Pirates of the Caribbean*-style sail, they were just yachts. 'The blue one' and 'the white one' is generally the best I can do to distinguish between them – and that doesn't narrow it down much. I could never be accused of being a boat-spotter.

I nodded and pretended I knew exactly where we were headed. Guy shuffled in his seat and I turned to face forwards again. I sneaked a quick look back at him as we passed the outlying yachts. He had changed a bit and that was a shock. When you don't see someone for a long while, you carry the memory with you of how they looked the last time you saw them. Even though we'd been in touch on Facebook and, once, on the phone, I hadn't seen him for three weeks shy of a year. I only had two photos on my phone of our week or so together in Thailand the previous December, so when I'd been daydreaming about this trip and this adventure we were embarking on, and also about this romance we were starting (or picking up – I wasn't sure which), I'd had to rely on my saved mental image of him.

Unlike my memory, in reality he had not stayed frozen in that moment in time eleven months earlier. His skin was the beautiful burnished bronze I remembered, his face as handsome, with its straight nose and full mouth, but his dark hair was longer, doubled over in a ponytail, and he was carrying a few more pounds. He had grown his sideburns and there was long stubble on the rest of his face. A tiny part of me wondered if my memories of who he was could be as disjointed as my recollection of what he looked like.

Mind you, I was hardly the same as I was when he met me either. My skin was paler, having spent time in the depths of an English winter. I'd dyed my hair back to brown, tiring of the orangey-blonde highlights that eighteen months of travelling in the sun had put into it. I'd just – and what a stupid idea that was, knowing I was about to go and live in a hot and sticky environment – had a fringe cut in. It occurred to me then that attraction is a very fragile thing. He might have invited me to come and live with him on his boat in Malaysia and go off on a sailing adventure around Indonesia for the foreseeable future, thinking he saw me as a potential girlfriend, and I might have accepted that offer, hoping the same, but we might find that, after taking such a big gamble based on a few snatched days together a year earlier, we didn't like each other after all. He might not fancy brown-headed, pasty British women when he was surrounded by tanned and tawny travellers. We might have got this wrong.

I met Guy when I was away travelling. A year and a half earlier I'd been working as a journalist on a newspaper in London until, looking around me at friends settling down, I'd not been able to suppress my feelings of restlessness any longer and I'd decided to go off and see the world.

A first attempt at this, answering a 'crew wanted' advert on the internet and buying a one-way ticket to Borneo to live with a man I'd never met on his yacht in the jungle, had ended disastrously. A second try had gone better and I'd spent a happy six months cruising through South-East Asia on a catamaran called *Gillaroo*, full of other free spirits. At one port we'd put into I'd met Guy, a fellow Brit, and we'd hit it off but had been forced to part when our yachts sailed in opposite directions.

We'd stayed in touch when I landed a job on a superyacht, *Panacea*, in Italy. Guy had been on his boat *Incognito* in Malaysia, living his traveller, boat-bum lifestyle, and while chatting on Facebook we had come up with this loose plan to sail together from the Malaysian island of Langkawi to Indonesia. But we had not openly discussed whether we considered ourselves a couple or not. I had a few little clues to go on – I dipped a toe into the water once or twice and told him I missed him and he didn't log off, instead sending me a smiley face, or coming back with an 'aww-shucks-you're-all-right-too'-type of response.

As I had mused about him during my daily evening jogs along the Naples' promenade, doing that thing that women do, whereby they plan out the next twenty-five years of their life based solely on a kind comment from a good-looking guy, I had felt close to Guy and excited to be going off on an adventure with him. Yet when my sister had asked me, 'So, are you two in a relationship?' I had answered, 'no.' How could we be, I reasoned, as we hadn't seen each other for months and hadn't been officially together the last time we'd met? But I wasn't interested in anyone else and I was – we both were – making quite a serious commitment. I was flying halfway round the world to live with him on his little boat and together we were going to sail, dive and explore some remote places in Indonesia. There would be no easy means of backing out. The only way to do this was to jump in with both feet, and that was what we were doing. Considering I'd never even lived with a boyfriend before, this was diving head first into a relationship with a hell of a heavy weight tied round my ankles.

Judging by the little kicks my stomach had done when he'd pulled up at the dock in the dinghy, I was still attracted to him, which was a good start. Guy was more than my friend but he wasn't yet my boyfriend. It was a strange kind of limbo to be in – both exciting and nerve-wracking, like a second date with someone you like, but at the same time it felt familiar. And I liked that combination.

The outboard engine slowed and I snapped back to attention, realising I recognised the outline of the yacht we were approaching. I reached down to pick up the painter rope, ready to tie on the dinghy. I hadn't quite got my seas legs back after my month-long shoreside break, so I propped one knee against the inflated rubber tube of the bow to steady myself against the dinghy's rocking motion as the wake rebounded off *Incognito*'s hull and bounced us around. I tied the rope around the cleat in the same way I had been taught with the superyacht-sized mooring lines on *Panacea*, climbed up the two brown planks that protruded from the transom and stood on the deck at the back of the boat. Guy killed the outboard and tilted the propeller out of the sea. The water made a rushing noise in the sudden silence as it drained quickly off and back into the waves.

He shoved up my bag and I pulled the other end. There was an open hatch behind me and I had to watch my step so that I didn't fall backwards down it into the boat below as I dragged my rucksack along until it lay flat on the deck. *Incognito* strained slightly at her anchor chain like a horse at its rein and I grabbed hold of the strong wire rigging to keep my balance.

There was no big welcome hug or kiss but there was a smile and an offer of a beer. Two hops and we were across the deck and into the cockpit; three more and we were down the wooden companionway steps and inside *Incognito*.

The sun sets quickly near the equator and it was dark by now – and still incredibly hot – and Guy moved around inside, turning on lights. He flicked a switch on the control panel and a fan mercifully blasted into life like a mini jet engine. I sat on the starboard-side sofa and sucked on the tepid beer I'd been handed. It was a Skol, the golden-orange can matching the colour of my old Peugeot 106. I hadn't seen a Skol since I was a kid. Who knew they were still making them and selling them out East?

'Are you hungry?' Guy asked. 'I'll make us some dinner.' He busied himself in the little galley next to me as I surveyed the boat from my seat. I'd sat in *Incognito*'s cockpit a few times when the catamaran I was travelling on, *Gillaroo*, was moored in the neighbouring spot in Danga Bay, a marina in the southern Malaysian town of Johor Bahru, but I'd been inside only twice – once when I bumped into Guy in Thailand, and we kissed and he invited me back for a tour of the boat, and a second time when I'd gone to visit him in Koh Lanta and we'd paddle-boarded out to fetch some equipment he needed. Both visits were brief and the boat had been packed full of boys' stuff, with equipment and tools covering every surface.

When Guy had given me that first tour, he'd explained that the one sleeping cabin, at the back of the boat, underneath that hatch I'd had to avoid falling through earlier this evening, was used for storage. And the bathroom, which contained only a loo and a sink, was used for storing things as well. That had effectively left just one room for Guy and his crew to live, cook and sleep in.

Now, the thought of that made me feel a little nervous – we'd never be able to get more than a few feet away from each other. I swallowed a mouthful of warm beer.

'Mind if I look around?' I asked him, as he diced onions and garlic.

He gestured with the knife. 'Go ahead'.

Most of the boat I could see from where I was sitting. Long, narrow sofas covered with natural-coloured calico lined each side. The saloon was so narrow that if I sat on the edge of one sofa I could just about touch the other with my toes. The mast came through the centre of the room and behind it was a large cool-box with a small towel laid across the top, turning it into a coffee-table-cum-foot-rest. Where the boat narrowed at the front into a point, the old internal wall had been cut away, joining the cabin to the saloon, opening up the interior and making it feel roomier as well as better ventilated, as a large hatch right in the front drew in the air. Originally there would have been a bed underneath that hatch but now it was bare wood covered with bags, planks of more wood, tools, equipment. The painted white floorboards were smooth and cool against my bare soles. I turned, standing, my eyes travelling over the small chart table opposite me to a wooden door fitted with decorative grilles, the kind you see on old-fashioned cane conservatory furniture. I opened the door. Inside was a small stainless-steel sink nestled in a white-and-brown Formica unit, and a pumping toilet. I backed out again, bumping the bottom step with my calf, and turned to Guy, who was opening a can of beans.

'Did you get the loo working, then?' I asked him.

He laughed. 'Yes. I didn't think you'd want to be using the poop deck all the time.'

I inched past the bottom of the stairs that led back up to the deck and squeezed behind him through the galley, which held a sink, a two-hob gas burner and a few small cupboards. The galley also served as a narrow corridor to the back cabin and was the only way to get back there apart from through the hatch. It was tight and I touched Guy lightly on his bare shoulder as I passed, steadying myself against the slight rocking motion of the sea, not wanting to fall into him and push him against the hot stove. His skin felt clammy in the heat. Steam bubbled from underneath the lid of a rice pan on the stove. He turned it down.

It was dark in the back and I couldn't see much. The starboard-side cabin wall, to my left, was covered in slats of wood painted white, like clapboard, fading into deep shadow ahead. A wisp of a breeze trickled down through an open hatch. I moved forward and reached a metal post, white paint flaking away at the height where hands had grabbed hold of it as people passed. Guy came through from the kitchen and stretched around me to reach across the dark to the wall on the other side. The space was so small, and we were standing so close, that I could feel his body heat and the dampness on his skin. He flicked a light switch. There was a bed! A double bed, mercifully clear of tools, dive equipment or bottles of paint. There was a big stack of stuff on the floor, including an air compressor and a petrol generator, which I'd have to clamber over to get to the bed, but at least there was one, with a sheet on it and pillows and even a blanket. A miracle.

'Did you clear this out for me?'

He nodded. 'I've been fitting lights and a fan this week.'

I was touched. I had mentally prepared myself for losing the luxuries I had become accustomed to over the last six months on the superyacht. I'd even managed to persuade myself that slopping out a bucket and having to read by torchlight would add to the sense of adventure; we'd be proper explorers. Guy had never mentioned in his messages what he had been doing on the boat. He had obviously spent time and effort getting ready for my arrival. He might have been playing it cool when we were chatting over the internet but he had gone to a lot of trouble for me. 'And you sorted the loo because of me?'

'Well, you are a girl. I thought you'd like some creature comforts.' And he flashed me a big white grin. A bubble filled my chest and I knew everything was going to be fine.

2

My Guy, no ties

Despite Guy's very welcome additions, after six months living the superyacht lifestyle *Incognito* came as a bit of a shock. At 36 feet she was small, but well designed inside, making the most of the space. If I'd been coming from another normal-sized boat I would probably not have even noticed the size difference. But my last yacht had been twice the length and twice the width, meaning *Incognito* had only a quarter of the space I was used to. Rather than six bathrooms, there was one – and the shower was outside, a cold squirt from a Thai-style 'bum gun' over the back deck. *Incognito*'s chart table, galley, bathroom and saloon could have fitted into *Panacea*'s kitchen. Gone were the creature comforts, such as a never-ending supply of drinking water, hot showers and air-conditioning. There was no washing machine or tumble dryer, dishwasher or chef, no wine cellar or ice cream on tap.

On the up side, there were also no guests to pander to, so on my first morning I slept late and Guy made us both a spicy Thai noodle soup for breakfast. We ate it in the cockpit, sitting opposite each other, leaning our plastic bowls on the sloping sides of the coach roof in lieu of a table.

It felt great to be back on the water, in the tropics and without a job. The superyacht deckhand position had been exciting when it was all new, but it quickly lost its fascination when it became apparent it was only a tiny step up from an unskilled waitressing and cleaning job, albeit a well-paid waitressing and cleaning job. Life as a domestic servant just hadn't been for me.

The idea of having months – possibly years – without having to report for duty on a daily basis was thrilling. Guy lived on his boat full-time and was used to this kind of freedom. He'd not had a 'proper' job for years and instead lived a nomadic lifestyle, moving from continent to continent, settling for a while in a place if he liked it and finding whatever work he could. He had a freelance IT project on the go now and needed to work on that for a few hours each morning. By lunchtime, however, he was getting stuck into renovation projects on the boat.

I was a newbie at all this compared to him. I had a few hundred pounds coming in each month from the rent of my flat in London and life was cheap in Malaysia and was set to be even cheaper in Indonesia. Guy wasn't charging me any rent and we were splitting costs for food, fuel and cooking gas. So I knew that if I was careful I could eke out my money for some time. I also had some savings in the bank – my *Panacea* earnings – for emergencies.

What a feeling it was, to know that I had nothing to worry about, financially, for the foreseeable future. Living like this allowed me to focus on the very basics: sourcing food and water, and making sure our little home was secure and comfortable – and water-tight. Beyond that, I made do and I spent the rest of my time enjoying life – watching sunsets, star-gazing, witnessing the world go by. All those old clichés are clichés for a reason. No stressing about the commute, about that thing my boss said, about if my clothes were the right style or my hair looked good. I wore what I felt comfortable in – bikini on the boat, to keep cool; trousers and loose tops on land for modesty's sake – and what was clean. On *Incognito* there was only one mirror, a small portable that Guy used for shaving, so I rarely knew what I looked like anyway. Lack of mirrors made me aware of how many times in my old life I unconsciously checked my reflection in a day – bathroom, bedroom, hallway, work toilets, shop windows, lifts. Here it was maybe once every three days, when I borrowed Guy's mirror to pluck my eyebrows.

That night we talked over beers while we ate. It was easy small talk, nothing heavy, nothing – god forbid – about our feelings. Just a nice, normal, friendly catching-up chit-chat over a bean-and-beer dinner. Afterwards, I went up on deck for a shower. It was pitch black, so I stripped off my T-shirt, shorts and underwear and steeled myself to fire forceful shots from the gun-trigger shower on to my naked skin.

As I dried off I secretly congratulated myself on how well things were going so far. There had been no awkwardness, as there had been a couple of years ago when I answered an advert for 'crew wanted' and flew to Borneo to join Steve, a stranger, on his yacht. Then there'd been no conversation to begin with, just awkward oh-god-what-am-I-doing-here waves of panic. I'd been green to the sailing-cruising lifestyle and horrified by the idea of showering outside, or naked swimming, or anything not 100 per cent prim-and-proper. But spending the best part of two years on boats had knocked that out of me and I had relaxed into the lifestyle and into myself as a person. Now here I was, in the nuddy, hosing myself down on the back of a boat owned by a man I liked quite a bit. Guy was a gent and stayed downstairs, giving me my open-air privacy. In that, he was a million miles away from the other boat captain, Steve, and I was thankful. The whole situation was much more chilled and I had more control. I dressed in cut-off shorts and a vest top and went back down.

We had another beer and I perched on the steps with my head high, almost out of the boat, to better catch the tiniest of puffs of wind as they blew backwards over the deck.

'Have you been running a lot?' Guy asked. He was sitting on the sofa next to the chart table, resting his feet on the cool-box. 'Your legs look amazing.'

I blushed, tickled literally pink that he was flirting. It seemed like everything was going well. We were getting on, comfortable in each other's company, happy in our silences but also keen to find out more about what the other person had been doing since we were last together. There was no kidding ourselves that we were little more than acquaintances but it was relaxed and felt right.

I made a mental note to wear those shorts frequently. They were an old pair of Seven jeans that I had ceremoniously cut off with scissors before I packed my bag to fly out to Malaysia to join Guy. Hacking away at the legs of my jeans – at £150, the most expensive I had ever owned – was a symbolic act for me. In my new life, living on boats in the tropics, I didn't need tight-fitting trousers or fancy labels. I just needed shorts, a bikini and a couple of faithful old vests. Removing the legs gave my body more freedom. The reason I was doing it gave *me* more freedom.

On the same day I took the scissors to my jeans, I had gone through all of my clothes stored at my parents' house and donated to charity anything black or grey, constricting or designed for being worn in an office. I stuffed clothes that needed to be ironed, that showed sweat or that were clingy into a white sack for the East Midlands Air Ambulance fund. I got rid of the few designer-labelled items I owned – a Marc Jacobs T-shirt that was far too fussy to be worn on a boat, a silk Balenciaga blouse that only suited an office environment. It was amazingly liberating to offload all that pointless stuff and I felt like I was finally shrugging off a sticky, annoying chrysalis and swapping an old, slow, plodding me for a new, fluttering, carefree one.

Before I flew out to join him, Guy had called me in England to ask if I minded taking on a boat project for a couple of weeks before we set off for Indonesia. The old spray hood and bimini, which protected us from waves coming over the boat and from the sun beating down, were so old and battered by the strong equatorial UV rays that they were shredding into pieces. The large fabric cover that protected the mainsail when the boat wasn't sailing also needed replacing. To buy these new would cost Guy thousands, he had said. There was a sailmaker here in Kuah town on Langkawi island, but she was fully booked up with work for a month. She would sell us the special fabric and thread that we needed, Guy had explained, and he had found some friendly local Malay women to do the sewing. So I would just need to be the project manager and make sure it all got done and worked well. Was I up for it?

I loved sewing as a teenager. I wasn't very good at it – in one textiles lesson I picked the trickiest thing to do, a pair of shorts, and promptly sewed them together inside out, which meant my poor mum had to spend hours unpicking the seams. Then I sewed them again the right way round, spent weeks finishing them off, added a button, ironed them … and hated them so much I never wore them.

I had had more success with altering garments. At fifteen I had a habit of raiding my dad's wardrobe, picking something I'd not seen him wear for a while, then customising it for my own use – all without asking him. An old RAF uniform shirt caught my eye – I liked the light-blue colour and starchy cotton – and I trimmed the bottom, hemmed it, put in darts to make it more of a feminine fit and lopped off the epaulettes.

I possibly only got away with my butchery because it looked so different that he never realised it was his old uniform. Another time – less successfully – I attempted to turn one of his old white M&S vests into an asymmetrical top. I just looked like I had a saggy, greying handkerchief draped over one shoulder.

I thought that all of this early experience plainly qualified me as a seamstress in the making, so I had agreed wholeheartedly with Guy's request and signed up for the job.

He didn't waste any time in putting me to work. He wanted to get things finished so we could head off to Indonesia, he explained. By mid-morning two days after I arrived, we were off the boat, on his rented motorbike and driving to meet the Malay women who were going to help us.

'Do they speak good English?' I asked him as he parked the bike in front of a shopping mall half a mile down the main road from the dinghy jetty. The smell of sewage had already started to rise thickly from the gutters under the pavement. I tried hard not to wrinkle my nose in disgust and give any onlookers the impression I was an English snob.

The mall was a tall concrete tower block set at a jaunty angle in the middle of a car park crazy-paved in pink and beige jigsaw tiles. Ahead of us a pair of grand smoked-glass doors slid open to let out a man in brown embroidered Malay robes and block hat. A welcome blast of air-conditioned air swirled around my calves.

'Yeah, pretty good English. You'll be fine,' Guy said, walking up a short set of steps and into the mall. I followed him into a lift opposite the entrance, dangling the motorbike helmet in my hand from the chin strap. Just as the doors closed, he said: 'Oh, and by the way, I've told them you're my wife.'

3

A stitch in time saves nine
(thousand ringgit)

The ground floor of the mall was set up to entice in stray tourists. There weren't many holidaymakers in Kuah. Most visitors to Langkawi stayed in exclusive resorts in Cenang on the west side of the island; Kuah was in the centre of a small bay to the south. I couldn't blame them. I had visited Kuah the year before, when *Gillaroo* had stopped there for a few days, and I had hated the place. It was busy and smelly, with open sewers running along the sides of some of the streets. In many places the sewers were covered with paving slabs, turning the drainage system into walkways, but holes in the slabs – some provided for ventilation, others the result of the concrete crumbling away – did nothing to stem the stench from rising in the 36-degree heat. The water in the bay off Kuah, where a hundred or so yachts lay at anchor, was a filthy green-brown and thick clusters of barnacles and coral choked anchor chains within a matter of weeks. They were probably well fertilised by all that sewage running out to sea.

Cenang bay, a good half an hour away by motorbike, was another world. While the water was not exactly crystal – the whole of the west coast of Malaysia is murky in varying degrees, from a green-tea shade in the north to a deep brown as thick as Willy Wonka's chocolate river around the industrial shipping port Klang – at Cenang it was just clear enough for a paddle or swim, there was a long beach, complete pavements and even – joy of joys in this dry country – a couple of bars selling alcohol. Westerners therefore congregated in Cenang. Those seen in Kuah town were either tourists who got lost after getting off the ferry from Thailand, or sailors.

The would-be entrepreneurs of Kuah failed to bear this in mind when constructing the five-storey Langkawi Plaza on the wrong side of town, far from where the odd lost tourist or cruiser strayed. They painted the outside of the tall mall lime green, but it still attracted no attention. They filled the ground floor with shops selling white cotton clothes, cheap pearls and plastic watches, to no avail. So they let out the first and second floor to local businesses: clothes shops and massage parlours that charged 50p for twenty minutes of therapy in a vibrating chair, who had one, maybe two, customers a day. To save money, the aircon only chilled the ground floor – another lost bid to attract the cash-rich *orang putih* who would never come. Floors three and four were empty and reported to be haunted; the fancy food court right at the top had effectively turned into a staff canteen for the workers who set up businesses in the cut-price rental units on floors one and two.

Our Malay seamstress, Zainab, had a corner unit by the lifts on level two. The whole front of her 2- by 3-metre cubicle was open and at night she pulled down an aluminium shutter to secure it. Pushed against all three walls were tables covered with patterned cloths. Small cubbyholes on the walls held threads in every colour imaginable and baskets on the floor and work surfaces overflowed with different materials. Clothes that had been made to order hung on wire hangers from poles above head height, traditional *baju melayu* slotted in between pairs of jeans and children's school-uniform shirts. It was an explosion of pattern and colour and at its heart sat three women in headscarves, giggling behind their hands.

Zainab was a grandmother but she was as girlish as her daughter Ana and her co-worker Nasreen. All three turned into little schoolgirls in Guy's presence. As we rounded the corner, she clocked him and looked up through her eyelashes and from beneath her headscarf, a fifty-something coquette missing her two front teeth. 'Hi, Guy,' she trilled. The other two tittered. He gave them one of his big smiles.

Ana and Nasreen introduced themselves to me, singing their 'helos' in the melodic tones Malay women seem to adopt from their teens. No matter the size of the woman – and not all Malaysian women have the stereotypical sparrow-like South-East Asian build – they have sweet sing-song voices that sound gentle, fun and feminine. I'd place a safe bet that there's no vocal equivalent of Davina McCall or Fearne Cotton in Malaysia.

I smiled back at them. At twenty-four, Ana was already married with two daughters of her own. She dressed daily in jeans and football T-shirts she accessorised with a headscarf in matching colours. In Malaysia the fashion for hijab – called *tudung* locally – is tight around the head and chin, with a small peak at the front, and then flowing out across the shoulders. It emphasises the roundness of the wearer's face – a style point that flatters some women but makes others look like a cross between a chipmunk and ET. The *tudung* can be decorated with a dangly brooch at the centre of the throat, looking like an elaborate zip pull.

Ana, tall and big-boned, loved her fried chicken, playing games designed for teenagers in the internet cafes and gossiping, especially telling the story of how she fell in love with her husband. But she was also a tough player, knowing how to stall for time if something wasn't going her way and to get what she wanted, and racing her bright-red motorbike around the island at top speeds.

Nasreen – who thought nothing of belching up sardine fumes in public – was the perfect foil to Ana's girlie-girl personality. She was the older of the two and smaller. A widow, she lived alone in Langkawi, while her family on the mainland looked after her three young children. She worked at the sewing shop a couple of days a week. As we spent more time together I learned she liked to suck on chicken necks boiled in broth at lunchtime and I think she secretly harboured a desire to be whisked away by a European gentleman. Whether, if push came to shove, she would actually go through with it, I wasn't sure.

We developed almost a kind of work routine. After breakfast each morning, Guy and I went ashore in the dinghy and he drove me to the mall on his motorbike. The idea was that Ana and I would work on our sewing project together and get it finished within a couple of weeks. First, I stripped the old mainsail cover, spray hood and bimini off *Incognito* and carried them to the shop, balanced precariously on the back of the bike. Then, to save Guy's money and Ana's time, I picked apart each piece by hand, stabbing holes in the sides of my fingers and my palms repeatedly with stitch-rippers until my hands resembled colanders. I laid out the new cardboardy Sunbrella material in the dusty corridor of the shopping mall and, on hands and knees for hours, drew round the old pieces, to make a pattern. I talked Ana through it and she sewed the new covers on her machine, finished them off and I took them back to the boat. Well, that was the theory.

The first couple of days went like that, while Guy was hanging around, watching and helping. Once he saw I was managing fine with the girls, he headed back to the boat and told me to text him later and he'd pick me up from the dock.

'Where your husband gone?' Nasreen asked me on the morning of the third day. It made me want to laugh every time one of the girls called him that. I wore no ring and, as I hate lying, I was careful to never talk about my 'wedding', although they constantly chattered about theirs. They befriended me on Facebook and never commented on how my last name was different from Guy's. They knew the word 'boyfriend', so I'm not sure why they never came out and asked me directly what our relationship was. All parties – Guy included – kept up the charade.

It was funny to think that, after several years of desperately wanting – and failing – to find a husband, I'd suddenly acquired one in the blink of an eye. Before I left my old job in journalism eighteen months earlier, I'd been full of self-pity over why all my friends seemed to be able to get married and settle down while I was stuck being single. At the time it was, privately, a real sore point, although the idea of marriage also freaked me out. My parents were still together after forty years, so it wasn't like I had a close family example of marriage not working out in the long-run, but I found it hard to believe that I would – or could – be with one person for the rest of my life. Maybe, I mused from time to time, when I felt like doing a bit of pop-psychology on myself, that was because all of my relationships had been short, or long-distance, or both. My longest relationship, right out of university, lasted five years – with a couple of breaks in between – and for all that time we lived at least a hundred miles apart; for several months we were separated by an entire ocean and four time zones. Other relationships limped on for six months or so before grinding, or plunging in some cases, to a halt. *It's no wonder,* I'd think, *that I have trouble picturing myself settling down with some bloke for fifty, sixty, seventy years.*

In my days as a cub reporter for a local newspaper I'd be sent out to interview couples celebrating their golden or diamond wedding anniversaries. I remember driving out to meet one couple in a village in the Oxfordshire countryside. Despite the blazing July heat, they had a coal fire burning in the sitting room of their low-ceilinged cottage. He was ninety-one; she was eighty-nine – they'd met as young teenagers living in the same village. He was deaf, so she answered for him while he made, shaking, a cup of tea for me. Each had their own armchair; there was no sofa for them to share. Their card of congratulations from the Queen sat proudly on top of a doily on the windowsill. I asked, as instructed by my editor, what the secret to a long and happy marriage was. Their answer – they always answered the same, these couples, whether they'd been married sixty, seventy or even seventy-five years, like one pair I visited – was 'a bit of give and take'. The old woman, who had lived with this man since she was nineteen years old, wore a purple dress and sat with her knees apart. Years of dropped crumbs and spilt tea had left oily spots on his well-worn trousers. Were they happy? I'm not sure they were anything any more, really – not happy, not sad, not elated, not proud. They just were; existing side by side in a stifling sitting room.

As I sat in the velour armchairs in these various houses that always smelled the same, balancing my teacup in its saucer and nibbling on a biscuit, and in the long pauses between my asking a question and the couples conjuring up memories long since filed away and repeating them back to me, I'd think about how different my life was from theirs. Age was the biggest difference, of course – I had most of my life left to lead and I didn't know where it would take me, while theirs was mostly a life already lived and known. And there was marital status. By the time they reached my age then, twenty-two or twenty-three, these couples had met, courted, married and set up home. Now they had spent three times the length of my entire life together. 'A bit of give and take', I knew, meant different things for different couples. To some it indicated that they'd had some settling in to do, for others it meant harsh words forgiven, affairs overlooked.

Back then I didn't want 'give and take'; I wanted perfect. At twenty-three, I wasn't able to imagine giving up my independence, my freedom, for a man. And to be with that man, no matter what he did, or what I did, for seventy years? It gave me the shivers, made me feel trapped. Sitting in those dusty living rooms, scribbling in my spiral-bound notebook, I went through the motions, said my polite congratulations to the couples, but inside I felt like a caged animal who couldn't wait to get out into the fresh air and freedom.

This cynicism stayed with me from me early twenties right through to nearly thirty, then something popped and I was suddenly fed up with being seemingly the only single one left. I don't know whether it was pressure society was actually putting on me to fit in, or if I perceived there to be some kind of pressure, or even if the old biological clock was ticking away, but I had a sudden need for a Big Romance with a Happy Ending. I went on countless dates and allowed friends to set me up with chaps they knew from their university days or the office or pals from their husband's football team, even though we had nothing in common other than our singleness and despite the fact that they were described by the setting-up mate as 'a bit socially awkward' or 'recently divorced but I'm sure he's ready to start dating again'. I tried hard – turned up, stayed longer on dates than I wanted to, tried to focus on their redeeming qualities, nodded and smiled at appropriate points. And yet, no matter how hard I looked, I couldn't find this Happy Ending I was seeking. So then, desperate, I'd agree to meet another 'man mountain' or a 'bit-shy-but-really-lovely-once-you-get-to-know-him' and the cycle would continue. It was miserable.

Then I travelled, and I removed myself from my old life and the associations that went with it, and, while I didn't go back to being so cynical about marriage, I didn't crave it, either. A Happy Ending, I knew, was not necessarily a marriage and a marriage was not necessarily a happy ending. I was content to just let things happen.

4

And the bride wore...

Once it was women alone in the small sewing shop on level two of Langkawi Plaza, and once Ana, Nasreen, Zainab and I had become friends, the work pace relaxed quite a bit. First thing in the morning we went upstairs to the fifth floor to buy drinks – instant, sickly-sweet 3-in-1 tea poured into a plastic bag with ice, a straw and an elastic band to fasten the two together. They were fine when being held, these drinks, albeit a bit wobbly, but were a bugger to put down. After mine tipped over on the table in the corridor outside their shop a couple of times, covering everything with a sticky residue, Zainab produced a stainless-steel cat bowl to keep it secure – and her floors safe.

After tea we'd gossip for a bit – Ana told me about life in her village and asked me questions about life in England. Her English vocabulary was amazing and I was constantly surprised about how similar topics of conversation Ana and I had were to chats I'd have with old friends in the UK. We were born six thousand miles apart in different decades: me in an industrial English city; she in a jungle *kampong* on a small tropical island. I went to university and then started a professional career. I was single, owned an apartment in one of the world's busiest cities and had travelled all over. Ana's life was more like those lived by the old married couples in Home Counties England than mine. She went to school and then started working for her mother's sewing company. She met her husband, who was from the same village, when she was little more than a baby and they married when she was still in her teens. She had travelled out of her *kampong*, to mainland Malaysia, but didn't own a passport. She and their two young daughters lived with her husband's parents in a hand-built house with pink walls. She never wanted to be anywhere else, she told me. 'I like it I hear the birds in the jungle in the morning.'

Yet she'd heard of Justin Bieber. She thought boys were 'cute'. She had a Facebook page and posted selfies after she'd done her make-up and she put up pictures of her daughters. 'Klik klik ... cheeese!' she'd trill. She asked me what I thought about boob jobs and when, laughing, I asked her if she'd ever have hers done, she was aghast. 'Nooooooooooo!', intoning all five notes of an arpeggio.

She told me how, when she was fourteen, she found she liked a boy in her village and sneaked out to meet him. They married three years later and their first daughter came within two years, her second three years later. Now, because her period was late, she was worried she might be pregnant with her third child. That would be 'big problem', she explained, because 'don't have money enough.'

All the way through every day, as she sat on a computer chair at a sewing machine, making *oterations* for other customers instead of working on my project, claiming this order was 'priority', and stretching out the pace of work sewing my three things from a few days to several weeks, she talked and talked in her dulcet tones and we became friends. She made it her mission to educate me in Malaysian life and culture and more than once I hopped on the back of her bike for a terrifying ride across town on a seemingly urgent mission that turned out to be shopping for pyjamas for her kids, sourcing material to make her grandmother a new outfit or going to see the bank manager.

Christmas came – a normal working day in Malaysia – and I marked the occasion by giving myself a one-day holiday from the sewing shop. Guy and I treated ourselves to a curry in town and passed plastic snowmen dotted among the stacks of plastic bins and tubs for sale outside the supermarket on the way to the restaurant. We popped open a truly awful bottle of fizzy wine in front of a movie back in *Incognito*'s cockpit afterwards.

New Year's Eve found me sitting in a gin-and-tonic-induced blur on Cenang beach. I dug a can of tonic out of the sand, where I'd buried it in an attempt to keep it shop-fridge cool. It was lukewarm and the sweetness made my molars throb and the sides of my tongue feel thick. I offered Guy a top-up to his plastic cup.

The beach was crammed full of groups of tourists sitting in dark huddles, waiting on the turn of the clock. There was no organised public event; a few friends wrote their names on the sides of Chinese lanterns that they released into the night sky to merge within minutes with the stars.

I checked the time on my phone screen, a startling blue in the night. For some reason I was feeling nervous – as anxious as I had the first time I'd spent an evening with Guy and had realised I liked him. When midnight came I didn't know what I was going to do. The New Year chimes ringing out was the time when real couples reached for each other and kissed them. Were Guy and I a real couple? Should I kiss him? I wiped away a sheen of sweat from my upper lip and fiddled with the ring pull of my can.

'Ten.' 'Nine.' Voices started counting down along the length of the beach, out of synch with each other to begin with, joining into one loud chorus by the time they reached five.

'Four.' 'Three.' I glanced at Guy but he was watching the beach, drink to his lips.

'Two.' What to do. What to do? I dabbed at my lip again, wishing we'd stayed on the boat. I didn't even hear the 'one.' Cheers broke out and calls of Happy New Year. I looked up again to see Guy smiling at me. 'Happy New Year, Em,' he said, and kissed me. Then a grinning stranger patted our shoulders, thrust his hand into our faces to shake and the kiss was broken almost before it had begun.

Days became weeks and started to risk delaying our departure. Guy got frustrated with Ana and I defended her actions.

'She's stalling,' he said. 'She likes you and she doesn't want you to go. She knows that once she finishes our project, we'll leave Langkawi.'

'She's busy,' I said, not liking the insinuation that there was something underhand about her actions and wanting to defend my friend in the face of his criticism, even though I knew there was truth in what he was saying. 'And she's not very organised. It'll get done. I'll talk to her about it.' I did, and she promised that she'd get straight back to it, and then an urgent trip to the supermarket came up and everything went on the back burner once again.

One morning, she told me she couldn't work on my 'projek' that day because her friend from her *kampong* was getting married. 'You want you come see make-up?' she asked me.

'Sure,' I shrugged. I didn't have anything else to do if she was away from the shop, and Guy had already dropped me off and gone back to the boat. We whizzed to another mall on her speed machine.

Inside the shop, once my eyes adjusted from the bright sunlight outside, I could see rack after rack of long, sequinned, bejewelled gowns. An ornate sofa, purple velvet trimmed with gold, was pushed against one wall, next to a small changing cubicle. So far, so bridal shop.

A small crowd of five or six people had gathered in the other half of the shop, which looked more like a hairdresser's salon. Smiling, Ana beckoned me over. 'Come!'

Her friend Hasni sat in a chair, head tipped back so that her face was horizontal. A white cloth covered her clothes from the neck down and, because she was in public, she still had her headscarf on. The make-up artist – a ladyboy, the first I'd seen in Malaysia ('He don mind if you call he or she,' Ana told me) – had blanketed Hasni's face in thick foundation and powder, replacing the natural darker Asian tone with a paler, sallow-Barbie-doll shade. Heavy false eyelashes stretched across her eyelids like caterpillars.

I was fascinated by the shading the make-up artist was doing. I inched forwards for a better look. He saw me and smiled. 'Does that work to thin the nose?' I asked him as he painted two dark smudges down the sides of Hasni's nose and a paler dot on the bridge. He blended and moved on to her cheeks, blending again, until he'd conjured cheekbones and contours from her flattish face. This was years before Kim Kardashian was tweeting pictures of her face outlined like a Hallowe'en skeleton and, even though I don't really like make-up, I was impressed by the effect.

With a slick of pale-pink lipstick that yellowed her teeth, Hasni was done and out of the chair – and I was suddenly in it, face tipped back. I shot Ana a frantic look – no one had told me I was next; no one had asked me if I even wanted to do it – and slimy goop was being sponged across my chin.

'Don worry!' Ana said (all of her sentences seemed to end in exclamation marks). 'Relaks!'

The making-up continued and I could feel the sponge getting damp when it swept into my sweaty hairline. Just as quickly I was whisked into another chair to have my hair piled on to my head, sprayed into a stiff tower and pierced with jewel-encrusted combs, and next I was dragged, by the hand, into the other half of the shop and shoved into the changing room by the make-up artist with an outfit to put on. He had chosen a floor-length ivory hobble skirt covered in lace and pearls. The matching top had a high neck and long sleeves and squeezed over my flesh to rest below my hips. Instantly my skin started to rash at the scratching unfamiliarity of tight-fitting polyester clothes secured with Velcro. I hobbled out of the cubicle and he thrust a pair of size-eight, five-inch-high ivory satin mules at me. I am a size five.

Smiling, he pointed to a photographer, who had appeared from nowhere, ready to take my picture.

'What's going on?' I finally managed to squeak.

'Take picture. For window.'

Ah. So that's what he wanted to do – add a token, dolled-up Westerner to the array of glamorous brides in the shop's testimonials and expand his business model.

Ana was beaming at me, a sparkle in her eye. 'Soooooooooooo beautiful!'

I was way out of my comfort zone but I decided to roll with it. They'd already dressed me up like a doll – why not just relax and enjoy it? I was posing with a sprig of plastic flowers in my hand, arranging myself on the purple and gold sofa – which was not that easy because the dress was so tight – and getting into my role a bit when the door opened. In my peripheral vision, I saw someone come in. I ignored them and smiled into the lens of the camera for a few more shots before looking up. It was Guy.

Ana had texted him to come urgently, apparently, and he had walked into a shop, not knowing what was going on, to find his friend-cum-crewmate-cum-kind-of-girlfriend he'd not known for very long, a woman he admired because she was a 'blokey girl' who wore shorts and got ready to go out in ten seconds flat, pimped up to look like some kind of extremely camp Disney princess bride. It was the stuff that single men's nightmares are made of.

He shot me a bewildered look. I tried to signal *sorry* with my eyes, without saying it out loud so I offended any of the others there, especially Ana. *I am not a marriage-obsessed Bridezilla*, I tried to convey. *This just kind of happened to me.* I am not sure he got the message. He left pretty quickly. He didn't laugh.

I wanted to wipe the gloop from my face and put my T-shirt back on but my ordeal wasn't over. I was, it turned out, to be a guest of honour at Hasni's wedding. I travelled to the *kampong* in the wedding car with the rest of the family because there was no way in that skirt I was going to be able to throw a thigh over the back of Ana's motorbike. I sat under a giant plastic gazebo in the centre of the village with other guests and ate rice and red chicken curry. I was vegetarian but felt I couldn't explain that to people who didn't speak much English, so I ate around the lumps of meat and bone with my fingers, hoping the sauce wouldn't drip on the white outfit so that I ended up having to buy it.

The whole thing felt surreal, like a dream, as I was pulled here, pushed there, poked and prodded and gawped at by Malay village children as if I were a toy.

A paper rose with a hard-boiled egg nestled in its centre, a symbol of fertility, was thrust into my hand. The whole village had turned out to celebrate the wedding and the children were fascinated by me. I wondered if some of them had not seen a white person before.

I was ushered into Hasni's parents' house, where the marriage bed had been prepared – covered in pale-blue satin, to match the bride's outfit, and decorated with fake fruits and flowers. Sisters and daughters and nieces crowded into the room with its wicker walls and bare floor, the smaller ones grinning toothlessly at me, the older girls shaking my hand and then running away, giggling, as if they'd just met a pop star.

Outside again, I watched the bride and her groom – a stern-faced young man dressed in a *seri* and turban, with a cutlass at his waist – process through the village to drum beats and settle at a covered trestle table to hold court. Ana shoved me into the official photos with them. 'They like it you in foto!' Hasni beamed to be pictured beside me; her angry groom glowered.

A white couple, a Dutch man and woman who had been visiting a home stay in the *kampong*, saw me as I sat at a long table under a makeshift gazebo that took up most of the patch of worn-down grass that served as the village green, and stopped.

'Is it your wedding?' the woman asked me. I could understand how she would jump to that conclusion, seeing that I was dressed head-to-toe in white satin. I tried to keep the shudder out of my voice as I told her no.

'You are lucky,' Ana confided to me as I hobbled down the dirt path in shoes that I thought were going to lead to a broken ankle, they were so high and loose. We were going to her parents' house so I could change back into my own clothes – she'd brought them from the shop for me in a plastic bag. 'These dress, they cost 200 ringgit to borrow.' That – about £40 – was a lot of money in Langkawi. She sighed and I sensed she felt envious that I'd been given them as a treat. I felt mean, then, for taking the piss, albeit only out of myself. It could be that becoming a Disney princess bride for the day would be Ana's idea of heaven.

At the house she proudly showed me her wedding album – pictures of her and her husband sitting on a bed, like Hasni's, matching their own chosen colour scheme (three photos and three colours, in fact – one for the engagement, one for a wedding at her parents' house and one at his). She tactfully didn't ask about my album – and the lack of it.

'Your husband, I think he like it when he see you today,' she said. *I doubt it*, I thought. Judging by the speed with which he shot out of that shop, it might well have scared him off, good and proper. I murmured a noncommittal reply.

Guy didn't mention it when he came to pick me up. I swept my embarrassment under the carpet and we carried on as before. In public, to Malays, he still referred to me as his 'wife'; in private, we both knew I was nothing of the sort. But Ana had a photo of me, which she could keep, which would have been worthy of the wedding album I didn't have. And, in her innocent, first-true-love Disney-movie view of life, that was perfect.

5

Cruise control

The early morning buzz of the first dinghy leaving a yacht and setting off ashore was my alarm clock, the hornet-like vibrations of the rotating propeller fizzing their way through *Incognito*'s steel hull and pulling me out of my deep sleep. It was relatively cool first thing in the morning – maybe mid-20s – but the high air pressure and humidity had a doubly soporific effect on me, keeping me asleep past dawn.

I stretched out in the bed, the printed *seri* from Borneo that I used as a sheet tangled tightly around my legs. I pulled it away and climbed over the precarious pile of generator, compressor and other assorted marine equipment, through the galley and into the saloon. Guy was still asleep on the sofa by the chart table. I peed as quietly as I could but the vacuum and pump action of the toilet made a horrendous racket as I flushed. He'd asked me a few times to try to be quieter. Wincing, I opened the bathroom door and tried to click it gently into its latch, so that I didn't disturb him any further. Picking up my Kindle and iPhone, I went upstairs to start my morning ritual.

The cruisers here in Langkawi were not early risers. One or two of the other sailors had jobs on the island, and were up and at 'em by eight, but most enjoyed a lie-in to either take full advantage of their retirement or to sleep off a hangover.

Guy and I had met a few of the other cruisers by now. On Wednesday nights a local woman opened a kind of pop-up restaurant where the sailors could have a social gathering. We had been a couple of times, lowering the average age by a fair few decades. Most of those we became friendly with were in their sixties and seventies and from the USA, Australia, Canada, Germany and Finland. They were almost exclusively couples. A handful of these had been like Guy and me, setting out for a life off the beaten track when they were young, and managing to find a way of keeping it going. The majority had the same back story: they worked hard until the kids flew the nest, then sold their business and their home and bought a boat to realise their dream of sailing round the world.

To begin with it sounded adventurous – I couldn't imagine my parents doing such a thing – but as I spent more time with these cruisers I started to realise that many of them had not been anywhere else for a long time – in some cases, getting on for a decade. They spent as long as they could, monsoon weather permitting, in Langkawi, only visiting Thailand, which was about half a day's sail away, every three months when their visas ran out. When the rains came, some flew home to see their children and grandkids. Others stayed put and toughed it out, drinking their way through the downpours and rolling waves.

Drink was a big reason why they chose Langkawi – and why there were a hundred yachts at anchor in this one bay. Malaysia is a cheap place in which to live – food is fresh, inexpensive and varied, with supermarkets selling imported pasta and American goods alongside noodles and pak choi; petrol and diesel are subsidised by the government to about 40p per litre and some places – including Langkawi – are duty-free, meaning normally prohibitively-priced beer, wine and spirits become reasonable, even on a cruiser's small budget. You just need to find a shop that will sell it to you.

And boy, do cruisers like to drink. They buy wine by the box, spirits by the litre and beers by the caseload. Think about how much alcohol you get through while you're on holiday – so much more than when you're at home, right? Maybe you have a refreshing beer late morning. A glass of wine with lunch turns into half a bottle, a couple of beers on the beach, G&Ts at sunset. Now imagine you are permanently on holiday, which is effectively what these people are. You need access to booze in big quantities. The storage space on your boat is limited, so it isn't easy to stockpile enough to feed your daily habit and head off into the wide blue yonder. And what if you ran out of limes for your gin? Best to stay within rowing distance of the off-licence.

In Langkawi, alcohol was available in some special duty-free shops but cruisers have a habit of sniffing out the best prices and suppliers around. For religious reasons, Malays are not really drinkers and therefore not big sellers of alcohol, either – but the local Chinese population is. Guy heard one day, on the cruiser grapevine, about a wholesaler where we could load up on booze and other provisions ahead of our upcoming Indonesia trip, when we might be out of reach of shops or markets for weeks at a time. It seemed like a good omen, that our adventure might actually happen, and the thought reinvigorated me. I cleared out the cupboards in the kitchen in preparation for loading up for months at sea and Guy designated an area in the loo for holding the beer stash. We got loose directions from a drunken German at one of the Wednesday-night dinners – 'go past town sign, turn right, go past fish market' – and the next morning we set off on the bike on our shopping mission.

The vague directions were wrong and it took us a few goes of passing the same widely spaced palms at the side of the narrow dual carriageway to work out where we were supposed to turn off. We followed a concrete road past some Chinese shops, the shuttered fronts of them wide open like garage sales, the stench of engine oil from a mechanic's place thick on the air. Ahead was an empty and open-fronted corrugated-steel warehouse filled with rickety tables, which we guessed was the German's 'fish market'. Long grass grew between gaps in the concrete slabs to tickle my ankles as we rolled forward on the bike. There was no one about to ask for directions. Guy accelerated and, just before we reached a road leading into a village, we spotted our wholesaler off to the right. We parked up.

There was no front desk and no security guard so we walked in slowly, waiting for our eyes to adjust from the bright mid-morning sunlight to the dim fluorescent strips. Stacks and stacks of tinned and packaged goods towered 4 or 5 metres above us: tomatoes and sweetcorn, beans and soup, pasta, Maggi noodle sauce, bottles of pop. Forklift-trucks whizzed their way along the dusty aisles, disturbing birds who were trying to roost on top of hundreds of jars of mayonnaise. On the floor, half-ripped sheets of cardboard, one side roughly peeled away to expose the corrugation inside, made me skid. This was no cash-and-carry – there were no trolleys, no check-outs. It felt like we had wandered into a working warehouse.

For Chinese Malays – at least, the ones whom I met – money is king, and the shopkeepers and traders are flexible when it comes to business. We saw a sack trolley resting against one of the stacks of crates and started loading up with tins of non-perishables that we'd need if we were going off to remote places for a couple of months. We filled it as high as it would go with beans, tomatoes, instant mashed potato, rice, pasta – even McVitie's Digestive biscuits. I ignored rat droppings to grab some boxes of soap and toothpaste. Then, as we wandered back to the entrance, carefully wheeling our load, we saw, near the door, a whole room packed full of booze.

'Blimey,' Guy said. 'They're well stocked in there.' We leaned our trolley against some steel framework to step inside the storeroom. There was rum and vodka, Passoa and fancy cognacs, beer and shandy. If I'd wanted Pimms, I probably could have found it in there, thousands of miles away from an English summer lawn party. Guy stared reverently at a bottle of Glenmorangie. He cradled it in his palm and angled it to the thin strip of light coming in through the dirty high window. 'I love whisky. This is a real find.' He bought three.

By the time we'd finished adding to our pile, there was no way we were ever going to be able to get it all back to the boat on the motorbike, even if we did several trips. We'd become skilled at cramming almost as much on to one bike as the Asians were – Guy often had rucksacks on his chest and back and plastic bags dangling like testicles from his handlebars. I'd be wearing a rucksack, too, while a box of something or other filled the gap between the bottom of Guy's backpack and my lap. I'd have three shopping bags in each hand, the thin plastic digging in so hard the tips of my fingers turned painfully purple. I had to lift them as we banked round corners so they didn't split against the high kerb. So much for 'safety first'. Holding on was out of the question.

Balancing this load was beyond even our skill – and my hand-muscle strength – so the warehouse manager, who eventually sidled up to us after we'd been there for an hour and it had become clear we weren't going to go away until we'd bought something, offered to deliver our goods to us in a van the next day.

It took four exhausting trips in the dinghy to shift everything from the dockside to the yacht. In the blistering midday sun, it was hellish work. Offloading from the truck on to the dock, from the dock to the dinghy, from the dinghy to the side of the yacht, from there down the companionway steps and finally into cupboards took a good two hours. By the time I'd finished, the small sliding cupboards that ran most of the width of the galley were filled with cans stacked three deep and two high, arranged in order of content and with labels pointing outwards, *Sleeping With the Enemy*-style. Guy lifted the floorboards to pack wine into the bilges underneath. He nestled his three bottles of whisky in the shelf he used as a wardrobe. He wrestled eleven cases of Skol into the cupboard next to the toilet.

'Better be careful – we might be listing to one side with all that booze stacked in there,' I joked. He laughed and popped one of the beers.

It was a significant moment for me. I'd been starting to wonder if we would ever manage to leave Langkawi or if we, too, would end up finding the lure of the easy – or easier – life here too strong.

Guy had said to me, one afternoon as he came into Ana's shop to survey the sewing project, 'If it were just me, I'd stay in Langkawi for six months and work on the boat.' I turned away quickly to hide the disappointment on my face. *Am I forcing him into making a trip he doesn't want to go on?* I wondered, confused. After all, he'd invited me out here to sail to Indonesia and I still wanted to go. Sure, Langkawi had its plus points – we had rented a cheap motorbike, so it was easy to get around; I had friends in Ana, Nasreen and Zainab; we had a social life with the old soaks – but that wasn't the reason I'd come back out to Asia. I'd returned because I wanted more travel, more adventure.

And I wanted more romance, too. Things between Guy and me were OK – they were relaxed and easy-going, most of the time, and we worked well together as a team – but our relationship, if that's what it even was – hadn't progressed much beyond how it had been when we'd spent a few days together in Thailand a year earlier. When I spoke to my sister over Skype in early February, two months after I'd arrived in Langkawi, and she asked again how things were going and if Guy and I were 'in a relationship', I couldn't think how to answer.

'What do you mean, you don't know?' Sarah said. 'You must know.'

I sighed. 'It's complicated.'

'Well, haven't you talked about it?'

There was a pause on the line longer than the standard international connection delay. 'Not really.'

'Perhaps you better had, then.'

Valentine's Day came and Sofia, a Scandinavian woman who ran a sail-making business in a vast loft near the dinghy dock, proudly sported a new vest top her husband had bought her as a gift.

Seeing it, Guy asked, 'Do you, er, want to do anything for Valentine's?' He didn't meet my eye. *So maybe he does think we're a couple, if he's asking about Valentine's Day*, I thought. Going out for a lovey-dovey meal didn't seem right – I'd hated the tackiness of Valentine's Day my whole life.

Romance, to me, was not about flowers, chocolates and overpriced set menus on one day of the year. I placed more value in a partner being, well, my partner, my equal. I'm not interested in expensive gifts or lavish displays of affection.

Guy didn't order a bunch of flowers for me for Valentine's Day (as it was, the only flowers on the island were the paper roses given out with hard-boiled eggs to celebrate Malaysian customs), nor did he take me out for a three-course set menu. Instead, he gave me the best present I could have asked for – if I ever asked for Valentine's gifts.

'How about we set sail and go on a trip?'

6

Flight or fight

Floating beneath me, a couple of metres down, was the ugliest fish I had ever seen. The restaurants in Langkawi often featured it on their menus and when you order *ikan* in Malaysia it tends to come whole, so I knew what kind of fish it was swimming beneath me – a grouper. This one was a monster. I wasn't sure if it was the magnifying-glass effect of the water, but it looked huge, easily the size of a small child or, more appropriately, given its rotund proportions, a piscine Buddha. Its down-turned mouth and heavy eyes gave it a mournful expression as it lumbered back and forth over the coral, inappropriately small fins only allowing its lolloping fat body to wobble slowly and inelegantly from side to side.

We had stopped, half a day into our journey, at Pulau Payar, a marine park made up of four small islands, to snorkel. When Guy had suggested we set sail, he hadn't, it turned out, meant we were heading off on The Big Trip to Indonesia. Rather, we were going 90 miles down the western Malay coast to the island of Penang to get the anchor chain re-galvanised. So much for romance.

Nevertheless, I was excited as we stopped at Pulau Payar – at least we were finally sailing somewhere – and I was about to go snorkeling for the first time since I'd done my scuba certificate in Italy in the summer. I leaned over the bow to catch hold of a mooring buoy and tied the yacht fast. We climbed into the dinghy, masks and fins in hand, and drove over to the beach, keeping a careful lookout for surfacing swimmers, and hauled the boat up the sand. Guy led the way as we waded back into the water again, fixing our cheekbone-pinching scuba masks to our faces.

This was no Mabul, an island the other side of Malaysia where I'd learned to love snorkelling for the way it opened up to me the fascinating and beautiful underwater world. There the water was so clear I could see for tens of metres, and the coral gardens and wildlife – turtles, clownfish, cuttlefish, schools of fusiliers and needlefish, cowries and nudibranchs – were incredible. Here, life under the sea might have been just as interesting but I couldn't tell because the water was murky and I could only see a couple of metres ahead. It was miles better than the water in Bass Harbour in Langkawi, which was so thick and dirty I would never have voluntarily got into it, but the overall effect was of swimming through a grainy old black-and-white movie, the particles in the water disturbing the light, draining the colour from fish and coral.

Not being able to see very far ahead also made me feel slightly claustrophobic but I could make out Guy in my peripheral vision to my right. He swam at a quicker pace than me, straight on, not stopping to look at this or that as he went. *He's dived in some of the most amazing places in the world*, I thought. *He must be really bored in here. I'm not that fussed, either.*

Just as I was finishing this thought, something large loomed out of the murk ahead of us. A pointy nose came first, followed by two beady black eyes and a snaking body. My heart leapt – it was a shark.

Guy was completely calm and I wasn't even sure he'd noticed it but I panicked and had the same automatic reaction I experience when I suddenly come across a dog – I put someone else between me and the potentially ravenous creature so it eats them first. Not very heroic, I know, and in no way fair, but in these situations I lose control of my reactions, as adrenaline takes over from rational thought. I reached out a hand to the right, grabbed a fistful of tricep and hauled myself, splashing, over Guy's back and on to the other side of him, further away from the shark. I wasn't exactly following the textbook guidance on how to behave when you spot predatory marine creatures but I didn't care. I just needed some kind of barrier – even if it was a soft, chewy human one.

Luckily my splashing about in the manner of a tasty treat didn't faze the shark – maybe it had just eaten a couple of paddling Asian children – and I felt calmer and braver in my new location and even a little bit curious. I watched it as it turned its nose from us and slowly eased away into the cloudy depths. Before it faded out, I got a chance to estimate its size – probably about the same length as me, but at home in the water, a stronger swimmer, able to breathe without aid – and by far the cooler customer.

Regularly, every twenty minutes, it felt like we were inside a washing machine. Chunky ro-ro ferries plied their trade from Penang island to Butterworth on the mainland from dawn until after dusk every day of the week. They were bulky, ungainly vessels, block-painted in garish colours and carrying such heavy loads that they displaced an awful lot of water every time they moved. Following the natural laws of physics, all that water had to go somewhere – and it chose to force its way through the Tanjong City Marina, where *Incognito* was berthed, creating an experience that was a cross between a spin cycle and a rollercoaster three times an hour. As the wash waves hit the side of the boat,

Incognito tipped right over and strained at her mooring lines to the extent of their stretch, then rocketed back upright and over the other way, momentum carrying her through like a weeble until she snapped on her ropes again and was thrown back in the opposite direction, the movements growing bigger and bigger until we worried she was going to break free and capsize. Then she would gradually quieten down for fifteen minutes of blissful rest until the whole cycle started again. Other cruisers asked us to slightly reposition the boat so our masts were staggered and couldn't whiplash into each other. I heard that a few months later the entire marina broke apart and is now closed.

The discomfort we felt in the marina was worth it to be somewhere as fascinating as George Town, the capital of Penang island. It's an old colonial city, full of narrow little alleyways that end abruptly, truncated by old temples. As we explored on foot we found that, like many Malaysian cities, it had a little India-town, close to the marina, with cobbled streets and shop after shop selling saris, strings of silk flowers and Bollywood videos. Cellophaned boxes of gelatinous sweets were piled on to tables outside shop fronts painted golden yellow. A few steps further on and we were on to Beach Street (there was no beach), a wide road lined with colonial buildings housing a pick-and-mix of businesses. There were modern travel agencies and air-conditioned banks between backpacker hostels and 7-Elevens. But it was the crumbling merchant shops that looked like they hadn't changed in a hundred years that fascinated me the most.

I popped into an old-fashioned perfumier, intrigued. The whole of the interior was made from panels of dark wood. A wooden counter lined each side of the small room, like a pub bar, and behind these were tiny pigeonholes that hadn't been revarnished for decades. Little bottles of perfume sat in an orderly fashion in each one, all with a hand-written label. The shop was busy with customers, Malay women in headscarves pushing past middle-aged Chinese men in short-sleeved blue shirts and light-brown slacks, ringgit clutched in their fists and raised in the air. Hassled-looking men behind the counters took shouted orders and sure hands reached into pigeonholes to retrieve the vials. From the confidence in their movements it was clear they knew exactly where each of the hundreds of perfumes was housed. I can't remember what clothes they wore but my imagination tells me they had on high-waisted black trousers, sharply starched shirts, and waistcoats, like Victorian shopkeepers from London. I doubt it, but that was the atmosphere of the shop. I wondered what elixirs these must be to draw such a crowd. Frankincense? Myrrh? I peered closer at some of the labels glued to the pigeonholes. Was that ... Calvin Klein Eternity? And Hugo Boss?

Guy and I went into the city museum one rainy afternoon – most afternoons were rainy that February in George Town and oh, how it rained! – to learn about the island's past. The museum was split into three sections, giving equal space to the three different cultures that made up the population: Malaysian, Chinese and Indian. As we walked through the quiet corridors, I stopped by a glass case in the Chinese section. Two red cloth baby's bootees inside caught my eye. (I love babies' shoes – anything miniature, really. It's something about the shrunken-down proportions.) I started to read the card next to the shoes and stopped, shocked. I looked at the bootees again – these weren't for babies; they had been worn by fully grown Chinese women. I knew about foot-binding, of course, but I had a vague understanding that it involved curling the toes under, to create a slightly shorter, Ugly-Sister-determined-to-get-into-that-glass-slipper kind of effect. This was nothing like that – these shoes were only 3 inches long at the most. It was incredible.

That is the charm of Penang – it is not only where East meets West, it is also where the old comes right up against the new. You could be examining a relic from a millennia-old misogynistic practice one minute and the next you could be heading off on a 12-hour unlimited drinking and gambling offshore cruise, or wandering through the charmingly crumbling new artists' district, eating at Pizza Hut in a dizzyingly tall 65-storey shopping mall or taking a dip in an infinity pool at one of the 5-star hotels nestled in the hills on the outskirts of the city. Not that we went to those fancy kinds of places, of course, but we had fun drinking with backpackers in the one pub we found, eating curries, watching knock-off *Twin Peaks* DVDs in the bowels of the boat when the rain got too much and taking hour-long bus rides to a suburban Tesco to stock up on cheese graters and table water biscuits and to experience a little nibble of home.

The artists' quarter was my favourite part of the city.

'This is all new,' Guy said as we wandered the streets one day. 'It wasn't here last time I was in Penang.'

By new, of course, he meant old – tall, romantic colonial buildings with balustrades and shutters that looked like the offspring of King George III (after whom the city was named) and a Chinese architect, all Classical lines with touches of the Orient in the upward turn of a corner or ornate carving of a screen. Some of the gently peeling buildings had been turned into backpacker B&Bs and as we strolled along the streets and ducked down alleyways we read chalk boards advertising painting exhibitions at galleries and live music. White women sitting out on balconies wore ethnic clothes in shades of purple and mustard and those particular knitted headscarves popular with long-term travellers. The atmosphere was of a destination in the making, as if a little community of travellers had settled in George Town and opened small businesses to cater for themselves – an organic coffee shop here; a vegan café there – and so more travellers had flitted in, drawn to the flame of something new and Western provided in an 'authentic' historic and foreign setting. Like Koh Phi Phi or Koh Samui in Thailand, or Ubud in Bali, I had no doubt it would become 'the' place for travellers in the near future. Where the hippies lead, commercial investment usually follows.

We still had the question of The Big Trip to Indonesia hanging over us. I'd been away three months by now and the return portion of my plane ticket was about to expire. A trip to Indonesia would be at least three months long and, after the provisioning trip to the Langkawi warehouse, I was feeling more confident that it would happen. Sailors had to buy a special licence to cruise Indonesian waters, which lasted three months and could be extended by a further three. So it seemed like a good idea for me to defer my flight back to the UK by at least another quarter of a year. It didn't cost much to do, compared to the price of the ticket, so my theory was that I could keep pushing it back. We went in search of the Air Asia shop.

The air-conditioning was up high inside. It had rained the afternoon and evening before, as it had for the past few days, turning the dusty streets of George Town pewter. The morning had been cloudy but the sun was strong enough – when it found its way through the clouds – to steam-dry the puddles in minutes, forcing the humidity up incredibly high within a couple of hours of dawn. As Guy and I stepped into the Air Asia agent's shop, the sweat that had beaded on our foreheads and the backs of our necks chilled quickly, hardening nipples and making our T-shirts feel like we'd mistaken a fridge for a wardrobe.

The inside of the shop, with its bright fluorescent lighting, uniformly sized and dazzling white floor tiles and plastic bucket chairs bolted to the floor, was a shock after the olde worlde street scene outside. Its bland design meant we could have been anywhere. I felt as though I'd been snapped back into 2012 from some dreamy other reality, a place where jobs and money didn't exist.

In the corner at the front a little machine dispensed tickets to waiting customers, as if they were queuing at the supermarket deli to pick up half a pound of luncheon meat and a good-sized wedge of Brie. I nestled a small square of shiny paper in my palm and sat in a chair to wait. Guy stood by the door, his back resting against the window. The other customers were all Malay couples, neat and tidy in smart trousers and *baju kurung*, and I felt self-conscious with my tanned skin, my yellow hair and messy, washed-in-a-bucket clothes. After ten minutes my number flashed red on a dot matrix board. I walked to the counter and explained I wanted to put my flight back three months.

'Not possible,' said the man in a short-sleeved shirt and tie, after consulting his computer.

'What do you mean, not possible? I understand there'll be an extra fee to pay but that's fine.'

'Not possible fly to London.' He folded his hands on his desk.

I frowned. 'Well, what about four months?'

He shook his head.

'Two?'

'Possible two months fly to London. Not possible three or four. Or five,' he added, heading me off at the pass.

I started to feel hot, despite the arctic aircon, frustrated by the language barrier. I wished I knew more Behasa, beyond my few basic nouns and greetings. I looked around for Guy, to see if he could help, but he'd left. I turned back to the man in frustration.

'Air Asia X not fly London after two month,' the man said, slowly, patiently.

His meaning slowly dawned on me. 'You mean they have stopped flying to London altogether? Stopped this route?' He nodded. 'But what about my ticket? Are you telling me I will lose it?'

'Not lose. Can fly earlier?'

'No, can't fly earlier. Fly four months, six months, one year!' I put my hand to my forehead in panic. Losing the ticket meant losing the equivalent of a whole month's worth of living money. It was a massive blow.

It was crunch time. This was forcing my hand quite considerably. I had two options: I had to make up my mind whether to cut my losses, use the ticket and fly home in a couple of weeks and try to work out what to do with my life. Or I bit the bullet, committed myself to *Incognito* and Guy and stayed for the longer term. I had only the remaining days in Penang to decide.

I backed away from the counter, without thanking the man for his non-help. Outside, Guy was drinking from a can of pop.

'It was too cold in there for me,' he said, taking a swig. He noticed my expression. 'What's up?'

I've always been a worrier when it comes to money. Living here without a job felt fun and relaxed because I knew I could survive on my small income if I budgeted well. So far it had been fine, even though I was pretty much living hand to mouth. In the past, if a sudden unexpected expense came up, my first reaction had always been to consider the financial aspect first. When you don't have a lot, preserving the little you do have becomes paramount.

As someone else on a restricted budget – and income – I knew Guy would understand. But it dawned on me as I told him what had happened that it wasn't such a big deal as I'd originally thought. OK, so I'd lost a return ticket home. But I didn't even know when I was going to go home – or even if I was going to go back at all. Maybe we would sail off to Indo and then Papua New Guinea … then Australia, New Zealand. Maybe things would work out between us and we'd just keep going, for years and years, like other cruisers I'd met. Perhaps we'd land some work offering day trips on *Incognito* to tourists, or maybe we'd settle somewhere, we'd stumble on the perfect place Guy had been searching for all these years and set up our own business. Money might not be an issue, then. And going 'home' might be something I only did every few years, to touch base and catch up. I remembered an epiphany I'd had a year earlier, when I'd had a kind of vision of myself in the future, living in the Caribbean, working with boats, enjoying a relaxed pace of life. Possibly losing that ticket was Fate stepping in and loosening one of my ties with the UK.

'It doesn't matter,' I smiled at Guy, realising that staying longer meant committing to him and our 'relationship', in a way. 'I can always buy another one – if I need to.'

7

Déjà vu

It was like we'd never left. We'd been back in Langkawi for two weeks, anchored just metres from where we'd been before, back of the pack, barnacles already clustering along the links of our newly galvanised anchor chain.

I was working with Ana, Zainab and Nasreen again, even though the waterproof covers had been finished and fitted to *Incognito* weeks ago. Guy had suddenly found other things that urgently needed making – covers for the dinghy and for the water and fuel cans to stop them degrading in the sun, a water catcher, a wind scoop. After chatting to other sailors in Penang he'd decided to try to build a hoist for the dinghy, to hold it clear out of the water off the back of the boat when it wasn't in use. His first design hadn't been quite strong enough and he was working on engineering a solution to shore up the A-frame that held the solar panels and dive tanks so that it could bear the weight of the dinghy and outboard engine as well. It was likely to take some time.

We were eating our way through our Indonesia food stocks, too. A couple of Kilner jars that we'd filled with half-decent Cheddar and preserving oil – a trick I'd learned for keeping cheese almost fresh when you haven't got a fridge or freezer – were already empty. Weevils had started crawling through the pasta packets and we had to lay them on the deck in the sun to kill the insects, then skim their floating bodies off the top of the water while the pasta was cooking. Guy checked the water tanks and realised the paint he'd applied just before I'd arrived was coming off and polluting our water supply. We spent a horrendous day crouched on the floor of the saloon, bent double to reach down into the water tanks located under the sofas, scrubbing away at the paint and trying not to inhale poisonous solvent fumes. A couple of days later, we were re-painting the tanks and crossing our fingers that the paint would stick this time. Then Guy noticed a problem with the rigging that held up the mast.

'We can't possibly go to Indonesia while it's in that state,' he said. 'The mast could fall down.'

I sighed. He was right – it could, and it would be dangerous if it did, and we might end up stuck, drifting in a place where there were no riggers to fix it, nor even any local workmen to do a patch-up job.

'It makes sense to get it fixed here in Langkawi, where we've got all these great resources,' he added.

He's doing the sensible thing, I tried to convince myself. *He's just making sure we're absolutely prepared for our trip.* But as the list of boat jobs grew and grew, no matter how many items we crossed off, I wondered if he didn't want to sail through Indonesia at all, or if it had been a half-dream that he didn't plan on making reality. There are two types of dreamers in this world: those who are captivated by an idea and do everything in their power to grab it from the ether and make it happen; and those for whom the dream itself is enough. I definitely fall into the first camp, and I'd thought Guy did, too. Now I questioned that – was this laid-back, so-cool-that-little-fazes-him guy actually the second kind? I couldn't help thinking back to his earlier remark, about how he'd be quite happy to stay in Langkawi for six months working on the boat if it were just him here.

It wasn't just him, though – I was here, too. And, interesting though it was living in another country and discovering a very different culture, month after month after month of sitting on anchor in filthy water, sanding and painting and drilling and scrubbing and patching and packing wasn't what I thought we'd be doing. And it wasn't what I wanted to be doing. I missed the adventures I'd had on *Gillaroo*, when we'd sailed thousands of miles in a matter of months, explored deserted islands, discovered beautiful beaches, met interesting local people, crossed an ocean, listened to dolphins exhale a breath in the dead of night. I missed moving.

There was another issue – we were running out of time. Not our time but the time of year – the favourable north-east monsoon season that we were currently in was soon to come to an end. Langkawi is to the west of peninsular Malaysia, which meant we were in the lee of the mainland and protected from the north-east monsoon storms and heavy rain. When the monsoon shortly switched direction by 180 degrees we would be right in the path of the fierce weather, and on a lee shore – a dangerous position if strong wind and waves make your anchor come free because you can be blown on to the land and shipwrecked. We were a fair way from the beach but instead there were plenty of other boats we could hit in a situation like that – and we'd already dragged anchor once and spent a horrible night trying to rescue ourselves. We really needed to be on the move – *I* needed to be on the move – and I muttered to myself every time I started a new task on the never-ending to-do list.

I'd like to think Guy sensed my annoyance – although it was more likely concerns about the weather and the possible damage it could cause to the boat that drove him – because he suddenly announced that we were setting off. But again, our destination wasn't Indonesia; it was to be Johor Bahru, a town on the southern tip of Malaysia, next to Singapore, where I'd spent a few weeks the previous year. We topped up with water, fuel and food, handed the motorbike back into the rental shop and set sail. Just like that, jobs' list on ice.

I say sail, but there was no wind, so really we were going to have to motor the whole way down the Straits of Malacca. I'd done this trip once before but in the opposite direction, and we'd sailed most of the way, staying a long way offshore and not stopping once between JB and Langkawi. But that was on a bigger boat, one that went faster and had a crew of four on board, which meant it was easy to rotate shifts so everyone got plenty of rest. The difference with *Incognito* was that she was smaller, heavier and slower and, as there were just the two of us, we'd need to stop at night to sleep. Guy had passed along the Straits a few times with a crew of two and had always used the stopping method, staying much closer to the mainland.

'There aren't so many big ships to worry about if we take my route,' he said, 'and there are small islands dotted along the coast that we can shelter behind at night. They're quite far apart, though, so we'll have to set off at first light, or even before that, push on for eleven, twelve hours – as much as we can manage – and make sure we reach the next island to anchor long enough before sunset that we can see where we're laying the anchor. OK?'

It sounded reasonable. I was itching to get going again and I kept my fingers crossed for some wind so that we could at least get a bit of sailing in on our week-long journey. I wasn't in the least daunted by the prospect of long days. *I've spent two weeks at sea before, out of sight of land the whole time;*

I've crossed oceans, I thought. *A few 12-hour stints is going to be easy-peasy. Nothing to worry about.*

The bucking motion of the boat was so bad you would have thought we were in the middle of an oceanic storm, when actually we were at anchor in a supposedly sheltered place, behind an island. Tall waves hit *Incognito* side-on, pushing her right over until she snapped back up again, sending cups, cushions and tools flying across the saloon. Guy's whisky bottles clanked glassily on their shelf. To walk forwards from the back cabin I had to hold on to the rim of the galley worktops or I would have skated from side to side on the wooden floor. The noise was incredible. I felt horrendously seasick. We were stuck for the night and it was a nightmare.

It turned out we'd departed Langkawi slightly too late and the monsoon was already on the turn. By day, the weather was calm and still – which meant, frustratingly, no sailing, only noisy motoring, the engine droning on and on, fraying my nerves – but at night great storms rolled in – and with them, huge waves.

These were the sumatras – lines of squalls that brewed up over the Indonesian island of Sumatra and at night rolled down the steep mountains to accelerate across the Malacca Straits towards western Malaysia and Singapore – and we were right in their angry path.

The island we tried to hide behind this particular night, the fourth of the trip, was really small and offered little in the way of shelter. We'd approached it before nightfall, as planned, and the seas were still calm then, but we'd seen dark, towering anvils forming in the air above us and so we'd had to guess which direction the winds would rage from later and how the waves would rebound around the island, and anchor according to our estimates. We'd got it wrong and ended up parallel to the waves, instead of rolling relatively easily over the top of them, and now we were having to deal with the consequence of our mistake – the knock-downs, the crashing, the nausea and the knowledge that we would get no sleep at all.

We were already exhausted. It turned out that long days but stopping at night was far more tiring than constant motion and two or three shorter naps through a 24-hour period. We were up at 5am, motoring non-stop, both of us on deck on the lookout for small fishing boats and the huge nets they cast across our path which, if we hit them, would wrap around our propeller in an instant and stop us dead. The only way to fix a problem like that was for Guy to don full scuba gear and dive, in this murky water, under the boat, knife in hand. It happened more than once. The stress of choosing a place to anchor in less-than-ideal conditions and worrying about the strength of that night's impending storm took its toll on our rest periods as well.

The rocking and the banging woke me about 11pm. I staggered, wide-legged for balance, holding on to every surface I could find, into the chaotic saloon. Guy was in the forepeak, rummaging through the locker, pulling out coils of long rope. Inches above his head, on the deck, a sickening clunk sounded every time the boat strained in the movement of the waves and the anchor chain tried to stretch beyond its full extent. I felt groggy and half asleep still.

'What are you doing?' I asked him, rubbing crust from the corner of one eye.

He raised his voice over the noise in the cabin. 'We can't stay like this. It's going to be impossible to sleep. I want to try that trick we were talking about with the second anchor and the winch.'

I knew what he was talking about – it was a technique we'd both read about and had idly discussed one day while we were on anchor in a sea disturbed by little more than ripples. It was adapted from a method used by boats in the Caribbean to make them extra secure in high winds. A boat on anchor will naturally lie pointing into the wind and will ride up and down over the waves like a fat pony taking part in a mini gymkhana. If the current is stronger than the wind, the boat will lie parallel to the current instead. This storm was blowing a hoolie but for some reason – perhaps a ripping current from the island – we were side-on to the waves, creating this puke-inducing rocking motion.

The theory was to drop a second anchor off to the side of the yacht and haul in the free end of the line on a winch, turning the boat to face the waves for a more comfortable ride. All Guy had to do was stick the kedge anchor in the dingy, motor out 10 or 20 metres, drop it, shout to me to crank away on the winch handle, mosey on back to the yacht, hop aboard and we'd sleep soundly in our bunks til the put-a-put-tut of fishing boats woke us just before dawn. Sounds easy, right? I've just explained it to you in a couple of sentences. When we had been chatting about it, relaxing over a lukewarm can of Skol, it sounded like child's play. Advanced anchoring technique, my arse.

Except in practice it was pitch black outside and chucking it down. The wind whipped away our words so communicating was hard. In addition, we'd proudly used the newly strengthened A-frame to lift the detached outboard engine from the back of the dinghy so we could tow the dinghy down the Straits without having to worry about it flipping and the outboard being ruined. As the engine weighed 50kg and the two of us manoeuvring it even in calm conditions always led to dints in both the yacht's paint and our egos, there was no way we were going to be able to get it back on the dinghy tonight.

Guy decided he'd get into the engineless dinghy and let the wind push it out, effectively drifting, paying out the anchor rope as he went. We tied a second line between the yacht and the dinghy for safety.

I watched nervously as he disappeared off into the black. Within seconds I couldn't see him any more; the only way I knew he was still attached to the yacht was by the vibrations on the anchor rope tied to the thick stainless-steel posts at the back of the boat. I shivered in the cold – the rain had soaked through my vest and knickers in seconds. The banshee howl of the wind, that particular eerie screech it makes when it shoots round masts and rigging, drowned out all other sounds. I strained my ears to try to hear Guy. Fragments of words forced their way through the dark gusts to me.

'What?' I screamed at full lung capacity, hoping he could hear.

Nothing came back. Guy was trying to talk into the wind, and his words were curving back past him, lost to the night.

I tried again. 'I can't hear you!'

Minutes passed and I clung to the rail at the back corner of the boat, peering out, one hand shielding my eyes from the rain. The deck light we'd turned on did nothing to illuminate the scene – mainly it just destroyed my night vision every time I glanced forwards.

'– not enough ... need more ... safety line.' His words came out of the gloom just before he did. He was squatting wide-legged in the dinghy, hauling himself back along the line towards the yacht.

'You want me to tie the safety line to the anchor rope?'

'Yeah.' He pulled himself along a bit closer. 'It's not working. I need more length.'

Kneeling, I pulled in the slack of the safety rope he'd untied from the dinghy's strong point. I untied the anchor rope to join the two lines together and felt it start to slip through my grasp – the force of the wind pushing the heavy dingy with Guy and the anchor in it was too much for me to handle. Shit. In an instant, I looped the rope around the steel rail and pulled with all my might.

'I can't hold you,' I shouted. 'The wind's too strong.'

'Fuck!' I could just about hear his exclamation over the clamour. 'OK. I'm coming closer in.'

I pulled on the line until the muscles of my arms, shoulders and neck burned and my quads bulged out of my thighs, and braced while Guy hauled himself back to the yacht. The rope sagged as he reached the boat and grabbed hold of the toe rail, still standing in the dinghy.

'Do it quick!' He still had to almost shout, despite being only half a metre away. I fumbled, my tired and burnt hands struggling to remember the right kind of knot. As soon as I had pulled it tight and tied the new end to the rail, he was flying out into the night again, but this time with no second line to keep him safe.

About a year earlier, when I was meandering happily through tranquil Thai seas, I'd received a sad email containing news about a friend. This friend, Simon, was a gregarious man in his sixties who was happily, giddily, newly wed to a thirty-something Thai woman, Nan. I'd met them sailing in Borneo. After we parted they sailed back to his native Australia. They had peacefully anchored for a rest in a calm bay, the email from a mutual friend explained, but when they went to start the yacht's engine to carry on, it was dead. Simon tried everything he could but had no joy, so he decided to lash the dinghy along the side of the yacht and use the smaller boat's outboard engine to potter both boats out of the lee of the land for half a mile or so until they picked up some sailing wind.

Simon was in the dinghy, without a lifejacket – because no one wears a lifejacket when they are cruising in calm conditions – and Nan was on the yacht. A squall blew up, really fast, and Simon was pitched out of the dinghy and into the water. Nan threw him a line and he managed to claw on to it but she was a small woman and he was a heavy man and she couldn't haul him on board. He clung on for as long as he could to that rope while the once-friendly waters weltered around him but eventually his strength gave out and he let go. They never found his body.

This story came back to me as I waited, helplessly, to hear from Guy out there in the dark, every muscle in my body gripping my bones.

They say that in moments of extreme stress your senses become heightened. That was the only way I could have heard a command from Guy to give him more length on the rope. I looked at it. There was an extra foot free beyond the knot I'd tied but that was it. I tested the part that led out to where Guy was: it was bar-tight. I was already exhausted from my earlier exertions and from crouching, tense, in the rain for hours. I wasn't confident that, if I untied the knot, the rope – and with it, the dinghy and Guy – wouldn't whip out of my control and slip away, just as Simon had. The safety line was gone and there was no way Guy would be able to paddle the dinghy back to the yacht against this wind and waves.

'I can't!' I screamed. 'There's not enough. I'll lose you!' I shouted the words over and over, not sure exactly where in the blackness he was. 'I'm not strong enough.'

Slowly, six-inch by six-inch along the line, all last reserves of energy spent, he made it back to the boat and crawled up the back steps and on to the deck.

Silently, feeling as though I'd let him down and cursing myself for my physical weakness, I took the anchor and ropes as he passed them to me. I felt like a complete failure – what should have been a simple procedure had turned into a disaster. As I climbed down into the relative calm of the cabin – it was still pitching wildly but at least it was dry and warm˙– numbness washed over me from mental, physical and emotional exhaustion. I looked at the clock as I took the ropes below – it was 4.30am. We'd been fighting against the weather for more than five hours. Neither of us spoke as we went to lie down, knowing that we'd get no rest in the remaining hour before we had to be up for another merciless 12-hour journey.

The yellow dawn brought calm to bleach away the horrors of the night. Looking at the rising sun and quieting seas, it seemed melodramatic to claim that I had probably saved Guy's life by not untying that rope. But I think now that it's a fair point to make. As well as being a salutary lesson in the foolhardiness of trying dangerous new tricks for the first time in difficult conditions, the episode also served as a reminder of nature's awesome power. We thought, with a couple of ropes and a clever theory found in a textbook, we could conquer nature, rein it in. The only spirit broken, it turned out, was ours.

8

Confused.com

Tampons. I needed tampons. They aren't easy to find in Malaysia but I had insider's knowledge. So the afternoon after we arrived at Danga Bay Marina in Johor Bahru, the pair of us as battered and frayed as *Incognito*, I set off on foot to stock up.

Danga Bay Marina was our old stomping ground, where Guy and I first met. It's not the most romantic of settings: fairly basic wooden pontoon moorings set beside an ageing old funfair imported from Brunei. The marina used to be free to cruising sailors, so people would stop there for weeks, months – even years – to do major works on their yachts and, like the lazy cruisers in Langkawi, many had been lulled into staying there long term. The appeal of being able to hop off on to land in one step, without going through the rigmarole of lowering a dinghy, strapping on the engine, filling it with the correct ratio of petrol and oil and motoring a quarter of a mile through choppy seas that doused your dry outfit, no matter how expertly you positioned yourself, probably had a lot to do with it. Don't forget – most of our neighbours were in their sixties and seventies. And I doubt they were there for the views of the major trunk road that formed the boundary of the marina.

I had stayed at Danga Bay for a few weeks with *Gillaroo* a year or so earlier and it was nice to be somewhere recognisable. I felt kind of at home here – I knew where I could pick up a bus to take me to a big supermarket on the outskirts of Johor Bahru; I even knew how much the fare would be. I could remember how to get myself across the causeway to Singapore if I wanted a taste of city life, and I also recalled where I could buy a pizza. These might not be the same things that make you, dear reader, feel most at home somewhere, but when you're a nomad the tiniest bit of familiarity or routine can be a great comfort when you're feeling like you need to lick your wounds. And comfort was what I needed after that horrendous week-long ordeal coming down from the north. Comfort – and tampons.

I set off on foot, jumping down on to the wooden pontoon we'd been assigned as our parking spot. I walked down the centre gangway, passing a clapped-out-looking purple boat that was our closest neighbour. Not all of the berths were taken, but I wasn't sure whether that was because business was slow or because the marina hadn't been well maintained and mud had settled on the once-dredged bottom, making the water closest to the edge too shallow to accommodate most yachts' keels.

A steel gate provided security of sorts but the guards who had sat in little wooden watchtowers on my previous visit had gone. I turned left to cross a patch of gravel towards the small complex that held the marina office and the pizza place. A steel staircase curved its way up the nearside of the wooden-clad building, shimmering in the sun like the pearlised spiral interior of a seashell. The building couldn't have been that old but the staircase was already condemned, with yellow-and-black tape.

I followed a winding footpath through the sleeping funfair, which only really got going on Friday and Saturday nights.

The rest of the time there were barely any visitors and the only people I saw as I followed the path were gardeners neatening up the edges of the lawn, trying to keep the oversized, rough blades of grass in some kind of order. I walked on, past the last of the cruiser yachts and through a deserted 'beach bar' – although there was no beach to be seen. At the edge of the zoo I kept an ear out for the resident gibbon's distinctive, squealing, tuning-in-a-radio call but he was silent.

I practically whistled as I walked – it felt so good to be on land and casually popping to a shop under my own steam. I idly touched ornate lampposts as I passed them, and any casual observer could have been forgiven for thinking I was about to burst into song and swing around one, so jaunty was my gait. I pottered onwards, thinking I'd be there any minute.

I passed the edge of the zoo and then a kind of weird kids' outdoor-play-park-come-Alice-in-Wonderland-statue-garden, with a giant concrete clock on the floor. I reminisced as I went: here was the corner where my crewmate Aaron and I had watched locals racing souped-up remote-control cars; there was the patch of broken pavement where I'd seen the biggest cockroach of my life, which had made my skin crawl for hours afterwards every time I thought of it; I was just passing the place where I'd bought a cup of sweetcorn from a street vendor. I walked through a car park, and I walked and I walked and I walked, until I reached the modern hotel on the junction.

I stopped, confused. I was pretty proud of my memory – look at all those things I had remembered just from this walk today. So how could I have mis-remembered the location of a large, brightly coloured shopping mall I had visited every day for three weeks, little more than a year ago? I frowned – was I having an early senior moment? Normally my brain was quite clear. I thought hard, tried to focus. *Come on,* I said to myself, *where was the mall with the chemist's shop in it? Closer to the road or nearer the water?* It was no use – I couldn't clear the confusion from my mind. I was utterly stumped.

It was then that I noticed the rubble around me. It wasn't piled high; there were no obvious signs of demolition. It was as if a giant hand had come out of the sky and plucked up the entire shopping mall in one go, leaving behind a few concrete crumbs of foundation. Gone was the chemist, the beauty salon, the waffle shop. There'd been clothes stores and places to buy luggage and a stall where I'd picked up a pair of knock-off Crocs that had come in handy when I was clambering over rocks in the Andaman Islands. The street-food vendors had gone, too, and the men selling whizzing little light-up toys for kids. Compared to the marina, the mall had been pretty vibrant. It wasn't like it was full of empty units, like Langkawi Plaza, where Ana and her mum worked. And it was reasonably new. There was no real reason to knock it down.

That's Malaysia for you: it has so much money to invest that things get built – fast and cheap – and then just as quickly they get pulled down again to make way for the next big thing. Nothing stands in the way of progress, even fairly successful businesses. Progress though, it seems, stands in the way of tampons. I sighed – I knew I could get some in Singapore but it seemed slightly ridiculous to have to cross a border into another country just to stock up on bathroom essentials.

That shopping complex was more to me than a convenient place to visit the chemist and stock up on clownish but practical rubbery shoes. It was also the place where I first met Azlan.

To be fair, it wasn't me that met him first – it was my *Gillaroo* crewmate Aaron. He'd popped over to one of the cheap food stalls one lunchtime to grab some *ayam goreng* and, as he'd been eating, a middle-aged couple who spoke immaculate English had stepped up to talk to him. They'd offered to show him Johor Bahru and Aaron came back from lunch bursting with excitement. The most interesting thing we'd found to do in Danga Bay until then was service the boat's winches, so I couldn't blame him for being stoked at the chance of getting out and about.

'Do you want to come along?' he'd asked me. I'd agreed.

Azlan and Yasmin were some of the happiest people on the planet. Now in his seventies, Azlan had joined the British Army before Malaya got its independence, signing up as an 18-year-old and finding himself the sole brown-faced recruit and the only Muslim in his shivering barracks in Cumbria. He loved it and he stayed. No one ever showed him any disrespect because he was different, he said. There was no racism. This might have been because he was the British Army featherweight boxing champion or maybe because he was too intent on enjoying himself to notice any nastiness. He served and got into drunken bar brawls all over the world: Hong Kong, Singapore, Malta, Northern Ireland. He guarded the gold stocks at the Bank of England – 'I seen it with my own eyes. Sooo much gold,' – and gave his various girlfriends the runaround before bumping into Yasmin during a spot of home leave and marrying her. It wasn't hard to understand why – she was a tiny, beautiful, graceful woman, even in her late sixties, always smiling and very content with her life. Their four children, each born in different countries, were given British first names and Malaysian second names.

Azlan and Yasmin had kind of adopted Aaron and me during our stay in Johor Bahru. His British Army pension went a long way in Malaysia and they were relatively well off. They bought us lunch, rice and chutney spread out on banana leaves, Azlan declaring with glee how little it cost in sterling – 'Is only £1.70. I can't believe it!' – and whizzed us around town like little dervishes. We met them for lunch that first day and somehow ended up in their car, being driven to their *kampong* house – a village property Azlan had built backing on to the river on land he didn't quite own. He was letting an Indonesian woman stay there. It was a one-storey, breeze-block-and-cement house, painted blue, the last in a row. Azlan let us into the house, proudly showing us everything: the washing machine, the sofa, the rugs. Outside he had built some brick-lined ponds. The murky water inside churned darkly – they were crammed with catfish. He nipped inside the house and emerged with some bundles of newspaper and what looked like a samurai sword.

'Frozen chicken,' he said. 'For the fish. You chop, Aaron.' He waved the sword around and placed the lumps on the remains of a tree trunk. Aaron gamely had a go.

'You want to try, Emma?' Azlan asked me.

'No thanks, Azlan,' I said. 'I'm a vegetarian.'

'O-o-ooh! Vegetarian!' Azlan and Yamsin had said in unison. That 'O-o-ooh!' is such a wonderful Malaysian sound. Everyone will say it to you when you answer their question, as if they need to convey the fact that they have definitely understood you. Even if what you said is not surprising in the slightest, the 'O-o-ooh!' still comes out. 'You already breakfast?' 'Yes, thanks, I already had my breakfast.' 'O-o-ooh! Already breakfast!' It starts low, rises in the middle and drops low again, full of wonderment. 'Where you from?' 'England.' 'O-o-ooh! England!' I think it is the equivalent of the American black woman's 'Mmm-hmm'. If I was eavesdropping on a conversation between two Malays on the bus and I couldn't understand a word they were saying otherwise, I'd still catch that 'O-o-ooh!' and it would make me smile every time.

Now I was back in Danga Bay for the foreseeable future and I was already as bored with the place as I had been before. I dug out Azlan's number and sent him a text.

'Hi Azlan. It's Emma from *Gillaroo*. You remember me? I am back in JB, on another boat in Danga Bay Marina.'

He rang immediately.

'Emma! Of course I remember you! You get my letter, with joke about the Queen?'

When we'd met before, we'd swapped addresses – actual addresses, since as a septuagenarian he had little interest in email, although he was better at text messaging than my mother (she once sent me a text written entirely in capitals with no spaces in between HAPPYBIRTHDAYEMMALOVEMUMANDDAD) – and he'd posted my parents in England a joke about the Queen and tea cut from a newspaper. It was nice to receive it, if a little bewildering. Now, I thanked him.

'So, you with same boat, with captain Mr Tyrone? Him I always remember as same name as another soldier in British Army with me.' He chuckled down the line.

'No, Azlan – I'm on a different boat this time. A smaller one.'

'How long you in JB?'

'Don't know.'

'Well, you want me come pick you up, show you around, take you my *kampong* house?'

'That'd be great, if you're not too busy?'

'Never busy, Emma. Retire on British Army pension!'

We arranged to meet the following morning out in the car park and, after I hung up, I went to find Guy to ask if he wanted to come along.

The to-do list was back. We'd only been in the marina for a day and he was already taking advantage of the dock space alongside us to plan jobs he needed to do. He wanted to examine the furler, do some work on the dinghy, have another look at the rigging. I found him on the foredeck, frowning, examining the base of the furler system that rotated to roll away the foresail. He had a tape measure in one hand.

I leaned over the guardrail to talk to him as he crouched over the sail on the dock below. I was used to seeing it furled nicely away around the forestay. Unrolled and taken off the yacht, it looked strange, like a big scrap of fraying material rather than a powerful tool that was capable of harnessing nature.

'I've arranged to meet my friend Azlan tomorrow – you know, the one I met with Aaron when we were here before?' I said. Guy grunted. 'He's going to show me round JB a bit. Do you want to come?'

He replied without looking away from the sail. 'Nah, it's all right. I've got stuff to be getting on with here.' He carried on taking measurements. I waited. He stopped what he was doing briefly to glance at me. 'You don't mind, do you?'

I was slightly surprised, since I thought as a traveller he'd be keen to get the inside scoop on a new town, but I supposed he had been to JB before and maybe he'd got to the point where one large Asian town was pretty much the same as another. And I found that actually I really didn't mind that he didn't want to come.

I needed a break – from both the boat and from Guy. It's always difficult spending 24/7 with someone, and it's particularly trying when you are trapped in a small space and you are facing conditions that alternate between being dangerous and boring. I was starting to feel like I hadn't had any fun for quite some time. I'd come away to travel and explore and experience new things and I hadn't been doing any of that. For weeks, all I'd seen was the inside of *Incognito*. Yes, we'd just done a 600-mile trip, but that had meant an entire week enduring the monotony of the Malacca Straits. It was the equivalent of driving along the A1 for twelve hours a day, seven days in a row – straight, samey and even less interesting than the M1. There were no sights to speak of – water brown enough to tempt Augustus Gloop as we passed Port Klang was the only remarkable thing I'd seen.

I know I sound a bit like a spoiled brat (call me Veruca Salt if you want to). On the surface everything should have been rosy. I'd been given this golden ticket: no need for a job, exotic travel, a free life on board a yacht, living with my 'dream' man. Surfaces often reflect things back at the viewer, though, and stop you from seeing underneath to the true workings that hold everything together. Did I really have exotic travel? I'd been away for four months and I'd barely been anywhere – and had certainly not seen a beautiful beach or clear water at all. It might seem like I had liberty but actually as a member of crew on a yacht you don't have that much freedom. Boats are demanding mistresses – of your time, energy, resources – and the captain always has the final word. His decision is absolute. I've never met a captain yet who understands the notion of consensus.

You could argue that I had no job to bring stress and tie me down all day, no mortgage to worry about (it was covered by the tenants renting my London flat), hardly any bills to pay. Life is cheap in Malaysia, for sure, and Guy never asked me to contribute to any of the boat's costs, despite all of the work he was doing. I had about £400 a month coming in – imagine being able to live off less than £5,000 a year! – which was 2,000 Malaysian ringgit. That was a small fortune in Malaysia, but it still seemed to have vanished come the thirtieth or thirty-first of the month. We had diesel, petrol, cooking gas and drinking water to buy, laundry to pay for and fresh food to get every couple of days. Some bills still needed paying back home – a gas-safety certificate or a new blind for a tenant's window – and one £40 or £60 expense like that ate into my income considerably.

Even being volunteer crew is still a job – you can't just swan off to the gym or the coffee shop when you feel like it (they don't tend to have those at sea, anyway). Number-one priority is always the boat – and, as I say, the captain is boss.

I'm not saying it wasn't wonderful to not have to set an alarm clock and trudge through a morning routine of shower-breakfast-dress-read newspapers-fight crowds-get-squashed-on-Tube. Waking naturally to the sun every morning, and the steadily increasing sounds of the city as it came to life, was a much nicer way to emerge from my slumber than to be jolted from my dreams by a tacky, tinny tune from my iPhone.

And yet – something was missing. I didn't feel as free as I thought I would. I was no longer the wandering sea gypsy that I had been for the six months that I spent on *Gillaroo*, travelling from country to country, island to tropical island and bay to secluded, beautiful, postcard-perfect bay. Perhaps, if Guy and I ever got our act together and made it into the far reaches of Indonesia, I could become that person again. The chances of that happening were seeming increasingly slim and not just because of the magically growing list of boat 'jobs'. I was beginning to put up a barrier to this trip, too. And it was a barrier I really hadn't expected: I missed work.

God, how I missed using my brain. In my old life, in a newspaper office, I was thinking, planning, dissecting, organising, creating, and managing twelve hours a day. My mind would start whirring with the adrenaline buzz of the first headlines as I rolled out of bed at 6.30am. All day, every day, I was surrounded by information. Press releases, news wires, reports from agencies, copy from reporters, articles in other newspapers, texts, tweets, emails, TV news' digests. I read tens of thousands of words a day and I learned endless facts about things I often couldn't remember by the time I got home, so overloaded had my brain become. My mind was still pelting along at 7, 8, 9pm, in the office. I only dropped down a few gears once I got home to my dinner or met a friend for a drink. It was as if my mind was running a marathon every single day.

When I initially left the UK, nearly two years earlier, and found myself on a boat in Borneo, it had taken a few weeks for my brain to relax and then it was almost as if it had emitted a great sigh and switched into another mode – chilled. I really enjoyed not having much mental exercise; I liked being lazy for a change. Instead of complicated, man-made information to process, I only had the natural world to consider – my surroundings, nature, the weather – and how they impacted on my immediate situation. I really was living in the moment. Freed from having to focus on getting the next day's newspaper out, my mind was also able to become more self-analytical and it was almost as if I could step outside myself and observe what I was doing and thinking from a distance. So far, so Zen Buddhist hippy.

My imagination enjoyed its holiday – and a long vacation it had been, lasting twenty months. But all holidays must come to an end and my brain was getting a bit bored with all this lazing around, navel-gazing and not really having to deal with anything urgent. It wanted to be a lean, mean, running machine again. It wanted variety. It needed stimulation and challenge. It demanded work.

I fought it. Oh, how I fought it. *You don't want to work,* I reasoned with myself. *Why on earth would you want to do that? You're in this great position – you can basically be on holiday for the foreseeable future. You're living on a boat – remember how you love sailing? And you're with this hot guy. What's not to like?*

You're right, I answered myself. (Possibly because I had too much time on my hands, my bored imagination was going into overdrive by this point, conjuring up alternative multiple personalities that argued with each other while I sat on the side of the yacht and stared into the murky waters of the Skudai River.) *But think about this: you're bored, you're never going to get to Indonesia. And you're not really 'with' this hot Guy. Face the facts. You're just roommates, really, friends with benefits. There's no deep emotional connection.*

*It's just not happened. So why not cut your losses? Go home –
start again, get back into journalism, feel the buzz of the
newspapers. You've had an amazing time – Christ, it's been
nearly two years – and you've seen some wonderful things,
had some incredible experiences. But it's time to get on with
things, to grow up.*

There was no let-up. *Deep down you're not really one of
these free-living, baggy-pant-wearing, chanting hippy types,
are you? You could never grow your armpit hair, for a start.
And you don't like tie-dye clothes. Incense makes you cough.
Do you really think you could live out the rest of your days
in a straw hut on a beach? You're having a laugh. You know
for certain that you're far too uptight for that. You'd worry
too much about money, about access to a good doctor in an
emergency, about whether you smelled a bit whiffy. You've
had a good time – just accept it as that and move on. Get back
to reality; get back to living and thinking and doing something
important. Get back to normality.*

I don't want normality, my mind squeaked in reply. But
it wasn't the firmest of responses and I increasingly found
my thumbs tapping on the Skyscanner app on my phone,
searching for info on flights to England. I told myself that
I was 'just looking', like hopping on to a dating site even
though you're in a relationship, just for a quick peek at what's
out there, if only to reassure yourself that you're not missing
out on anything, that you've made the right choice, that the
grass isn't always greener.

The problem with that, though, is that all it takes is for one
thing to catch your eye and suddenly everything changes.

9

She wants to be a Paperback Writer

Azlan was waiting for me by his car the next morning, shaded by the overhanging branches of a tecoma cherry tree. I recognised him immediately. Although his hair was greyer and longer than I remembered, forming a wiry halo around his head, his flat, broad Malay nose, neat beard and thick glasses were the same. He wore a short-sleeved cotton shirt, undone at the neck, the type of slacks loved by 70-year-old men the world over, and sandals. We shook hands.

'Where's Yasmin?' I asked, suddenly panicking that she might have died in the eighteen months since I'd seen them last. She had been on serious medication when I met her.

'Yasmin gone,' he said, his expression unreadable.

Shit, I thought. *I've completely put my foot in it. Why didn't you think of this possibility yesterday, Bamford? He didn't mention her on the phone.* 'I–.'

'She gone England. Few weeks. She go see our daughter in Brighton.'

I breathed out, relieved.

'So, where you want to go?' Azlan asked, as I buckled myself in to the Proton's passenger seat. 'You want to go see my *kampong* house?'

'Sure, Azlan.' I smiled at him. 'I'd love to go see your *kampong* house.'

Once again, it was a whistle-stop tour of Johor Bahru.

From the *kampong* house he drove me to their other rental apartment, high up in a damp-stained concrete tower block, from which the last tenant had taken even the light switches. From the rental apartment we went to a café run by a friend for an iced tea in a plastic bag. From the café we drove to a fishing village, a shopping mall, a park, the bus station and an enclave where the original people of Malaysia, the Orang Asli, lived, ghettoised, a bit like the Aborigines in Australia. I watched through the car window as small clusters of children and young adults walked aimlessly across a rough patch of gravel. It was the first time I'd seen anyone who actually looked like the description 'dirt poor' – a coating of dust caked their black hair and their grimed faces, which looked sort of off-kilter, as if either malnutrition or inbreeding (or likely a combination of both) had caused mild facial deformities. Their T-shirts and shorts were worn through and smudged with grey. I felt ashamed to be there, looking at them as if they were exhibits in a zoo, and Azlan quickly turned the car around and back into the bright, neat streets of Johor Bahru with their pristine high kerbs as white as skirting boards.

As we went on our daily outings, he proudly filled me in on the history of the city – how it used to be part of Malaya, which at that time included Singapore; how when he was a boy the stretch of water where the scuttled marina was now wallowing in dingy mud was lined with brilliant ivory beaches; what it was like when the Japanese invaded. We got a taste of 2012 JB when we dropped in on a *Fast and Furious*-style souped-up car show, where young Malays parked their polished and customised wheels inside a giant room to proudly show off their bodyshopping skills. Some had dozens of trophies – also highly polished – displayed next to their cars. In spending just a few days with Azlan, I learned as much about urban Malaysian culture as I had about village life from Ana over those months in Langkawi.

One afternoon he took me to his flat – the one of his three properties that he, Yasmin and their youngest son actually lived in – and we had *limau ais* – pressed fresh lime juice – with his son while admiring the view from the twelfth floor. They didn't have aircon so Azlan took off his shirt, stripping down to his sensible old man's white vest, and I saw his upper arms were covered in huge scars.

'What happened?' I asked, expecting a story about bullet wounds or shrapnel. He liked to regale me with macho tales from his army days: stories about arm wrestling and training and being posted overseas.

'Tattoos,' he said. 'I didn't like them no more.' He shrugged.

'So you cut them off?' My voice rose. 'Yourself?'

'Yeah. They were ugly.' I stared at him. At only 5 foot 5 inches or so, with his halo of hair, laughing eyes, glasses and beard, I couldn't imagine him as a British soldier. But he must have been a brave man to carve the flesh-deep ink stains off his own body, doing one arm and knowing he had a second to go.

Throughout our hours and hours of conversation, Azlan never once asked me about my relationship with Guy – in fact, he mentioned Tyrone, my previous skipper on *Gillaroo*, more times than my current 'captain'. It was a relief, as I didn't really feel like talking through the situation with anyone, let alone a small ex-Army Malaysian grandfather who'd been happily married for fifty years. I was glad he respected me enough to not pry.

They say that if you need to make a difficult decision in your life, you need to get perspective on it. During these simple outings with Azlan, having to do little but laugh at his stories and express wonderment at each place we stopped, my subconscious must have been getting the breathing space it needed to process my thoughts. The pull to return to England, to familiar things, to work, grew stronger, without my even really noticing it, and the draw of Guy, the boat, and this messy, unknown life path got weaker.

There was another element to wanting to go back home: writing. When we'd been in Langkawi, Guy had left me on my own for a couple of days while he went on a visa run to Thailand. Idly browsing the web on my first night on the boat alone, I came across an advert for a short-story competition. The theme was 'journey'. *Ooh*, I thought. *I'm on a journey* (I'm sometimes one for stating the obvious). *I might have a crack at that.* I bashed out a thousand words on a train trip I'd taken in Sri Lanka through the tea plantations, stuck in some waffle and lots of adjectives like 'verdant' and 'vast' (I hadn't heard of 'kill your darlings' back then), checked it for typos and emailed it off. *Hey, I'm a journalist, a professional writer,* I gloated to myself. *It's in the bag.*

Needless to say, it wasn't in the bag and I didn't win. I didn't even get an email acknowledging my entry. But that didn't matter. Because entering that competition brought back to life something that had been lying dormant deep inside me for years – the desire to write. All of a sudden, I couldn't stop ideas and words and characters and settings and phrases and paragraphs and pages and pages and whole, entire chapters from pouring out of me. I scribbled in two notebooks and typed away at my little netbook for hours. I was prolific.

When I first moved to London when I was twenty-three, to work for an internal communications agency, I had an idea for a novel. A comment my boss made about taxis often being booked for one-way journeys to Beachy Head, the notorious cliff-head suicide spot in East Sussex, intrigued me and I churned out a novel with an anti-hero at its centre, a chap so utterly useless at everything that he couldn't even manage to top himself. I had him try to kill himself three times and each attempt ended in hilarious (or so I thought) failure.

Agents I sent the finished manuscript to apparently didn't find suicide a laughing matter. I'd come home from the office to find manila A3 envelopes on the doormat, and my heart sank when I turned them over to see my address written in my handwriting and stamps affixed that I'd paid for with my own money and wasted my saliva on.

'While I like your writing style, I find the mix of subject matter and tone doesn't work for me,' wrote one of the kinder agents. What – suicide and gags? (It worked for Nick Hornby a couple of years later.) Eventually, after five or six rejections, I filed the floppy disk (yes, really) in a drawer, and forgot about being an author. By that point I was working as a news editor for the *Daily Express* and I was reading tens of thousands of words every day, and re-writing thousands of words of other people's copy. All of my creative energy was spent conjuring up intros to agency-filed stories about cats getting stuck down potholes and suburban grandfathers building life-sized replicas of the 4468 Mallard locomotive entirely out of matchsticks.

I wrote so much at work over the next few years that I was in no way interested in putting fingertips to laptop keys when I got home, in much the way that after I finished my English Literature degree I didn't pick up a book for at least three months and it took me a good year of girding my reading loins before I was able to tackle another classic.

And now this little short-story competition had turned on all of the taps plumbed into the left hemisphere of my brain. Every morning, when I woke, I climbed out of *Incognito*'s rear hatch and settled myself on the cockpit cushions under the shade of the bimini and typed on my netbook, hands cramped inwards like claws on the tiny keyboard, until it grew too hot to concentrate any more and I could barely see the screen in the glary mid-morning light. I started to write a novel based on tales that I'd heard from the old-timer cruisers while we were in Langkawi.

Then I switched from the novel to a memoir. Diary propped open on my knees and resting on top of the computer screen, I recounted my adventures on board the yachts *Kingdom*, *Gillaroo* and *Panacea* that had started when I answered a 'crew wanted' ad on the internet and quit my job in London. Reliving those times, all the places I'd been to and the people I'd met was great fun and I looked forward to my writing session each morning.

I wrote in Langkawi, I wrote in Penang, I wrote in Danga Bay. By keeping my head down and writing fast and furiously, I managed to keep the fear demons at bay, the ones who, while I was working on the Beachy Head novel, had whispered, 'This is dreadful. This is cheesy. You might as well stop right now' – and been proved right. I got enough words down on paper (well, in a .doc) that I started to feel that it was taking on the form of a real book and that it might be an OK one at that. I loved the fact that my creativity was flowing again and I took my writing very seriously.

I'd told Guy what I was doing one night over dinner on the boat.

'Am I in it?' he asked.

'A bit. When I met you in Danga Bay and spent time with you in Thailand.'

He nodded.

'Do you mind?'

'No. It'd be kind of cool to be in a book. But can you change my name? People I know in Thailand will probably still recognise me, but it'd be better if I had a fake name.'

I smiled inwardly at the confidence he had in this project of mine – he saw no reason why it wouldn't become a real book one day, printed and bound, something friends of his might pick up at the airport on their way back to Thailand for the dive season or that might populate the sandy shelves of book-swap stations at backpacker resorts all over South-East Asia.

'Sure. Who do you want to be?'

He had an answer straight away. 'Guy Incognito.'

I laughed at the pun. 'That was quick. I like it. But why that name?'

'It's from *The Simpsons*.' He took another mouthful of the ravioli we'd made ourselves in the pasta machine that was rusting fast in the salty marine environs. Luckily, any rust particles were camouflaged by the tomato sauce.

'But you're not going to go into great detail about us, are you?' he asked. He chewed. 'Not sure the "us" bit would be a great read, anyway.'

He had a point. There wasn't really an 'us bit'. I had thought there was going to be one, when I was in Italy, working on the superyacht and daydreaming about him and when he asked me to come away sailing with him. I believed in the 'us bit' when I arrived at *Incognito* and found that the chemistry was still there between us. Gradually, over the weeks and months that followed, it fizzled out (perhaps damp sea air will do that to a spark?) and now there was no exciting relationship – and no exciting trip to Indonesia, either. What there was was this pull to return to the UK to work and, in particular, to write.

In the end, I think sheer boredom proved the straw that broke the camel's back and it was quite easy to come to a conclusion to leave. Sheer boredom and the fact that Azlan slipped into idle conversation that he'd managed to bag a £300 Qatar Airways flight to the UK to collect Yasmin. It was

the final shove from the universe I needed to make the leap.
I went back on Skyscanner to look for flights.

Telling Guy was hard but once I'd said the words, made
it real, I felt relieved. I'd taken action and it was all decided.
I've always been a person who cuts their losses and moves on
quickly. No regrets. I'd be leaving in two weeks.

Once he'd gotten over his surprise – 'It's a real shame,' he
said – we made the most of the time we had left and explored
the city, going to watch the appalling movie *Battleship* at the
cinema, our teeth chattering in the fierce air-conditioning
that was turned up to the max. We learned our lesson after
that first outing and when we returned to see *The Woman
in Black* the following week we packed socks, trousers,
hoodies and blankets so that we could maintain living body
temperature for the 2-hour screening. We couldn't work out
why the cinema needed to be so cold – surely the locals,
acclimatised to year-round 36°C heat, would struggle even
more than us? Or maybe there was a ticket option that meant
you got a heated seat but we hadn't realised, due to our only
elementary Behasa?

We took city buses everywhere – cramped, belching
dented Spam tins on wheels that queued by the side of the
road. Come nightfall, each one had its own tout who shouted
to potential passengers and tried to persuade them that his
bus was better than any of the other clapped-out vehicles in
the queue. A bus wouldn't leave until it was full – I guess it's
a private enterprise out there that doesn't enjoy the luxury of
public funding to pay for empty vehicles to run the routes,
and so needs to be profitable.

In an upper storey of the mall we sampled the delights
of the vegetarian 'mock' stall – dozens of meat dishes
recreated in fake meat, otherwise known as seitan, a form

of protein made from wheat gluten. Mock frankfurters, mock ribs, mock steaks – there wasn't much you couldn't get mocked up. It made a welcome change for me from the usual noodles but, as I tucked into a meal of salad and mock chicken nuggets, I wondered if they might have just used the real thing – it looked, tasted and smelled the same as the little birdy finger foods I remembered from my childhood, and there's probably not much more meat in a real chicken nugget, anyway.

Two days before I left for home, we took a day trip to Malacca, the famous trading port that used to be a Portuguese and a Dutch colony. We wandered around cute little side streets lined with colonial buildings that looked really similar to those in Penang. There were health-food cafes and knick-knack shops and all the usual suspects. *It's weird that I'm not going to be exploring places like this next week, that I'll be back in the land of the familiar,* I thought as we stepped off the main road and into a side street.

Dawdling along, we passed what looked like a gym. What gave it away was the fact that there was a statue of a bodybuilder outside. Not an army general, nor a king, nor even a horse, those more usual subject matters for sculptors. No – a bodybuilder. We walked over to take a closer look. Technically speaking, it was a bust of a bodybuilder, in massive proportion, so his head was probably 60cm across. He flexed two muscled arms in the air, cocked, the better to show off his bulging biceps. A seven-pack (no mere six here) extended down the front of his torso and a big smile was fixed on a face that was topped with neatly side-swept hair. His lats were so enormous that they looked like fish's gills. The bust stopped at groin level but, from a cheeky bit of carved metal hip, it was plain to see that he'd posed in his scanty undies. Oh, and he was painted gold.

'Datuk Wira Dr Gan Boon Leong,' I read out to Guy from the placard underneath. 'Look – he was Mr Universe, Mr Asia, Mr Melaka and the Father of Bodybuilders in Malaysia.'

'Yep, and he certainly had some guns.'

Golden statues of bodybuilders in quiet side streets, fairground rides, supermarkets selling live fish, souped-up car competitions, young women in hijab running their own businesses, old men who carved off their tattoos, overenthusiastic ladyboy make-up artists, endless restructuring, mock duck, ice-cold cinemas. Ah, Malaysia.

I thought back over it all as I sat in the departure lounge of KL airport two days later. It was all so alien to this middle-class, single English woman. But at the same time, when I had been with Ana and with Azlan I had realised what similarities there were between our two cultures: families living and loving together, the daily routine of work, play and eating, and people striving with their business ideas, wanting to carve out their own place in the world.

And now I was off to do that, too. I was going back to England, to be A Writer. I didn't have much of a plan, other than to stay at my parents' house in Derbyshire while they were away travelling themselves, and to try to eke out my savings so that I could get down as much of this book as possible. Writing had gotten under my skin – I even had a name for the book, *Casting Off* – and I was itching to get stuck in, free from all distractions and all responsibilities.

Of course, thoughts of Malaysia were deeply entwined with those of Guy. This was where we'd met; where I'd returned to him, to have a shot at becoming a couple; and where we'd journeyed together and battled the elements.

He had carried my bag to the taxi in the morning, given me a hug and leaned slightly in to the back seat of the car, one hand on the door frame.

'Keep in touch, Bamford,' he said with a smile, and I was glad there was no awkwardness – just a simple parting of friends who had spent a good time together.

I felt a small sadness at the thought that things hadn't worked out between us, but I also recognised, deep down, that that aimless way of living wasn't really for me – not right now, anyway. I still had too much energy to put into building my own life. I wasn't sure what that life was going to entail, exactly, but I felt strongly that I was making the right decision.

'Flight 625 to Doha is now departing.' The tannoy announcement brought me out of my reverie. I picked up my bag and walked down the concourse.

10

The green, green grass of home

England, late April 2012

My parents are the kind of people who pack for every eventuality. When they go to visit my sister for the weekend, they cram bag after bag into the back of their car. My dad is in charge of loading the boot and he approaches the task like a three-dimensional mathematical puzzle he has to solve. He takes pride in making the most efficient use of the available space. Every single square inch ('mil' to him – he's an engineer) is accounted for, and there's a strict packing order to the cases and bags and boxes and wind-up torches. The process starts a week in advance, with cases laid ready and open on the single bed in the spare room.

At the last minute, the timing chosen so it's easily to hand as well as to keep it cold, my mum always shoves in four litres of milk. Four litres. 'Well, we don't want to get stuck without any, do we?' she says, in answer to any queries. (My dad has already been informed multiple times about the milk and has allowed margin in his packing-volume calculations.)

I'm all for being prepared, but my sister doesn't live thousands of miles away in the middle of nowhere; it's a 4-hour run down the M1 and A34 to Southampton. She lives in the city centre. I'm fairly sure they have milk there.

I'm quite the opposite when it comes to packing. For two years I lived in pretty much the same clothes, all packed, unpacked and repacked over and over into the same bag. The night before I was due to take an international flight to start my next jaunt in an exotic location, I rolled everything up, layered sausages of clothes on top of each other in my waterproof North Face rucksack and zipped it up. Packing took me five minutes and I had it down to a fine minimalistic art.

Now, struggling with the single-digit temperatures of a British spring and so wearing three jumpers as well as a pair of tights under my leggings, I was standing in the front room of my parents' house, surrounded by bags and cases. Barely an inch of wooden floorboard or floral rug was visible between their luggage, and the blue cord sofa resembled more a giant game of Jenga than a relaxing place to sit. Judging by the amount of stuff my parents deemed to be absolutely necessary for a weekend on the south coast, I was slightly worried about how they were going to cope with being away for six months. They were off to Scotland from April to October, they had said when I rang them to tell them I was coming back from Malaysia. The woman who needs four litres of milk at hand for a 120-mile car ride to Southampton was about to drive for twelve hours to the Highlands, where the nearest shop was 78 miles away. It was their version of challenging themselves.

It did cross my mind that they'd need a trailer to transport six months' worth of belongings and emergency milk provisions across the border but to their credit they managed to get everything into the car, much the same as usual. My offer of assistance was dismissed by my dad.

'No, not that one; it's the big case next. Just leave that one there, in the hall, and I'll come back for it in a bit.' He was perspiring. I decided it was better not to mess with genius.

After receiving an in-depth, last-minute run-through on how to turn off the stop-cock, where the window keys were kept and how frequently to clear the fluff out of the filter in the condenser-dryer, I waved them off from their gravelly driveway as my dad bumped the back-heavy car down the kerb on to the road and they set off on an adventure of their own.

I turned back to the house and closed the front door behind me. It was so quiet I could hear the fridge humming in the kitchen.

I made a cup of tea and took it through to the living room, to ponder my immediate future. My mum and dad would be away for nearly half a year and they'd said I could stay at their house for as much of that period as I needed to – with the bills all paid for.

'You're actually doing us a favour,' my dad had said. 'The insurance company doesn't want the place empty for too long.' It was kind of him to make it sound like I was helping them, rather than the other way round – that they were supporting their layabout 33-year-old daughter who hadn't had a proper job for two years.

I was feeling pretty content. I had a place to stay, all of my own, and it seemed vast after sharing a poky 36-foot boat with someone else. Here I had rooms that I didn't even use! I had a table to eat from! I had as much hot running water as I wanted! I no longer had to scrub my clothes (or someone else's underpants) in a bucket of cold water! And – best of all – I had a shiny new car parked in the drive. I had a drive!

My parents live in a normal, three-bed brick house in a village in Derbyshire. It is on a bus route but it's one that goes round the houses – for real: it shuffles down one housing estate after the other, stopping so frequently that the

OAPs who have just got on barely have time to park their backsides on the seats before they're being pitched forwards by the momentum from the driver hitting the brakes at the next lamppost sign. To get to the nearest city, Derby, takes fifteen minutes by car but by bus it's an hour. That's OK if you want to go to Derby city centre but if over the next few months I wanted to visit friends who lived in other towns and villages I'd have to take a bus an hour into the city, wait for another and then take a second bus to the friend's place, then repeat the whole thing in reverse a couple of hours later. An invitation to 'pop round for a cuppa' could end up taking the best part of a day.

When I was overseas, we took it for granted that things took a long time. A trip Guy and I made to the supermarket in Penang formed an entire afternoon and evening's entertainment because the travelling took so long. It's all part of the experience. Yes, it's a bus, but it's an Indian bus; OK, it's Tesco, but it's a Malaysian Tesco. Ooh, look – they've given me a receipt. Printed on a piece of paper. A piece of Thai paper! How wonderful! The interest comes from the spot where familiarity and difference meet. I'm sure the Indian bus passengers and Malaysian supermarket shoppers we sat with didn't share our sense of wonder. It's just not the same when you're on home turf.

I'd decided I needed a car and I'd spent half of the money I'd earned in Italy as a deckhand on one – and had ended up with an 8-year-old blue Mini Cooper with two white stripes down the bonnet. I'd heard Minis held their value pretty well – and was even more pleased with my choice when a mechanic told me that whenever he'd had to tow away concertinaed vehicles from the scenes of road accidents, Minis always seemed to come out the best of the small cars.

My previous rides had always been quirky – and by quirky, I mean shit and, quite frankly, embarrassing. My first was a clapped-out 998cc Austin Metro that only fired on two cylinders, so top speed up a hill with a couple of passengers was 15mph. Next came an old lady's Mazda 121 (not even the type that looks like a mid-1990s Ford Fiesta, but a more hideous, boxy version) with a smiley-face sticker on the back; then a phlegm-yellow 1974 MGB GT; and, finally, a gold Peugeot 106. Most of these car selections were dictated by penury rather than free will. The Mini Cooper was the most expensive car I'd ever owned. Modern and slightly cool as it was, it had a Union Jack covering the whole of the roof. See – quirky.

I didn't mind the Union Jack that much, though, because I'd landed back in an England that was slap bang in the middle of a strong upsurge in patriotic pride. The new Duke and Duchess of Cambridge, Kate and Wills, had married the spring before and in a few weeks' time the Queen was to celebrate her diamond jubilee. Union flags were all the rage: embroidered on to cushions, fashioned into rugs, criss-crossing from lamppost to lamppost in strings of fluttering bunting up and down the land. In buying that car I had accidentally stumbled into the middle of a big trend.

It was heart-warming to see the UK being proud of itself for once. Technically, I suppose it was proud of two people who had managed to get hitched (wowzers!) and an old woman who'd stuck at the same job for a considerable amount of time (not that she had a choice, but then who was I to talk, with my capricious attitude of late?). The country was also getting itself into a lather over a bunch of fit people who were about to descend on London and throw themselves over horizontally-placed sticks and dash like maniacs round in circles. For no money. Actually, I'm not sure which is more impressive to me – being brave enough to commit to spending the rest of your life with just one person or pedalling like the clappers around an Olympic velodrome. Lord knows I've done neither.

When I'd been out and about on my travels, I'd noticed that other countries were very openly and proudly patriotic. In Malaysia, a huge number-one symbol – representing unity between the majority Malay, and Indian and Chinese populations – was pasted everywhere. I saw men and women wearing polo shirts with the number 1 logo embroidered on to the left breast, above the heart. In the Andaman Islands, orange, green and white Indian flags were everywhere, and when I was in Naples people hung *il Tricolore* from their balconies and it was hard to find anything that was not *prodotto in Italia*.

A couple of years back, when I was still living full-time in the UK, it had been almost as if displaying a flag was a kind of protest. It whispered of jingoism, of *Daily Mail*-subscriptions, of 'send them back' mutterings over coffee and fondant fancies. And as for flying St George's cross – well, you might as well have worn a T-shirt declaring yourself a member of the BNP. It's possible, of course, that some people hoisted their flags on their front-yard poles because that was exactly what they meant. But I thought it was sad that it was seen as almost shameful to celebrate being British or English and to take pride in the country, whatever your origins. I know being overly apologetic is a traditional British trait, but being apologetic when there is nothing to be sorry for? It was ridiculous.

Now, in spring 2012, it was almost as if the country had been plunged back into the immediate post-war years. As well as the Union Jack everywhere, there was a definite upsurge in quaint tea rooms and vintage furniture shops. You couldn't turn round without bumping into an artfully 'distressed' repainted chest of drawers that used to belong to someone's grandmother. Women wore dresses and heels and red lipstick. They curled the ends of their hair instead of ironing it poker-straight. My, how things had changed in the two years I'd been absent. From every shop window, posters and birthday cards, plates and teapots (usually displayed on a tastefully whitewashed piece of reclaimed furniture) and urged me to KEEP CALM AND CARRY ON. *Carry on what?* I wondered. And as for keeping calm – well, I was as relaxed as I had ever been in my life.

My days were wonderfully free and unburdened with no boat jobs to tick off a list or other person to have to factor in when deciding what I wanted to do. It was the first time I had ever lived by myself and all fears of being lonely vanished within the first day (although I did often find myself talking to inanimate objects such as the cooker, telling them to 'hurry up' – but I wasn't particularly embarrassed by that, since I was the only person around to hear myself). I established a loose kind of lazy routine over the next few weeks. My bedroom faced east, so I woke after sunrise as the dawn filtered through the voile curtains and took my time to get up. After breakfast I'd settle in the living room with its large picture window that framed a beautiful view of the Amber Valley. I'd sit on the sofa, cup of tea by my side, feet on my mum's footstool and blanket over my knees (I was still feeling the cold as I hadn't yet acclimatised back from tropical temperatures), and get out my netbook. I'd faff about for a while on Facebook and email, then get down to working on *Casting Off* at about 10am. I'd plough on for a few hours, losing myself in my memories of my adventure, and only come out of my writing trance when my stomach rumbles became too distracting. After lunch I'd get back on to the sofa and work through again until 6pm. Some days my word count would hit 4,000. Then I'd get out my mini trampoline and Tracy Anderson DVDs, work up a sweat, cook dinner from scratch, and sink, mentally and physically tired, back on to the sofa for the rest of the evening, watching the sun sink slowly beyond Crich Stand.

After months of living near the equator, with its short sunrises and sunsets, I was mesmerised by the long light of the late-spring twilights. The shadows of the trees lengthened diagonally across the valley towards me, stretching themselves so thin they eventually melted into the grass of the fields. The sails of Heage windmill rotated with the wind so I always knew which direction the weather was coming from. Birds sang in the apple tree until ten or eleven at night and, as the window faced west, I had watercolour-thin mauve and lavender skies long after the sun had sailed off towards Australia.

Every now and then, to prevent myself from getting to the stage at which I would begin to believe the washing machine was talking back to me, I'd go out to visit a friend or my brother. But for the most part I was perfectly content to stay put, following my little self-imposed timetable. Sometimes days passed without me leaving the house or verbally talking to anyone, but I never felt alone. I had robins, wrens and a curious dunnock for company on the other side of the pane of glass and the other kind of tweeting when I felt the need for human interaction. After years of living in small spaces with other people, I relished the freedom of being on my own and completely in charge of my life. And whenever I got bored, there was always internet shopping.

When I was in Malaysia with Guy I was living off about £5,000 a year. Things were cheap in Asia, and the budget was manageable. After the essentials there wasn't much worth buying anyway. I was far too big for most of the women's clothes, and blingy jeans and floral polyester knee-length blouses aren't really my bag. I did have to 'go local' and buy some underpants at one point, and to my shame I couldn't fit into medium, large or even extra-large. In Malaysian sizes, I needed XXL. And, as if the humiliation weren't enough, the only styles they carried were proper belly-huggers in shades of pastel green and orange. So I didn't really bother venturing into the shops and my bank balance stayed healthier as a result.

Back in the UK there were lots of things my size. And my size, after a six-month diet consisting primarily of rice and green vegetables, was an eight. Single digits! With no exercising or real effort involved! I weighed less than I did as a 17-year-old, and without suffering a single case of Delhi belly. As any woman who's lost weight or reached a size target well knows, the natural thing to do to celebrate is to go on a shopping spree. So I did.

I hadn't quite abandoned all of my South-East-Asia-traveller parsimonious ways. I was constantly shocked by the price of things in the UK. Fuel was four times as expensive and it seemed an absolute scandal to spend £50 on a dress. When I wanted to scare myself into not buying something, I converted back to Malaysian ringgit: 250MYR for that? It's just a mere scrap of a thing! Conversely, if I wanted to persuade myself that something was worth it, I stuck to sterling.

Through a mixture of penny-pinching measures, such as shopping in the market and going on eBay, plus telling myself that I 'really deserved' an item that I was coveting 'because you worked bloody hard on that Italian boat to earn this money', I soon ended up with drawers and closets stuffed full of giant bath towels, garishly patterned leggings, electrical beauty gadgets, pointless workout equipment and weird-sounding foodstuffs like water kefir grains and rapadura. I told myself that it was all in the name of self-improvement, that my travels had turned me into an orange-paisley-wearing, kefir-gorging, hairless thin hippy who was at one with herself and the universe. In truth, I was just a bit bored and giddy on commercialism after going cold turkey for such a long time.

And so it was that I quickly burned through my savings. Of my Italian earnings, half I'd spent on the car and the other half I'd stuck in a savings account, which soon morphed into a second current account. With no rent or bills to pay at my parents' place, and still with a few hundred quid a month coming in from the tenants in my London flat, I'd originally figured that I'd be able to spend months and months working on my magnum opus before I'd have to abandon literature and lower myself to finding paid employment again. And then another shiny sparkly thing I didn't need caught my magpie eye on Amazon and I'd hit 'Buy-now-with-1-click' before you could say 'broke'.

One morning, about two months after I'd waved off my parents, and supposedly only a third of the way into my half-a-year writer's retreat, I logged on to my bank account and realised I had £144 to my name. I gulped, did a quick mental calculation of how much longer I had to live if I had water kefir as my only sustenance, bit the bullet and rang my ex-boss in London to beg for my old job back.

11

London's Calling

Like a giant mound of marshmallow, the duvet spilled over from the passenger seat and obscured the gearstick. I shoved a corner sharply out of the way with my left hand and shifted down to fourth, slowing as I came off the M4 and into the start of the London traffic. I shuffled about in my seat as I slid to a halt in the first city traffic jam, trying to find a more comfortable position on the pillow I was sitting on. The car in front started to move forwards and I realised I was in the wrong lane. I glanced in my rear-view mirror, and cursed under my breath as I remembered that the back of the car was piled high with so much stuff that I couldn't see a thing. Feeling handicapped, I glanced quickly in my wing mirrors, which I've never really trusted that much, gritted my teeth and pulled out into the right-hand lane.

This so wasn't in the plan. Actually, let's not call it a 'plan', since I had supposedly been trying to learn, over the past year or two, how to let go and be more impulsive and less of a planner. Let's say instead that this so wasn't in the epiphany. According to a wake-up call and particularly realistic daydream I'd had about a year ago, I was supposed to be living bare-legged and fancy-free on a boat in the Caribbean by now. And yet here I was, sitting in my car, which was packed to the rafters with my worldly belongings, like a student going back to uni after weeks of holiday, burning through fuel in a west London traffic jam, on my way back to my old flat, job and life.

Weirdly, I didn't feel that deflated that I'd not yet managed to achieve my dream of beach-side, tropical living. 'Yet' was the operative word. I'm a fairly practical person and if I'm faced with a problem, I tend to be able to calmly work out the best way to solve it. Here was my problem: I was broke. The solution: get work. My skills, experience and contacts were all in journalism in London, so that's where I was headed. I'm not sure why it never occurred to me to get a job – any job: bar work, office temping – in Derbyshire and stay living at my parents' house. When my bank balance got dangerously low, I rang a couple of newspaper ex-colleagues and they offered me a bit of temporary work. By fortunate timing, the tenants in my flat were moving out as their lease was up. *If I do a bit of part-time work at the newspapers and rent out my spare bedroom I'll have time and space to write my book,* I thought. *I'll still be broke but it'll only be a matter of time before enormous amounts of publishing royalties start rolling in (enough for me to live off on a tropical island), won't it?*

I didn't yet have a publishing deal but, ever the optimist, I was sure one would come. And I did have reason to believe that. A friend who was the winning skipper in the 2009/10 Clipper Round the World yacht race, which I'd taken part in as media crew, had written a book on what winning yacht races could teach you about leadership in the business world. It wasn't the kind of book I'd normally read but I knew no one in publishing so I had travelled down to London to attend the launch, at the headquarters of Bloomsbury in a townhouse just behind Tottenham Court Road. A thrill went through my chest as I walked through the front room of the publisher's building, set out like a large, old-fashioned drawing room (which is what it probably originally was), and through to a narrow, long conservatory. Brendan Hall, the author, gave a speech and, somewhat emboldened by glasses of lukewarm white wine, I approached his editor, Liz, and started harping on about Borneo, strange men, elephant pygmies, pirates and billionaires. After a few minutes her frown of concentration eased as she realised the slurring woman in front of her with oddly yellowed hair and wearing some kind of vaguely Indian costume was pitching a book. She smiled as I mentioned my old job at the *Independent*. 'Your book sounds really interesting,' she said, kindly, handing me her card, 'and as you're a journalist, that gives me confidence that you can probably write.' Of course, I emailed her immediately, sending through a few sample chapters. She asked for more, so I forwarded everything I had – two-thirds of the rough first draft of *Casting Off*. It all seemed so easy.

I was determined to write all the way to the end of my story once I moved back to London. *Even if I no longer have all day, every day, to write, I'll still do it*, I vowed now, as the traffic light changed to green and, almost in automatic mode, I turned left down the King's Road in Chelsea, then indicated to turn right over Battersea Bridge to cross the Thames into south London.

It's almost as if nothing's changed, I mused as I sat at another traffic light, pushing the bedding on the front seat out of the way of the handbrake while I waited for a red double-decker to clear the box junction ahead. *The shops are the same, I don't have to think about where I am driving, I know the short-cuts. Did I really go off on those exciting adventures? Did I actually visit exotic lands and learn a lot about the world and about myself?* I kind of felt like the past two years had been a particularly surreal episode of *Dallas*. Except without the spurs and shoulder pads.

It's strange how the memory of smells can evoke such strong feelings. At my block of flats in London, after I'd held my fob to the heavy front door and heaved it open while the familiar beep tone echoed loudly, a specific odour hit me: a combination of old cigarette smoke and wet brick, tinged with a trace of old-vegetable-peelings-stuck-in-the-rubbish-chute and an underlying hint of earthy curry spices. It was a distinctly human smell: the smell of lots of bodies living stacked on top of each other. It wasn't very pleasant; if I'd been anywhere else, I'd have wrinkled my nose in distaste and possibly held my breath. But it smelled particularly of home.

I know what I said earlier, about familiar things not being interesting, about normal being boring, but as I stepped inside the hallway and moved towards the staircase, I felt almost a sense of wonder at being back. How could it be that nothing – not one thing – had changed? Here were the same reddish-black floor tiles and concrete steps with their black handrails that I'd walked on when I first came to view the flat with an estate agent five years earlier. The same tiles on the corridor walls, lining the stairs, covered in slightly peeling magnolia paint, so many layers of it that only the faintest impression that there were gaps between the tiles remained. Here were the scuff marks the upstairs tenants had made on the wall when they carried their bikes up the stairs every night after work. Here was the stainless-steel lift that no one ever used as it was barely big enough to fit one person inside. And here was my front door, dented in one corner where, presumably, a visitor coming to call on the previous owner had forcefully applied a boot. The large chrome numbers two and six that I had screwed in at eye level were still slightly skew-whiff.

I put the key in the lock and pushed the door open and the clunky 'thwack' of the back of the door hitting the wall welcomed me just the same as if I'd come back after a

2-minute trip to take the recycling to the communal bin, when really I'd travelled thousands of miles and hadn't set foot in the place for two years.

I dropped my armload of belongings on the carpet of the nearest bedroom and walked around the empty flat. My heart sank as I looked through doorways and the illusion of having been gone only a couple of minutes popped. Everything was filthy, covered in a film of dust and, worse, mould. Thick black forests of it lined the windows. It spread across walls in bluey-green swathes, inching its way into every nook and cranny. I ran my hand over a wooden chest of drawers I'd spent months worrying whether to buy, such a relatively big investment did it represent at the time. The oak surface felt mottled to the touch. My fingers hit a rough patch and I stooped closer to look – a dent had been roughly sanded into the top. An angry black burn mark stuck out of one end of the valley that guilty hands had furiously sanded away. Slowly, I pulled out the top drawer. Velvety mould bloomed across the dovetailed joints at the back. Recoiling in disgust, I put it down. The tenants had gone but the mess they had left behind created a really strong sense of other. Home wasn't so sweet after all.

Hours later, after I had bleached, dusted, scrubbed, mopped and vacuumed, the things from my car piled out of the way in a corner while I worked at removing the last traces of strangers and returning my flat to me, I paused in front of the mirror that hung on the wall in the corridor. The face that looked back at me was grimy and streaked with sweat. Beneath the dirt, the features were the same but the details had changed so much since I'd last stood in front of this glass, as a 31-year-old journalist about to embark on her first solo trip abroad. My hair, bleached by two years in the sun, was a brighter colour and stained nearly white-blonde in parts. All traces of brown dye I'd occasionally applied were gone. My skin was still slightly tanned, the English summer having maintained some of the colour I'd built up in Malaysia on Guy's boat. Arcing around my hairline were dark-brown and shell-pink marks – freckles burned into my face by the relentless equatorial sun burning down on to my forehead every day for months and little scars left after a bout of sunscreen-induced acne. The lines curving underneath my cheeks from the side of my nose were deeper, and rays of fine lines fanned out from the corners of my eyes when I smiled. It was a face I knew so well, but a face altered by time and, very quickly, by the sun. A dermatologist would probably scream at the obvious damage I'd done to myself. My skin – so used, after thirty years of being inside for twenty-two hours a day – had aged rapidly in two years of outdoor living. But I wasn't horrified by the lines and blemishes. To me, they were battle scars, earned from being outside, in the world and the sunshine, from really living. The reflection in the mirror was me, but a changed me. They have a saying for it in Thailand, reproduced on the fronts of souvenir T-shirts worn in the beach bars and restaurants by hundreds of backpackers and holidaymakers: 'same same but different'. And here I was, standing in my familiar flat, about to go back to my old job, with memories of sun-drenched beaches and sea-voyaging adventures burned into my brain. Same same but different.

'Bammers! How the devil are you, old bean?' The voice of Swifty, my old boss at the *Daily Express*, had boomed down the phone as I rang him from Derbyshire a couple of weeks earlier.

'Not bad, Swifty, thanks.'

'Still enjoying the high seas? Shacked up with any drunken sailors yet?'

'Not exactly.' We caught up for a few minutes, while I waited for the opportunity – and the courage – to ask for work. It's a bit embarrassing, really, to announce to everyone that you're off on the adventure of a lifetime and are probably not going to come back, and then to have to ring up and beg for a job.

Niceties over, I took a deep breath and went for it. 'The thing is, Swifty,' I began, 'I'm a bit broke.'

Silence. I swallowed, tried to keep my voice nonchalant. 'Got any shifts?'

I'd known Greg Swift long enough to not have to beat around the bush. I knew he'd be busy and, while there's no ideal time of day to ring a hectic newsroom, I'd picked the hour that was likely to be slightly less pressured than all the others. He had had no idea what I was ringing for – I could have been phoning to ask if he wanted to meet for a beer, or to tell him I'd set myself up as a freelance journalist – a stringer – in the South Pacific and had a cracking story about cannibalism he might be interested in. I sincerely doubt he expected me to be ringing him up to ask for my old job back – a job I'd left four years earlier.

I could hear the humming buzz of the newsroom in the pause before he spoke again.

'I thought you'd left all that behind.'

'Yeah, well, so did I – but, as I said, I'm broke.'

He paused again. I knew I wouldn't have his full attention – the nature of the job meant he'd be scanning the news wires, flicking to and from his email account and checking out the rolling news on the TV bolted to the ceiling above the news desk at the same time.

He exhaled noisily, like a plumber about to deliver bad news. 'The thing is, Bammers, I'm all set for news desk staff these days.'

I was prepared for that and had my answer ready. 'What about reporting shifts?'

'Where are you?'

I had told a little white lie. 'Back in London.' Well, it was almost true – I was about to be back in London. I waited. 'I can do Sundays, nights – anything you've got going, really.' I tried to keep the desperation out of my voice. *I'll do all the really shitty shifts that no one else wants to touch with a barge-pole. Come on – just say yes. Please. Pretty please.*

'All right. Drop Becky an email, and I'm sure she can sort you out a shift or two.' It was a concession on his part, and a demotion on mine, to midnight sessions re-writing celebrity paparazzi picture captions and re-nosing Reuters copy, but it was a lifeline, and he'd thrown it to me.

'Great. Thank you. I'll email Becky.'

'All right, Bammers.' He was already putting the phone down.

'Oh, and Swifty? Cheers.'

The conversation with the *Independent*, where I'd worked after the *Express*, but before I quit to go on my travels, had been slightly easier. Oly Duff, the home news editor, told me they were looking for extra help on the news desk during the upcoming Olympics. I balked a bit – I know sweet FA about sport – but he reckoned he could get me eleven shifts over the two weeks, and we'd see how things went from there.

And then, just like that, I was back in my old life. I did a quick round of catching up with friends. Despite the odd new baby here and there, not much had changed in two years. It was weird to think how much I'd seen and done, how much sheer distance I'd covered, and yet here everyone else was carrying on just as before.

From the outside, I suppose, it might have seemed like my life was just as before, too – if you ignored my yellowed hair and sun damage. Some people didn't even have a clue I'd ever been away.

At the *Daily Express*, on my first day back, I sat at the desk I'd first chosen as my favourite spot on quiet Sunday shifts eight years earlier. One of the routes into national newspapers is to do the graveyard shifts that the staff reporters don't want to do: the late-nighters and Sundays (daily newspapers don't work on Saturdays, since they don't need to get an edition out on Sundays). I'd done my apprenticeship on local papers in the provinces and then I'd taken a job writing the Home Office's staff magazine to get me to London. I'd had a Monday-to-Friday job but I'd been desperate to break into the nationals, so I'd printed off twenty copies of my CV, written twenty individual covering letters and rung up the news desk of each paper, asking for the name of the person to apply to for shifts. The *Daily Express* got back to me within a few weeks, while I was in Guernsey visiting a friend for the weekend, asking if I'd work the next day. I remember my heart hurtling out of my mouth, past my shoes and through the floor as I thought I'd just missed my one opportunity for a big break. I'd rung up the next morning and explained that I was sorry but I'd been away, and the news editor offered me a shift the following Sunday as well. From then on, for a year, I had two jobs: Monday to Friday at the Home Office magazine and Sundays at the *Express*.

The first time I pushed open the enormous blue-framed glass door to the *Express*'s lobby, I'd been so excited. The newspaper's parent company, Northern and Shell, which also published the *Daily Star* and *OK!* magazine, had recently moved into a former bank building right on the River Thames, between London Bridge and Tower Bridge. It was a boxy 1980s Lego building, built of steel and glass tinted blue like reflective Ray-Ban lenses, wedged between an old church and the Palladian grandeur of the Old Billingsgate fish market.

The impressive limestone lobby contained a fountain – indoors, in an office block! – and stretched nine floors up above my head, the cavernous empty space a blatant waste of prime retail estate that screamed, in yuppie fashion, 'I am considerably richer than yow.' Richard Desmond, the billionaire who owned the publishing company outright, and whose beetle-black Bentley with its RCD 1 number plate was often parked outside, really *was* richer than yow.

I've been inside a few national newspaper offices in my time and they often have grand entrances. The Derry Street entrance to Associated Newspapers' offices, which now house the *Daily Mail* and *Independent* range of titles, has two long escalators that deposit visitors into a first-floor atrium vast enough to house artworks, pot plants, a coffee shop and canteen and a bust of Viscount Rothermere. The *Daily Telegraph*, hidden behind tall iron railings near the Victoria train station exit used by coach passengers, has similar escalators that whisk reporters and sub-editors up and away from the grime of the central-London streets.

The *Express*'s newsroom was the best office, physically, that I've worked in (if you ignored the occasional mouse). It had the standard coffee-stained bluey-grey carpet tiles and recessed fluorescent lighting, but there was plenty of space and a clear-desk policy and half of the reporters sat at a bank of desks that lined the window, with a view straight out, at second-floor level, over the River Thames. High-end hotels would have paid top dollar for that view. On winter days I could watch the sun rise in the east over Tower Bridge and then set over London Bridge in the afternoon, red rays being bounced back and forth off the mirrored surfaces of the buildings on the South Bank to dazzle us as we rushed towards deadline. After dark, the camera flashes of tourists posing for riverside shots strobed into the office through the floor-to-ceiling windows like disco lights. Many times, once

I'd gotten over my new-girl nerves, I'd find myself watching the boats ply their trade up and down the Thames and slip into a daydream.

Now, back at those desks again, I couldn't get the computer I was using to log me on properly, so I rang down to the basement.

A woman's voice answered. 'Hello, IT.' I glanced at the ID screen on the phone. Sue. She'd been working there when I'd started eight years earlier.

'Hi, Sue, it's Emma Bamford.'

I expected a note of surprise in her voice to hear from me, but she was totally neutral. 'Oh hello, Emma, yes. What can I do for you?' She didn't seem to have realised that I'd left the company ages ago and had just reappeared. Maybe she just thought I'd not had a single problem with my PC in all that time.

A week or so later, Arthur, the octogenarian duty lawyer – dapper former attorney general and all-round good egg – hobbled slowly into the office. He'd always had a twinkle in his eye and Arthur and I had had lunch together a couple of times when I was full-time at the *Express*.

Now I smiled as I walked towards him. 'Arthur! I'm so glad I managed to bump into you.'

He frowned and his forehead, topped with his neatly combed back slick of white hair, moved down closer to his nose.

'Are you? Why?' He had that specific kind of accent and tone to his voice that belong to a BBC broadcaster from fifty years ago.

'Because I've not seen you for years. I've been away.' With the look he gave me after each successive short sentence I felt more and more like I was making things up, piling fantasy on top of lie like a 6-year-old trying to cover her tracks. 'Now I'm back.'

'Have you really?'

'Yes, Arthur. I've not worked here for four years.'

'Well!' he chuckled, a bit like a doting grandfather indulging a slightly slow child, and wandered off.

But I have! I wanted to shout at Arthur's retreating back, still remarkably straight despite his years. I wanted to yell it at Sue, the IT woman, too. *I've lived in a Borneo jungle. I've watched wild pygmy elephants swim in a treacly river. I've sailed across oceans, swum with turtles, waved at lost hunter-gatherer tribesmen. I've lunched with multi-millionaires, climbed to the top of a smoking volcano and gazed down on hot red coals being spewed into the night. I've been mistaken for a bride at a Malaysian wedding, run away from pirates and flown halfway round the world in pursuit of love. I have! Honest! Please believe me!*

It was like I'd stepped into a time warp, except there were no little Willow-type bandit dwarves coming barrelling towards me. I'd been to all these places, seen all these things and experienced so much and it had changed me – but to everyone else I was still the same old Emma Bamford.

What's worse, I was starting to get the impression that people really weren't that interested in hearing about it. It was too far removed from their normal lives and they couldn't necessarily relate. I was a little bit concerned I was becoming a bit of a joke. When someone said 'I like your ring,' I altered my answer from 'Thanks. I got it in this cute little shop on Koh Lanta in Thailand, when my crewmate Aaron and I took a motorbike tour,' to just 'Thanks,' and then I started to shove my hand, embarrassedly, into the pocket of my jeans, hiding the three tiny polished seashell domes from view. Every time I caught myself saying 'When I was in—' I cringed and stopped mid-sentence. I didn't want to turn into a real-life version of a parody of a traveller. I hated the idea of becoming a bore.

That's the thing about travelling. It does broaden the mind, and you have amazing experiences that touch you so deeply you want to share just the tiniest bit with other people, however you can. And it had taught me to let go, and not care so much about what other people thought of me. Going away to an utterly alien environment helped me to really become me – at least, when I was in that alien environment I felt I could be myself. I really wanted to be able to hold on to these new recognitions and this self-awareness. At first I wore my Indian tunics, I chatted to strangers, I happily shared my stories.

As time progressed, the tribe started to close in. No one pointed at me and jeered, politely suggested I put on a pair of jeans or told me to 'stop harping on, Bammers – we get that you had a bloody lovely long holiday' but, subtly, slowly, I started to feel the pressure to conform again, to fit the pattern the same way everyone else did. With a sigh, I packed my Indian tunics away at the back of my bottom drawer. And when I pulled on my smart new office appropriate clothes, the old, pre-travel me came back a bit stronger and the new, lighter me got pushed down a little.

With every Tube journey I took, glass of overpriced wine I drank and cynical joke I cracked, my vision of a life on a Caribbean island, driving a ute and working in the boating industry moved a little out of focus until eventually, as if it was three, five or ten years earlier, while I was laughing at a nasty jibe and draining the dregs of another 250ml before hopping on the last Northern-line train home, it went out altogether, with a gentle hiss and a thin stream of black smoke, like someone holding a wet finger to a candle.

12

Howdy, pardners!

London and Houston, Texas – November 2012

It's funny how the universe provides things for you, sometimes. I'm not much of a hippy and, before I went off on my travels, I was certainly a sceptic. If someone (who, in this daydream, is wearing multi-coloured flares and a little headband of beads jammed down over long, centre-parted hair) said, 'Just trust. The universe will provide, maan,' I'd have snorted, raised my eyebrows and marched away pretty quickly, possibly to immerse myself in something logical and to dress in modern, man-made fabrics.

Then, after I did go on my travels and – here comes the cliché – it opened my eyes, I kind of began to partially accept some of the things that people like my friend Aaron believe. Manifestation was beyond my comfort zone but a loose idea that the universe provides for you I was OK with, especially since the logical part of my brain was able to make sense of it all. I didn't think that when good things happened it was because some kind of anthropomorphised benevolent god was tossing out favours. *You've just opened your eyes,* my brain reasoned, *and that means you notice these opportunities when they come along.* When these lucky breaks cropped up from time to time, in my new-found spirit of living in the moment I went with the flow, smug in the knowledge it was all just a coincidence. My heart, meanwhile, enjoyed the magical element to those surprising instants that life seems to throw into your path, just when you need them most.

On a grey London morning, when I was sitting in a grey office staring at a grey computer screen, reading yet another story about how a dog had had to be rescued by the coastguard after jumping off a cliff at the seaside and landing on a ledge, and simultaneously wondering if I, like Fido, should just do the same, so dull and routine had my life become, a message popped up on Facebook from my friends Ben and Vicky, who I'd sailed with on *Gillaroo* from Thailand to Sri Lanka.

'What are you doing in October/November? Fancy helping us deliver a yacht from Texas to St Lucia?'

Boom! Like that, my Caribbean epiphany was back on track. Far out, maan.

Say 'Texas' and you'll think dry, dusty plains, nodding oil donkeys and JR's giant white Stetson. Houston 'we have a problem' mission-control centre. Tight-trousered cowboys riding rodeo in sandy arenas. What probably won't spring to mind is sea or sailing. Texas has a coastline? Who knew?

It actually has quite a lot of coastline, spanning 360 miles and curving round from the north-east corner of Mexico to the south-west tip of Louisiana. And it was down to that coastline that my American Airlines flight dipped on what had been a cold November day in London but was a scorching-hot one in Texas.

It'd been scorching-hot for a fair while, judging by the darkness of Ben's skin and Vicky's near-platinum hair. It was late by the time I'd passed through immigration and the arrivals waiting area of Houston airport was all but deserted, apart from two very bored people who looked like they'd welded their behinds to the plastic buckets seats. Their faces split into wide smiles when they saw me and I waved.

I hadn't seen Ben or Vicky for nearly two years. I'd met them on a catamaran in Thailand, and the three of us, half of a crew of six, had become good friends in the month and a half we sailed together through the Andaman Islands and across the Indian Ocean to Sri Lanka. Being British, we shared a sense of humour. I'd been slightly in awe of them when we first met, as the kind of life I was seeking, so far removed from the rat race it was difficult to comprehend, appeared to come easily to them. They'd worked at exclusive dive resorts through Asia and the Caribbean and had set up a dive business in Mozambique. They seemed to me to have led a charmed life, full of fun, adventure and the odd bit of danger. It was like meeting characters from a story.

Why they wanted to be friends with dull little old me, I had no idea. By this point, l suppose on paper I'd led a half-interesting life myself. It probably sounded quite glamorous from the outside – national newspaper journalist who took up sailing, quit her life and headed off to Borneo on a whim. Some-time superyacht hostess. Freelance reporter who was free to head off on travels at the drop of an email. It's different when it's your life, though. Everything then, because you're living it day in, day out, becomes normal – mundane, even. You can't be glamorous to yourself because you live underneath all that veneer. At the end of the day, you are just plain old you. And I was back to being an office worker, albeit an office worker with sailing skills.

I'd picked up a bit of background info from Ben and Vicky before I flew out to Texas. They'd done another big sailing trip the year after I'd met them, helping a guy deliver a boat he'd bought from Pacific Mexico to the Panama Canal. What was meant to be a fun trip had turned into a bit of a nightmare as horrendous wind and sea conditions put them in fear of their lives for several days. 'I never want to go through anything like that again,' said Ben, with touching honesty. Being a northerner, he usually brushed off any suggestion of difficulty with a sarcastic remark.

They survived it and came out of it with a business model – Ben and Vicky were going to buy an identical yacht to the one they had helped deliver and both boats would base themselves in St Lucia, where they'd offer exciting 'match racing' events to tourists and holidaymakers.

Earlier that year they'd popped into a marina in California, had a quick look round a boat, bought it, and left instructions for its mast to be taken off and for the whole lot to be trucked overland to Texas and put back in the water, waiting for them until they were free to return to the States in the autumn. Then they'd dropped me a line, asking if I wanted to help deliver the yacht to St Lucia over the winter. They made it seem so simple.

I'd spent the past two Christmases in the heat of the tropics and I'd loved it. I was feeling bored, uninspired and a bit trapped in London, and Ben and Vicky didn't have to work hard to talk me into spending two months in the States and island-hopping through the Caribbean. I was freelancing, so could take the time off. All I had to do, since I wouldn't be earning while I was away, was watch the pennies and make sure I had work lined up on my return. Apart from that, it was a simple case of opening my bottom drawer, lifting out all my old travelling and sailing gear, and dropping it into my holdall.

'She's a one-tonner,' Ben told me now, after we loaded my bags into the back of their grey Japanese rental car and pulled out into Houston's snaking and confusing highway system. 'She's called a Choate 40. Built for offshore racing. Did quite well in the early Eighties.'

I hadn't heard of a Choate before. I'm not much of a boat nerd, as I've said, and tend to describe boats by their hull colour rather than their designer's or builder's name. Unfortunately, 'Over there, by that white boat,' usually doesn't help narrow things down. So all I could tell from Ben's description was that my new home was a sailing yacht that was 40 feet in length, which was 4 feet longer than *Incognito*.

It was dark as we pulled into the car park of Seabrook Marina and the streetlights cast pools of orange on to the ground around us. Ben took my large bag and I grabbed hold of my hand luggage and the two bottles of champagne I'd bought in duty free as a present. Vicky led the way up a small grass bank and on to a narrow path and I followed her, excitement bubbling up in my chest.

'That's our toilet block,' she said, as she strode along the wooden dock in wedge-heeled espadrilles, her hair gleaming in the artificial light. Yachts and motor boats were moored on finger berths either side of us. There was no one else around. We walked on another 50 metres or so, then followed the dock as it did a dog leg round to the left then right. Vicky tapped the lid of a large plastic storage box that sat on the edge of the water, just level with the tip of a boat's bow. 'That's our box. And that's our Hoover.' She sounded as giddy as I felt. Turning sharply right, on to a wooden finger berth that rocked precariously with the motion of her steps, she extended a slender leg on to the deck of a boat, grabbed a metal stanchion post in each hand and hauled herself up in one giant, gymnastic movement. I shuffled along the wobbling dock and carefully placed my bags on the yacht's side deck before copying her move to get on to the boat. It took a huge push-off with my left leg and a strong pull with both hands to step up. I dropped my shoes in the cockpit, as she had done, and followed her down the companionway steps into the boat.

'And this is our boat,' she was saying.

I paused at the bottom of the steps and looked around the inside.

By this point I'd sailed and lived on quite a wide variety of yachts, from a 68-foot racing yacht that slept twenty-four people to a 24-metre superyacht with power showers, air-conditioning and a live-in chef. I'd spent six months on a large catamaran that the captain had built by himself and I'd lived for another six months on the small, very masculine-styled, *Incognito*. I'd showered from buckets, hunkered down with cockroaches and learned to engineer useful bits of boat equipment out of odds and sods. All that, I now realised, would stand me in good stead on *Papagayo*.

Ben and Vicky had chosen to name their yacht after the strong wind that blew off the Mexican coast that had beaten them to within an inch of their lives. They'd survived the storm that *Papagayo* brought, and naming their yacht after it was almost like a peace offering. Looking around, I wondered what this *Papagayo* would have in store for me.

Ben had told me that she was an offshore racing yacht, and I could see that in her stripped-down interior. There were no niceties here – no hull lining or prettying up of things. The ceiling and the walls at the back of the boat were exposed whitish fibreglass – rough, not sanded to match the smoothness of the navy hull outside. All of the through-deck fittings were clearly visible. I could tell where the winches were on the deck above me by the circles of four or five washers and the back ends of the sturdy bolts that slotted through them.

Behind me, in the aft of the boat, were four metal stretcher-type bunks – rectangular steel frames with curved corners that held stretched blue canvas. These bunks were bolted to the walls of the boat and were stacked two high. Past them I could clearly see the steering mechanism of the wheel and the exhaust pipe from the engine. The engine itself was hidden in a large, cream-coloured, bungee-corded box immediately behind the steps.

In front of me was the main saloon. There was a 'sofa' on either side of the boat – upholstered benches with removable cushioned seat pads and backrests. Above each of those was a narrow shelf, about 2 feet deep, again with a royal-blue seat pad on it. The clearance between the top shelf and the ceiling of the saloon, and a line of exposed bolts, was about 2 feet.

The bench seats and floor were made of dark wood, and further forward on the port side was a small wooden chart table with a flip-up lid, and then a two-burner hob. On the starboard side there was a small, square Formica counter with a lip around it to stop plates from sliding around, and a sink. A wooden cupboard on either side completed the saloon. Ahead of that was a cut-out archway. I walked the 3 metres to the threshold and stuck my head through into the bow of the boat. To my left was a sink; to my right a place where, judging by the loose pipes, a toilet should have been. There was a couple of feet of wooden floorboards and then the rest of the forepeak was a large raised platform, clearly meant for housing sails and little else. It was currently full of buckets, fire extinguishers, a large cool-box and dive equipment.

And that was it. No doors, I realised. No privacy. The three of us were to live for two months in a space little more than 3 metres by 3 metres, with no doors. No doors – and no toilet. No shower, either, from what I could see. I'd lived basically before. On *Gillaroo* we had a bucket for a shower, but there was a bathroom we could use to wash in private. With doors. And a toilet. Here there was nothing. Would the bucket have to serve a double purpose as a shower and a loo? It was all right for the other two – they'd been together for twenty years. But I hardly knew them, really. What was I going to do?

'So, what do you think of my boat?' Ben asked from the saloon. I turned round, gulping to stem my panic. His wide Wallace and Gromit-style grin stood out bright white against his deep tan.

I knew I couldn't hesitate in my answer, not even for a split second, in case he detected any hint of reticence.

'Great!' I said, and forced a smile. 'It's great.'

13

Lone Star state of mind

We were in the wild, wild west. Nineteenth-century wooden stores lined both sides of a dusty street, hand-painted signs on tall frontages sticking up above like two-dimensional top hats. A veranda spanned the length of the wide avenue, its roof held up by ornate posts that curved prettily where the filigree brackets met the ironwork, and bathed the sidewalks in shade. The street between them, hot under a dry November sun, was almost empty. We could have been in the 1800s; only the cowboys here had Harley-Davidsons for steeds, rather than horses.

After a week of boat jobs – fitting an autopilot, a furler for the foresail and grab rails on the deck; adding a reef to the mainsail, lee cloths to the top bunks and, thankfully, a toilet in the forepeak and a curtain for privacy – we'd taken the day off to visit the nearby town of Galveston, a quiet dock town and, this weekend, host to the Lone Star Rally.

Hundreds of thousands of Harley-Davidsons, plus owners and enthusiasts, arrive in Galveston for four days every November for what is the largest motorcycle event in North America. Row upon row of bikes, their chrome polished to a competition-standard gleam, fill every spare patch of side street and huge bike parks are set up in readiness. And with the motorbikes come the easy riders.

It looked like the cast of a Mad Max movie had taken over the town for the weekend. There was a standard uniform, and everyone, bar us, was wearing it. The men dressed in black leather boots and jackets or vests emblazoned with their club colours, their stonewashed jeans buckled under bulging guts and their waistcoats displaying hairy upper arms in which the muscle had long since turned to fat. Beards and moustaches were the norm and those who were able to wore their hair long in defiance of any thinning at the temples or crowns. With these big, stomping beasts of men came wives and girlfriends, also in uniforms that varied not so much from their partners': blue jeans, diamante-encrusted black T-shirts stretched so tightly across surgically enhanced breasts that you could see the colour of their bras underneath; over-dyed dark hair teased out for volume; a definite brown line inked around the edges of their lips and a steely look in their eyes that said, 'Back off, bitch – this hunk is mine.' Everywhere we turned was a sea of blue denim and black leather.

I'd never been to anything like this in my life, and I was loving it. It was completely and utterly American, down to the warm bottles of Bud being served from makeshift bars in shop doorways, the enormous deep-fried turkey legs and corn dogs on sale on every corner and the 'promo' girls sporting thong bikinis fashioned out of the star-spangled banner. Speaker systems blasted out country music, punctuated by the throaty rumble and loud coughs of motorcycle engines. Everywhere was noise, dirt, hair, grit. It was great.

Ben walked ahead of Vicky and me as we slowly moved through the crowds on the streets of Galveston, wondering where we were supposed to be going. I'm 5 feet 7 inches, and Vicky is only a couple of inches shorter than me, but I felt dwarfed by the size of these giant men around us. They looked intimidating, but every now and then one would politely step aside to let us past and we'd realise they weren't all as surly as they looked.

The souvenir shops were all selling beer, so we bought a round of Coors and three 'koozies' – the Texan name for what Aussies call 'stubby holders'. We don't have much call for them in the UK, partly because we tend to drink pints rather than bottles of beer, and also because the weather rarely gets hot enough that the amount of condensation forming on the outside of a bottle would form a minor inconvenience. Or maybe we just drink more quickly.

We sat on a window ledge and watched Americana go by. I'd been to New York before, and Florida a couple of times, and they didn't feel as foreign as this. For a start, all of the people were huge. Absolutely gigantic, with calves not far off the size of my waist. Everything was supersized – the cars, the roads, drinks, the meals in restaurants. If you chose the healthy option and ordered a chicken salad, it came with two giant breasts. In McDonald's they sold deep-fried chicken drumsticks in a 'biscuit' – a soft white roll – for breakfast, and if you asked for tea you got two pints of overly sugared icy brown water. Asking for a 'to-go box' was the norm, and often there were enough leftovers from my dinner to feed both Vicky and me for lunch the next day.

The Texans drove absolutely everywhere. As well as drive-thru restaurants (and I always think it's strange that fast-food places call themselves 'restaurants'), there were drive-thru chemists and drive-thru banks. Main roads, even in the city, were four or five lanes wide and there were so many sets of traffic lights that the thick black power cables they hung from formed a veritable web at crossroads. The cars were huge – lots of shiny pickups that would put even the biggest Chelsea tractor in the UK to shame – and gas was cheap, some of the cheapest in the country, seeing as how we were so close to where the oil came out of the ground.

As well as eating, Texans are big fans of drinking, but in Kemah, where the marina is, there is no public transport infrastructure to support that. The state is designed around the car and there are few pavements. We were there in winter, when it can be 28°C in the day, but in the summer temperatures can hit the 40s. The advent of air-conditioning was what helped the development of these southern states; before it was common, they were far less populated. At a time when air-conditioning units were becoming accessible to everyone, so were cars (and then air-conditioned cars) – and the newer Texan towns were partly designed with keeping cool in mind. And so everyone drove; and everyone drank and drove. The drink-drive penalties are on a par with those of Britain but that doesn't stop them.

'Quick! Cops! Act normal!' urged one chap when we were on a night out near the marina. He meandered a zigzag path across the parking lot into the shadow of some trees. He was on foot – not even driving at the time.

It wasn't just a couple of bottles they'd have before getting behind the wheel. Beer came in pitchers of about three pints, large plastic jugs with a shot of sealed ice through the centre to keep the lager cold. It was the cheapest – and most popular – way of ordering. After the beers, and during them, even, came the shooters – shot glasses of tequila or whisky. Texans take their drinking very seriously. They don't just start with a friendly beer and see where the night takes them; they are on a mission to get drunk from the get-go. Beer, shooter, beer, shooter, shooter, beer, more shooters. There's no watering down the spirits with mixers. That'd just slow down the inebriation.

Then, whooping loudly, they get behind the wheel of those enormous five-litre pick-ups, shift the automatic gearstick to 'drive' and head home. It's a wonder there's any of them left.

For the three weeks I was in Texas with Ben and Vicky, we went to the supermarket almost every day. There was no fridge on *Papagayo* so we needed to buy fresh food regularly. The Walmart in Kemah was big enough that you could have put at least four British hypermarkets inside it. It had an area inside selling car tyres. It had a fishing and camping aisle – and one where they sold guns. The clothes section was about the size of the entire ground floor of a Debenhams. It was massive.

The fresh produce aisle, where we did most of our shopping, was always empty. The places with the trolley traffic jams were the processed-foods aisles. Here was all manner of weird and wonderful foodstuffs that I had never realised my kitchen was missing. Spray cheese. Pink or green breakfast cereals. Eighteen different varieties of chilli in a can. Chicken in a Biscuit – not like the McDonald's version, but actual chicken, dried and ground into a powder, mixed with flour and treatment agents and god knows what else, and baked into a cracker. There was no such thing as a single bag of crisps. There were single *sacks* of chips. One packet was bigger than a 12-pack variety selection at home. One sack of Cheesy Puffs (Ben's favourite) would last us nearly two weeks.

The milk aisle was confusing beyond belief. Milk came in gallons and there were far more than the three or four varieties we had at home (and I'm talking just cow's milk here). I thought half-and-half sounded closest to semi-skimmed, but it turned out it's a mixture of milk and cream. It's pretty revolting in tea.

Still, it was fun trying to work things out and what made it even more fun when we went to the supermarket was the knowledge that we were buying things for our journey. There was no *Incognito*-style procrastinating here – by the time I'd been in Texas for a fortnight Ben and Vicky were already apologetic about the delay in setting off. Workmen they'd commissioned to add things to the boat – autopilot so we didn't have to steer all the time; a furling system for the front sail, to make using it much less labour-intensive; a second reef in the mainsail to make it safer in strong winds – were very much operating on 'Texas time'. I don't think they saw a lot of business, and the business that they did get in Kemah was mainly from people who had boats and talked big about sailing them away on trips – but never actually did (it sounded familiar). But we weren't like that. We were definitely going, and soon.

Within just a couple of days of the last bolt being fixed in by the professional yacht services people, Vicky and I had bought and stowed enough food and fuel to last us till Florida and Ben had returned the hire car. In true British style, with little pomp and ceremony, we motored out of Seabrook Marina, past Kemah boardwalk, where a few hardy tourists rode funfair rides, and pointed *Papagayo*'s bow out to sea. We still had to make one more stop, in Galveston, to file some paperwork with the Department of Homeland Securities, but that would just be one night in the marina, a quick morning visit to the town hall and then we'd be off on our adventure.

14

Weathering the storm

The water was grey and oily, sitting heavily in the marina like concrete-y sludge, so it was almost a surprise that we cut so easily through it. Up on the bow, I coiled the line that had a minute before held us fast to a tall wooden post, and watched to make sure *Papagayo*'s hull wasn't about to bang into anything as we pulled out of our berth and as Ben turned her 90 degrees to the right to get us out of Galveston and into the Gulf of Mexico.

'All good?' he called from his position at the helm.

'Clear,' I shouted back, thinking how calm he looked. I was a bag of nerves because I was about to start my first official responsible role on a boat, as navigator. Ben and Vicky had asked me to take on the job of getting us from Texas to St Lucia shortly after I arrived in America. I had been daunted by the prospect – the most I'd done before was get a boat from one island to another in Croatia or Greece, something that took just a few hours in water so deep there was no chance of running aground, and the next island on the itinerary had always been visible from the one we were leaving, so all I'd had to do was double-check with a compass that I had the right one, give a course to the person on the helm to steer and go. This time I was being asked to take us more than 2,000 miles, including across the 800-mile-wide Gulf of Mexico, and to multiple stops in more than ten countries. There were major shipping routes, famed shipwrecking areas and notorious rough passages on the way to St Lucia. I tried to convince myself it was 'just' island-hopping – well, once we left mainland USA, the Florida Keys and the Caribbean were all islands – but I knew I was kidding myself.

I dropped the two lines I had coiled through the hatch in the deck and made my way towards the back of the boat, untying a plastic fender as I went. Vicky, ready for sailing in white shorts, bikini top and Ben's green baseball cap, was untying fenders further back. We took them below and tied them to the rail at the front, adding the lines I'd thrown down and two from the back that Vicky had coiled. It wasn't easy tying them to the stainless-steel rails that were suspended horizontally from the ceiling. There was plenty of length to fit all of the fenders, mooring lines and spare ropes we carried; the difficulty was being able to reach far enough forward to find a clear section of pole to tie them to because the raised bed of the forepeak was absolutely stuffed to the brim with gear stowed for our crossing: spare sails, Ben and Vicky's dive kit, a vacuum cleaner, fire extinguisher and the giant cool-box that served as our fridge and was packed with ice, vegetables, ham, cheese and milk that would only keep fresh for a couple of days. There was no door to the forepeak, only the roll-down toilet-in-use privacy curtain, so the whole lot had been tied in place for the journey with a long piece of plastic string that weaved back and forth, up and down at all angles, looping round handles and through fastenings, as if a giant spider had got drunk in a hoarder's house and forgotten how to make a proper web.

The last mooring line I had to stow felt damp and claggy against my palm as I reached up to tie it to the pole. By wriggling the outer edge of one bare foot into the restrained mass of tied-up stuff I managed to find an inch of surface – enough to heave myself up and on to the pile, the rough surface of a dive bag grating my knee caps, so that I could extend my arms and tie the rope away.

Everything stowed, I jumped off the shelf and stood, rubbing my palms together like a builder celebrating a job well done. Tiny specks of salt, sand and shell felt gritty on my skin but I didn't bother washing my hands. We were off to sea for a week on a boat with no bathroom. There wouldn't be much washing going on.

The bright Texan sky blinded me temporarily as I emerged into the cockpit of the boat. Ben had just steered us out of the marina. The loading cranes of Galveston docks stood tall and black in the morning sun, looking like praying mantis' legs.

The three of us had bright, wide smiles. This was it – we were off on our adventure. Compared to all that procrastinating on *Incognito*, it seemed so easy. I was finally going to get to see the Caribbean – and not just view one island from the safety of an all-inclusive resort; I was going to visit places I'd barely heard of, to dig my toes into the soft, white sand of countless beaches while sipping piña coladas, swim in clear blue waters, dance to reggae and eat a lot of jerk chicken. I'd be living in cut-off jeans and a string bikini top and I'd be brown as a nut. I'd probably meet lots of handsome, tanned men at beach parties who'd invite me to glamorous parties on verandas where I'd be introduced to people who'd offer me jobs working for their boating businesses, impressed with my skills navigating a yacht all the way from Texas. I'd end up living in a little condo on a beach somewhere, eating barbecued fish for dinner that I'd buy from one of my fishermen friends, and I'd become accepted as a local and sometimes accidentally slip into a little Creole. It was going to be amazing.

The floor of the cockpit poked sharp holes into my cheekbone, stopping me from sleeping. To make the surface safer and non-slip, tiny granules of glass had been mixed into thick paint and so it felt like I had a bed of nails for a pillow. I tried resting my cheek on my hand, but the prickling sensation started up in my palm instead. It was no good – I was never going to get any rest.

I opened my eyes, resigned to the fact I wouldn't sleep, but I didn't stand. The boat was heeled over so much that it was too much effort, and I had pretty much zero left in the way of energy reserves. I would need every once of strength I had left for steering the boat on my next hour-and-a-half shift, which was about to start any minute. So I stayed on the floor, dressed in full oilskins and lifejacket, my lifeline clipped to the D-ring by the hatch, and wedged myself more firmly into the small gap on the cockpit floor. Curled on one side, crossways across the boat, I pushed the top of my head into the base of one bench and my bare feet into the opposite one, trying to stop my body from being thrown around quite so much. It didn't make any difference.

Everything had been great when we left Galveston. We were barely out of the harbour when a dolphin came to play in our bow wave, its sleek grey back cutting through the surface of the water as it raced to keep up with us. I took it as a good omen and, to start with, things were fine. Then the problems began.

As navigator, I'd been given the task of planning our route from Galveston to Key West, the island furthest south in the chain that hooks down from the tip of Florida. I'd chosen that as our point of departure from America – from there we'd go to the Bahamas and then into the Caribbean proper.

The first thing I'd done was unfurl the paper charts of the Gulf of Mexico that Ben and Vicky had bought. I smoothed out the large sheet of paper on the floor of the gym at the marina and drew a pencil ring around Galveston and another round Key West. So far, so good. Then I looked at the expanse of water between those two points – some 800 miles, about a week's worth of sailing – and doubt started to creep in. More than half of the enormous bay was peppered with thousands of the same little symbol: a black dot with a black square around it. It was like someone had fired buckshot at the chart. There were so many that in places I couldn't see clear sea between them. The symbols, I knew, stood for oil rigs. Huge, tall, dangerous things that we could crash into. And our line from Galveston to Key West went straight through hundreds of them. I gulped. This was going to be a nightmare.

The thing with maps and charts is that symbols are shown out of proportion. In reality, there were hundreds of oil rigs in our path, but they tended to be fifteen minutes or half an hour apart, and we had plenty of time to steer out of their way. That was when we could see them, though. Some of them had lights on, so at night we were able to spot them from a long way off and ignore them. But some were unlit, and others were hidden under the surface of the sea, proving an invisible danger because the keel that extended 7 feet down from *Papagayo*'s hull meant we could still hit a submerged rig if we miscalculated our position and tried to pass over it. And if we hit something like that, we'd probably gouge a big hole in the boat, and sinking, hundreds of miles from land, would become a reality.

Most of the oil rigs were marked on the chart, so we knew that there'd be another one coming up shortly, but sometimes there would be a rig where none was marked on the chart and a few times they were on the chart but we couldn't see them in reality. Our eyes started to strain with the effort of constantly looking around us for three days, especially in the dark, desperately trying to find something that was no longer there.

The rigs themselves were all different from each other. Some were from the earliest days of oil extraction and looked like they were made out of wood. Of these, generally little remained other than four posts and a bit of a rickety platform. It's difficult to gauge the scale of things at sea, but I'd guess that the older rigs had a footprint the size of a large room.

The seabed of the Gulf of Mexico remains quite shallow in the northern part – too shallow for *Papagayo*, with her draught, to call in at places I longed to visit because they sounded so cool, such as Mobile, Alabama, and Pascagoula, Mississippi. The older oil rigs – they started boring in the 1890s – sit on this shelf. Once you move south, the water gets deeper and this is where the newer rigs were drilled. The really enormous ones, such as Deepwater Horizon, which was drilling for BP when it exploded in April 2010, spilling (according to the courts) more than four million barrels of oil into the Gulf, are located further south and east, in the deeper water. Deepwater Horizon was capable of drilling in 8,000 feet of water. If it had still been operating when we sailed past, it would have marked the halfway point of our journey. According to the chart, the second half of the gulf was mercifully clear of rigs – but we weren't quite there yet.

On our fourth day, just as we were getting towards the end of the oil fields and looking forward to a bit of an easier time of it, not being constantly on high alert, a big storm blew in – and took with it our autopilot.

I was helming, sitting at the back of the boat by the steering wheel, as we sailed along in increasingly high winds, when there was a bang below me and the autopilot alarm started beeping. I crouched down by the console, trying to work out what was wrong. Ben stuck his head up from below, woken by the noise.

'What's wrong?' he asked, rubbing sleep from his eyes.

'I don't know. The alarm won't switch off.'

He staggered up in his underpants and I steered the boat by hand while he crouched into the small space beside me, pressing the buttons on the autopilot.

'Shit!' he muttered, and dashed below. I watched the back of his head as he shot down the steps in one bound, a feeling of worry starting to build inside me. Within a few minutes, he was back in the cockpit.

'It's busted,' he said. 'The bracket's snapped clean through.'

'Can you fix it?'

'Nope – it needs welding.'

It wasn't the end of the world but I knew it was a significant blow for him and Vicky. They'd spent thousands having the autopilot fitted because they knew how invaluable it would be. Sailors often call the autopilot 'the extra crew member' because if you've got a machine steering the boat it frees everyone up to do other things. I like hand-steering but it can get very tiring when you're doing it for hours on end.

We were running a shift pattern, which meant each of us would be on watch – in charge of running the yacht – for an hour and a half while the other two rested, and then we'd get three hours off before we were on for another ninety minutes. Using Autohelm meant that we could do things like nip to the loo, make a cup of tea, go below to fill in our position on the chart and in the log, and check on the computers that our course was good. Without it, we'd be effectively chained to the wheel for an hour and half at a time. It made everything more difficult, but not impossible.

Then the storm got worse. Ben had very sensibly decided to have another reef put into *Papagayo*'s main sail in Kemah. Because she was a race boat, designed to be sailed by eight crew or more and constantly pushed to her limit, she only had one reef in the sail, which meant that when the winds got up we could only reduce the sail area, and therefore slow down the boat and make it safer, by a small amount. Adding a second reef meant we were able to reduce our sail area a bit further but we were lacking the third reef that most yachts have. If there is too much sail up in very strong winds you can become overpowered – effectively losing the ability to steer the boat. There's also a heightened risk that the boat will broach: tip over so far that her side is in the water.

With growing winds, we reefed the mainsail down as small as we could, and furled away some of the jib to match, but that was all we could do. We just had to hang on and hope the boat would cope.

The boat coped fine. I, however, did not.

I've not got the strongest build in the world. I'm by no means Twiggy-thin, but I do have pretty weedy arms. They're fine for doing most things but, it turns out, not so good at wrestling with the helm of an ocean-going race yacht when she's caught in a hoolie. After my first hour-and-a-half shift hand-steering through the storm, all the muscles in my body were screaming with pain. The wind was so strong that I had to use my entire body weight to force the steering wheel to go where I needed it to. I had to take my hands off the edge of the large steel wheel and wrap them around the spokes instead, gripping vertically and pulling with two hands with all my might. At the same time, the boat was heeling over so far that the only way I could stand was with one foot on the floor and the other braced against the side of the seat next to me, so that I was effectively in a wide-legged squat, pushing away with the extended leg, for the whole shift. Every time I felt the pull of the rudder as the water pushed it away, I braced my legs, leant with my whole body and yanked with my arms, trying to get *Papagayo* to stay on course. It was utterly punishing. Vicky is slighter than me, so it must have been even worse for her.

Seeing Ben's head pop through the companionway to take over from me at the end of my first watch like this brought a feeling of relief like no other. That didn't last. Below, the boat was heeled over so much that standing on the wooden floor, which was slick with salt water leaking in through one of the deck fittings, was hard, to say the least. The toilet was on the high side and the only way I could remain sitting on it was to reach forward as far as I could and grab the sink on the other side of the boat. My face was pointed at where the floor would have been, had the boat been level. To stand, and pull my trousers up, I had to follow the rhythm of the boat and effectively guess when I thought we were in the trough of a wave to make a grab at my waistband and find a handhold again, double-quick. Time after time I misjudged it and pitched head forwards into the opposite wall, my bare bottom sticking up in the air.

Taking off full oilskins likewise took an age, and climbing into bed was tricky also. Once I was thrown so violently off the settee when I was trying to climb into my bunk that I did a backwards somersault through the air and chipped a piece of bone from my shin when it struck wood as I landed. By the time I'd come off watch, struggled downstairs, filled in the log, checked the navigation, called the course up to Ben steering, gone to the loo, brushed my teeth, taken my kit off, hung it up, worked out which of the bunks on the low side was free, retrieved my sleeping bag and pillow and crawled into it, all while wearing a head torch with its red light on, I'd have maybe an hour and a half to sleep at best, before the struggle to get dressed would start again.

As the storm raged into its second day, and our strength ebbed further (we effectively gave up eating and drinking, as it took up too much time and probably would have ended up over the side anyway), Ben cut the watches to forty-five minutes, which meant only one and a half hours off, and possibly just forty minutes of snatched sleep each time. Hence the reason I was lying fully clothed in the cockpit of the boat, with glass paint digging into my cheek. I thought I'd try it, to see if I got more sleep that way. Obviously I was wrong.

We had no idea how long the storm would last and how much of this hell we could endure. At my lowest ebb, lying on the cockpit floor, I asked myself what on earth I was doing, voluntarily putting myself into situations like these. But most of the time, especially when I was on watch, I was so busy concentrating on not killing us that I just got on with it as best I could.

After two days, the winds died, leaving a clear, pinkish dawn overhead. Within hours, the waves died down too. With no wind, Ben went to start the engine – and we discovered that that had died as well.

It was almost funny. After a 48-hour living nightmare with winds so powerful they threatened to destroy us, we were now effectively drifting, becalmed, in the middle of the Gulf of Mexico. We'd gone from one extreme to another.

All three of us were on deck, in the cockpit. No one had washed for five or six days – and I knew I hadn't even changed my underwear – but I couldn't smell anything because we were all wrapped in so many wind- and water-proof layers. After the incessant noise of the storm, screaming round the rigging and thwacking the sails, and the motorway-like roar of the water behind us, it was calm. There were no ships as far as the horizon, and the oil rigs were long past us, so Ben lashed the steering wheel, fixing us on our course, and we had a team meeting.

'Right,' Vicky said. 'Let's take stock of what we've got and make a plan B. And first of all, let's have something to eat.'

The other two had been suffering from bad headaches. I suspect these were caused by dehydration, as we'd barely drunk anything for a couple of days. I was fine, and I didn't even feel that hungry, since I'd managed to shove a couple of broken granola bars down my throat just before each watch. But once the smell of real food hit me, I realised I was starving.

Vicky went through our food stores, throwing away vegetables that had started to rot in the melted ice in the cool-box, and I mopped the sludgy salt-water residue from the floor of the inside of the boat, rolled down the privacy curtain, stripped off and had a wet wipe bath. Changing into clean leggings and T-shirt felt amazing. My hair was matted beyond belief by the wind but it'd have to wait until Florida and a hot shower.

We ate in the cockpit, shovelling noodles into our mouths like there was no tomorrow and downing great draughts of water and tea, then I went to bed, continuing to drift gently east towards Florida with the current, and slept like the dead.

15

Pete'll fix it

'What's your decision, then?' Ben asked, a few hours later, after I woke and started to come to terms with our situation. There was still absolutely zero wind and the calm conditions made the storm feel like a nightmare dreamed of years ago.

I turned round the spiral-bound book of charts I had in my lap so he could see it.

'I reckon Vicky is right – we go to St Petersburg. We're bound to get some wind sooner or later, and this is a pretty big town, so there'll be mechanics and people like that there.' I pushed my hair back off my forehead. It felt grainy. 'It's in Tampa Bay, and I've been there before. Tampa's a bit of a dump but needs must and all that.'

He nodded. 'OK. Can you do us a new passage plan to there? I'll go and have another go at the engine.'

After hours of trying everything he could think of, he finally got the engine going by filling it with half a can of starter fuel – a risky procedure but one we were glad he tried once we heard it chug back into life. I normally hate the loud clack of a boat's engine – it reminds me that we're not sailing, and they're unbearably loud – but this time it was a welcome sound. Vicky gave a little cheer. As long as it held out and we had enough fuel to get us to St Petersburg, there was no way any of us was going to switch it off, even if the wind rose enough to give us perfect sailing conditions.

I chose St Petersburg because it was the closest large port and made the most sense but privately I was gutted we wouldn't be going to Key West. I hadn't liked Florida at all both times I'd been before. I'd found it ugly and full of drunks on holiday, not that far removed from some of the sadder seaside towns in the UK, just on a larger scale. I bit back my disappointment and didn't tell the others.

They call Florida the Sunshine State but if the sun was shining when we arrived, we couldn't see it because we were in thick fog. We all had to don extra jumpers and woolly hats in the cooling damp and Ben gleefully sounded the fog horn every two minutes to signal to any other ships that we were nearby. It was just after dawn as we passed under the not-so-sunshiney Sunshine Skyway bridge that spans Tampa Bay and turned off towards St Petersburg. The fog burned off quickly once the sun rose and, despite the dreary start to the day, we were all smiles as we followed the navigation channel into the unfamiliar town and headed towards the marina. We slipped into a berth, tied up, turned off the engine and went in search of food and a well-earned beer, the stresses of the trip quickly dissipating and turning from horror stories into interesting anecdotes to store up for the future.

Despite my reservations about Florida, St Petersburg turned out to be a beautiful city. It was the antithesis of Kemah and so much more than a body of water separated them. There are two universities in the town and the marina we pulled in to was located a little way out of the city centre, on the far side of one of the campuses. To get into St Pete itself, it was a 20-minute walk down a straight road lined with trees and green areas.

In Texas, the car was so pivotal that there were barely any pavements and the furthest we went on foot was from a car park to a store entrance, round the shop and back again. In St Pete there were sidewalks everywhere, some running through landscaped gardens, and cycle tracks and jogging routes. In contrast to the enormously overweight Texans, the St Pete inhabitants seemed to flaunt their good health. Everywhere we went there were people – thin people, not at all what I'd become used to – running and working out, enjoying outdoorsy lifestyles in this green city by the sea. And they were friendly, too. When we accidentally gatecrashed a private party on a rooftop bar the hostess welcomed us and posed for photographs with us. We quickly made friends in the marina and were invited to barbecues and out for sunset cruises on motor yachts.

I could see myself living here, I thought as I helped myself to a free Krispy Kreme donut in the Captain's Lounge – a room with leather sofas, TVs and wifi that was provided for anyone staying in the marina to use. *There are running clubs that meet in pubs, art and community events every weekend, thrift stores, cute little cafes and coffee shops, boats and even yoga classes held on stand-up paddle boards. All my kind of thing – apart from possibly the paddle board part. But who knows? Maybe I'd enjoy that, too.*

It was a good job I liked St Pete so much. Because we ended up being stranded there for quite a while.

'That's it!' Ben whooped, relief obvious in his voice. 'We have autopilot again.'

After we'd limped into St Pete, taken ourselves off for a seared ahi tuna salad and a beer and had a long-overdue shower, Ben and Vicky had wasted no time in calling in the experts to tend to *Papagayo*'s wounds.

'That's your problem right there,' said one burly chap, tapping the top of the steel fuel tank that was hidden under the port-side bunk. His fingers made a hollow sound. 'You're plain out of diesel.'

We knew he was wrong – we'd motored all the way here after the storm – but we topped up the tank anyway and, following much coughing and spluttering, the engine finally started. It was odd but we shrugged it off and happily accepted it.

Next a whiz of a rigger managed to weld our autopilot bracket, strengthening it in the process, and repair the baby stay – one of the steel cables that help support the mast, which had also broken in the storm.

Vicky and I cleaned the inside of the boat, bailing out bucket after bucket of salt water that the storm had left behind, wiped everything down and re-provisioned. It was all done extremely quickly and we felt smug that we'd been held up for only a few nights in the marina while all these jobs were done. I planned out our route to the Bahamas, we waved goodbye to our neighbour on his boat on the next pontoon and then we pulled away from the dock.

'Shit!' said Ben, as the engine died. He managed to get it going with almost a whole can of starter fuel and it had just enough power to get us back to the berth we'd just left.

'It's definitely not the diesel,' he said.

Mechanic after mechanic after mechanic came to look at *Papagayo* and none could work out what the problem was. None could even figure out how the engine worked in the first place. She was fitted with a truck engine, a VW tractor motor re-jigged with a seawater-cooling system to 'marinise' it.

Mechanic number three actually scratched his head as he looked at the engine.

'I just can't see how it even lifts fuel from the tank to the engine,' he said.

I was getting more and more frustrated with these so-called experts by the minute. The engine obviously could work – it had been running (not including recent events, of course) for the best part of thirty years. Just because it was slightly different from the motors they more commonly saw, they didn't have the brains to work out the mechanics of it. If they could do that, they should be able to fix it. Mechanics who don't understand mechanics? As the Americans would say – go figure.

Ben and Vicky were far more sanguine about it than I was. Really, it should have been the other way round. This boat was their property, their home and their future business.

'I don't have a pension,' I had told Ben one day, as we were chatting about the future.

He had spread his arms wide. 'This is my pension. You're sitting on it.'

And he was about to invest heavily in it. They took the decision to buy a brand-new engine and have it fitted in St Petersburg, which meant we'd be stalled here for some time.

While we waited for the new engine to arrive and for the mechanics to crane out the old one, crane in the new one and get everything going again, I formed my own mini work routine. I'd had an email from Liz, the editor at Bloomsbury publishers, about my book. I held my breath as I saw her name in my inbox and I paused for a moment as I hovered the cursor over it, issuing a little prayer that it would be good news, that she'd be saying she loved *Casting Off*, that she wanted to publish it immediately, and that she wanted to pay me a great big advance. Time standing still, I clicked.

She fed me a praise burger (that silly business-world phrase works well for me, since I can't stand beef patties). The first bit of bread: she liked it. The chewy middle part: it wasn't really flowing well; it needed work. The bottom half of the bun: 'If you want to have a go at re-writing, I'll take a second look at it.'

As rejections from publishers go, it was a brilliant one – and only half a rejection, at that. So every morning we were in St Pete I settled myself down on one of the battered tan-leather sofas in the Captain's Lounge, did my best to ignore the 24/7 CNN coverage that was blasting out of the TV in the corner, the smell of burnt coffee as the percolator ran dry, and the temptation of the free Krispy Kreme donuts (I didn't always manage that last part) and got down to re-writing, honing and crafting my story into something I thought Liz would accept.

As much as I liked this city, I was still itching to get away. The Caribbean was so close now. We couldn't feel it in the culture, which was resolutely American – there were none of the Cuban influences here that you get on the Miami side of Florida – but I could almost taste it on the warm salt winds that rippled off the bay. More prosaically, I wanted to get a move on because I was running out of both money and time. I had a return flight booked from St Lucia at the beginning of January and it was now early December. As a freelance, every week that I wasn't working meant I wasn't earning and being on land rather than out at sea meant we were spending more. My bank balance took a nosedive and I started to panic a little.

Every day, while we waited for the new engine, I fetched out the books and charts and went over the route again and again, looking for any shortcuts to help us reach St Lucia in time for me to make my plane. I measured out distances, consulted my diary and wrote dates next to destinations. I pushed it as hard as I could but there was no way we were ever going to get there by 4 January, even if we never stopped and just pushed straight on.

And it seemed like it would be such a waste to do that – to have to sail past wonderful tropical islands, never pausing to experience the Caribbean for real, just viewing the white beaches and palms from afar like a moving version of a postcard. So I raised it with Ben and Vicky and rearranged my return flight for a month later, thinking that if I was careful with my dwindling resources, I'd just about scrape through. Pleased with myself, I looked at the list of destinations I had written in my pad – Bimini and Long Island in the Bahamas, Providenciales in the Turks and Caicos Islands, the Dominican Republic, Puerto Rico, the Virgin Islands, Guadeloupe, Martinique – and the 'best-case scenario' and 'worst-case scenario' dates I had written next to them. It was going to be a fast and furious Caribbean tour, but it was possible, and with two or three stops listed for some of the larger islands, we were going to be able to see quite a lot of places. Much as I enjoy hanging around boats and marinas, three weeks in Texas and a fortnight in Florida was going to be nothing compared to six weeks spent Caribbean-island-hopping. I smiled to myself.

Vicky gasped loudly and sat up straight, bringing her feet close in towards her, blue-painted toenails disappearing under the hems of her jogging bottoms. 'What's that?'

I followed her line of sight to the semi-transparent hatch that slid over the steps that led down into the yacht. A small shadow scuttled quickly from left to right, its outline blurred.

'Oh shit!' said Ben, scrambling to his feet and shutting the ceiling hatch above Vicky's head in one move, kicking the fold-up chair behind him in the process.

'What?' I asked. I was still lying on my bunk, half lost in the film we'd been watching on a laptop perched on the stairs.

'Rat!' they both shouted, a blur of action.

When it was decided *Papagayo* was to have a new engine, the marina had asked us to move her to the yard, since the engine would have to be lifted in by crane and the lorry carrying the crane wouldn't be able to use the dock we were currently moored alongside. With a lot of finger crossing and praying, and with other yacht-owners on standby in case we needed a tow if our dying motor packed up again, we stuttered our way half a mile to the yard: out of the marina, across the harbour and up and into a creek full of green water. What we found was not a yard in the traditional sense – no hardstanding covered with boats in various states of repair – but a couple of dodgy-looking wooden posts by short tumble-down jetties and some filthy warehouses. We eased *Papagayo*'s nose into tall weeds growing on the water's edge and tied ropes around the posts, hoping they'd be strong enough to support her. To get ashore we would have to walk right to the front of the boat, grab hold of the furled headsail with one hand and climb over the metal rail that carried the navigation lights, step down on to a ledge only an inch or so wide and then leap on to the precarious jetty. It was cumbersome and not something we could do easily.

'Lovely spot,' said Ben, sarcasm heavy in his voice.

Workmen were around in the day but at night we were the only people there. There were no electric lights and the nearest road was a good five minutes' walk away. We were pretty isolated and alone.

Apart, it seemed, from the rats.

When Vicky spotted the first one on our first night, she and Ben moved round the boat at lightning speed, closing hatches and stopping up any entry holes with old towels and weighted bits of board – anything they could find.

'We don't want it getting in,' Vicky said. 'They're a nightmare to get rid of.'

It sounded like she spoke with the voice of experience but I was too creeped out to want to know any of the details.

The ironic thing was that no part of the boat was touching land, which made it more difficult for the rats to get on board.

This one we saw must have scurried along one of the two lines tied to our bow and then scrambled the rest of the way along the deck to the cockpit. In the split-second flash I'd had of its shadow, it had seemed a hefty size. Not as big as a cat – but big enough to revolt us.

'They can probably smell the food on board,' Ben said. 'We'll have to get rid of all our rubbish before the sun goes down.'

For the rest of the week, it was battle stations. Whatever we were doing in the marina or in St Pete, we dropped everything to race along in the dinghy to ensure we were back before sunset – the witching (or ratting) hour. After dinner, we bagged up any rubbish, threw it into the cockpit and closed and locked every hatch and stopped every hole. Then we hunkered down, until dawn, pretending we couldn't hear the tell-tale scratching of pattering paws above our heads in the dead of night. It was pretty gross, being held hostage by a bunch of rodents, but our plan worked, and we never saw a rat inside the boat, nor at all once we left the creek.

After three weeks in St Pete, the old engine had been craned out, the new one craned in and the engine tried and tested. Ben and Vicky's bank balance was considerably lighter and, because I'd been inspired by all the active Floridians I saw everywhere, I was a little bit fitter, having put on my running shoes a few times and gone exploring the city on foot.

Christmas had been a milestone date for me. I hadn't been relishing the prospect of spending Christmas Day boxed inside the yacht, hiding from rats. As it drew closer, and staff at the supermarket took to wearing full Santa costumes and beards, despite the summer-style temperatures, I found myself getting as antsy as I had been when I was stuck in Langkawi.

This time, though, Ben and Vicky were as keen to get on as I was, so they did everything they could to get us ready. When Ben announced we would be leaving on 23 December, I slipped a few turkey breasts and some cranberry sauce into my shopping basket on a final run to the supermarket, so that we could attempt to celebrate the big day in some kind of a traditional way, even if we were at sea. We had no oven, just a small two-hob burner – so I wasn't quite sure how I was going to achieve it – but I decided I'd be able to work something out.

I think we were the envy of the marina as we slipped our lines and headed out back under the Sunshine Skyway bridge – for all their talk of trips, voyages and adventures, the other sailors never seemed to actually go anywhere on their boats but just used them as an (expensive) extension of their backyards. We had an overnight passage to Marathon, in the Keys, where we'd check out of the States, and then it'd be a hop into the Gulf Stream on Christmas Eve and, like the surfer-dude turtles in *Finding Nemo*, a fast and free ride north up to Bimini, the closest island in the Bahamas and my first taste of the Caribbean.

16

Party at the end of the world

The heavy baseline of dance-mixed reggae boomed out into the wooden shack, sending vibrations through my bones and into the centre of my body.

I dug my heels further into the cool sand, marvelling at how soft it was. The fingers of my right hand trailed a pattern in the grains, piling them up with a stroke away and raking them flat again as my hand moved idly back towards my leg. Someone leaned over me, their torso briefly blocking out the orange glow of the outdoor lights.

'Here,' a man's accented voice said. I took a plastic cup and held it to my lips. A blast of fumes filled my nostrils; a sweet tang worked its way backwards along each side of my tongue. Rum.

I was sitting in the outdoor area of a Bimini nightclub, a fenced-off square behind a wooden shack, filled with soft sand carried over from the beach. There were a couple of chairs in the corner but I'd opted for the floor, digging a comfortable seat in the sand with my bum and resting my back against the wooden planks of the wall. The coolness of the sand was invading the seat of my jeans but it wasn't cold enough to be uncomfortable. I was warm from the rum, which had thrown everything into mellow soft focus. The guy sitting next to me tapped the back of my hand with one finger, to emphasise a point he was making. I watched it, noticed the way the brown of his skin faded out along a line around the side, changing to a shocking pink. I took another sip of rum and half listened to the timbre of his voice, following the tones without really taking in the words. It was two o'clock in the morning on Boxing Day and I was at the End of the World.

Two days and a couple of hundred miles had transported us to a very different place. On 23 December we'd left St Pete, sailed down the west coast of Florida, slipped between the Keys and stopped briefly at a marina in the town of Marathon to get some more diesel and ice and to catnap ahead of our overnight passage. On the afternoon of Christmas Eve Ben had hauled up the anchor, bent double over the rail, muscles in his shoulders straining as he pulled the chain and anchor up from the white sandy seabed and stowed it below decks. We were all quiet as we motored gently out of America and pointed *Papagayo*'s bows north-east towards the Bahamas.

We sailed non-stop through the night, taking it in turns to be on deck as we counted down the miles until we reached Bimini, the first in the chain of 700 Bahamian islands that stretch 600 miles through water so blue you can't believe it hasn't been Photoshopped.

As the morning passed, my excitement rose. In three hours … two hours … thirty minutes we'd be in the Caribbean, after just a mere hop out from the States. I scanned the horizon for any signs of land, hoping to god that I'd got my calculations right when working out our course to steer, and that the strong Gulf Stream current hadn't swept us along and past our mark like a travelator in the sea.

What will it look like? I wondered. Will there be a beach? Will there be palm trees? Will everything be painted bright colours and will people pass by and smile big white smiles and say 'mon' at the end of every sentence?

Bimini didn't disappoint. The Bahamas are, in the main, low-lying islands, so we were almost there before we saw it. As we took down the sails and got out the lines ready to tie *Papagayo* to the dock, Ben asked me to go on the VHF radio and call Browns Marina.

It took a few goes before anyone answered, then I got through to a man who gave me some rough directions.

'Will we be starboard or port-side to?' I asked him over the radio.

'Whichever you wan,' he said, his accent thick.

'And what number berth?' I asked.

I thought I heard chuckling from the handset, although it might have been the static. 'You jus' look for me. I be wavin' at you.'

I nipped up the stairs back into the cockpit and saw that we'd turned the corner of the island and were very nearly there.

I'd visited marinas in lots of different countries by now and I knew they could vary considerably. Many are enormous concrete constructions with thousands of boats of all different sizes squeezed together in uniform rows. Others, like the one we used in Sri Lanka when we were on *Gillaroo*, are old naval facilities, pretty rough and ready, with old tyres slung over the sides of high concrete walls on long chains and ship carcasses everywhere. I hadn't seen any photos of Bimini Marina in our pilot book but I had a mental image that fell somewhere between these two versions – large, lots of concrete, boats everywhere. What I saw now was nothing like that at all.

We were motoring down a channel between two islands that were only a couple of hundred metres apart. The water was a bright, deep blue, lightening to turquoise at the edges where it shallowed on to white beaches. In front and to the left were a few ramshackle wooden buildings with tin roofs. Past those, a little way further into the channel, tall planks of dark wood rose vertically from the water, some standing straight up like masts, others nailed diagonally across at haphazard angles. They seemed to stretch for metres above the surface of the water, and on top of them were horizontal planks of the same dark wood, none of it uniform but more like hand-hewn planks roughly hacked from spindly trees and quickly tacked together. The whole lot looked not dissimilar to a matchstick tower, scaled up and black in contrast to the bright sunlight that made the water underneath and around the structure glow. A silhouette moved across the precarious pile and started to wave.

'*Papagayo*!' a voice called out from the radio, which I'd left on below. 'Welcome to Bimini, mon!'

'This was Ernest Hemingway's favourite marina,' Browns' manager told us once we'd tied up *Papagayo* and gone to check in. 'He liked to stay here an' go fishin'.'

I could see why. The water was incredibly clear – swimming-pool clear – and an astonishing iridescent colour, with ripples of light arcing their way through its depths, reflected off the surface waves. I know little about fishing but it looked like it might yield something.

I was still struggling with the word 'marina' to describe the place. It was really just a few wooden jetties jutting out of the sea and looked old enough to have actually been used by Hemingway to tie up his boat *Pilar*.

Papagayo was moored closest to the shore and only metres from her side deck was a square wooden bar with a thatched roof that was shielding us from the sun while we chatted to the friendly marina manager.

'You have all the facilities you need here,' said the manager, the short sleeve of his cotton shirt flapping as he leaned across the wooden counter to gesticulate at the marina grounds. 'You have the shower block over there, the barbecue over there, the sunbathin' area over there.' As he spoke, I looked over towards a couple of cute sheds (housing the showers and toilets – and probably quite a few mosquitoes), a patio with gas grill and table and chairs and – hooray! – a sandy area with sun loungers on it.

'Everytin' that the sailors want,' he said. His mega-watt smile faded a little. 'Unfortunately, the bar is closed today, for Christmas.'

Ben, who had been squinting in the sun to look at the facilities, turned back to the manager.

'Seems pretty quiet. Is anywhere open?'

The smile was back. 'Yeah, it's quiet today. Las' night everyone was celebratin' at End of the World Bar. So now they all restin'.'

Vicky spoke up. 'I suppose that means it's closed tonight as well?'

I wondered if she was thinking what I was thinking – a cold beer would be a great way to celebrate Christmas. The ice we'd bought in Marathon had half melted by now and our food was paddling around inside the cool-box.

'No, mon.' The manager laughed. 'Bar openin' tonight, all right. They just restin' now.'

'Where is it?' I asked.

He pointed across a small beach to a wooden shack a couple of hundred metres away that looked from this distance like a dilapidated old garage. His smooth forearm gleamed in the sun like it had been basted with butter.

'Right, well maybe we'll go later.'

Ben and Vicky echoed my nod and we finished off the paperwork and headed to the white plastic sun loungers for a well-earned afternoon snooze.

Once the traditional Christmas Day afternoon naps were over (for once, real tiredness was to blame, rather than an overconsumption of turkey and twenty-five different types of vegetables), we set off exploring. North Bimini is a narrow stick of an island, snapped in two, and the marina was tucked just inside one end. The main road ran parallel to the sea, lengthways, and as we turned out of the marina we found ourselves in a little village called Alice Town that had spread itself, one blocky concrete building deep, along the street. The marina manager had been right – pretty much everything was closed, apart from a hotel bar a little way down, the Bimini Big Game Club, which also had a marina that claimed to have been Ernest Hemingway's favourite. A little further on was a third marina, proclaiming the same thing.

'Seems like he was a pretty fickle chap,' I joked to Vicky.

As we walked, we passed few cars but did see a couple of parked golf carts, a popular method of getting around this tiny island, which was only one kilometre long and had just two roads – the main street that lined the eastern side of the land and a rougher, empty track that ran along the western, exposed shore, raised above the long beach.

I noticed that the soft tarmac beneath me was pitted with small marks that glinted in the sun. I bent down to take a better look.

'They're beer-bottle tops!' Golf carts and sandalled feet must have pushed them down into the melted tar on hot days. They were concentrated around the entrances to bars and convenience stores like the remnants of a steel hailstorm, petering out in the emptier stretches of Alice Town and clustering together again at the next shop or bar we reached. I imagined locals, in the heat of a summer day, popping the top off a beer or a soda and tossing the lid aside in the rush to quench their thirst. The sun had faded many to a silver-white but some still bore the coloured remnants of branding and they looked a little like a collection of semi-precious stones embedded in the ground. The closet thing we have to this in the UK is flattened globules of spat-out chewing gum blackening in the doorways of nightclubs and around bus shelters. In the Caribbean, even the litter is pretty.

It didn't take long before we were past the shops, hotels and small businesses and into a residential area, where washing flapped in the afternoon breeze in the scratchy front yards of poor-looking stucco houses that weren't much different, in their construction, from the shops. At the end of the island we looped back along the northern road, and here it was wilder, with fewer buildings, and exposed to the weather. We passed an enormous pile of empty plastic Carib beer crates stacked man-high on a worn patch of grass. We looked, but they were all empty.

The sun was getting low as we wandered slowly back through the gates of Browns Marina and we decided to have a (slightly warm) beer in the cockpit to celebrate Christmas.

'I'll see if I can do something later with those turkey steaks,' I told Ben and Vicky, secretly worrying about the risk of botulism and salmonella in 5-day-old supermarket meat that had been soaking in cool-box water for the past twenty-four hours.

As the sun dipped, the temperature dropped surprisingly quickly. Even though this was the Caribbean, it was still winter, and we needed jeans and hoodies in the evenings. I went below to add layers and came up to find a stranger in the cockpit, talking to Vicky.

'So, there I was, in the water, and I saw this huuu-uuge fish and ... oh hey,' the man said, breaking off from his story to acknowledge me. He wore a fleece and his dark hair curled over the collar at the back.

'Hi,' I said, expecting him to introduce himself. He didn't.

'... so, as I was saying,' the man continued, 'I thought to myself, *Time's up, buddy*, and I shot it with my spear gun ...'

I turned to Vicky, raising a quizzical eyebrow. She grinned back, mischief in her eyes.

'... and then the next day I went out again and there was like three of them the same size as the one the day before and I thought, "Oh man, this is great!", and I dove down with my spear gun and ...'

Ben was listening, too, but not as politely as Vicky, so I caught his eye and asked him quietly, through the side of my mouth, 'Who's this?'

'Jean-Paul. He's on that boat over there.' There was a small yacht tied up two berths out from *Papagayo*. A maple-leaf flag fluttered from its backstay. I hadn't noticed it when we'd come in.

'He's French Canadian,' Ben continued. 'A spear fisherman.'

'So I see.' I sipped my beer and grimaced. With no fridge to cool it, it had a strong metallic taste.

'... and I got four in one day – and two huge lobsters, too. All with my spear gun, obviously. And ...'

'Been here a while, has he?' I asked Ben. *Looks like he's bedded in on* Papagayo *for the evening, too*, I thought.

'Seems like it.' He shot me a cheeky grin.

Long-term cruising is a funny thing. Most people do it because they are opting out of the rat race. After busy city lives and the stresses of the modern-day jungle, they crave quiet, solitude, contemplation. And most people cruise with their partners, which means that when you're in a remote spot for weeks on end, you only have one other person to talk to. No matter how much you enjoy each other's company, no matter if you never fight and even if you are true soul mates who are on exactly the same wave length, sooner or later the conversation is going to get stale. There are only so many times you can discuss that dinghy ride that you took earlier over to that immaculate beach, or the time the labels came off the food cans and you had no idea whether it was going to be chicken curry or creamed corn for dinner. Stories lose their magic when everyone already knows what happened.

In a cruising situation, when you come across someone new the variety is an incredible relief. And for single cruisers the effect is even more marked. Hence Jean-Paul's total verbal vomit right now. He probably watched our every movement in our approach to the marina from half a mile out, itching with impatience while we tied up and then disappeared into town, waiting for our return and chanting 'Fresh meat! Fresh meat!' to himself inside his head.

'... Yeah, so when the Swedish guys get back, maybe we can have a party,' I caught Jean-Paul saying. That got my attention.

'Wait. Party? There's another boat?' I asked.

He turned to me and drained what looked like one of our beers.

'Yeah – *Swallow*. There are three Swedes on it. They've been gone a couple of days but they said they might be back today. They're cool. They like to party.'

'What time do you think they'll be back?'

'I don't know. Not long. Sun's going down soon. Hopefully they'll have some fish with them. Or some lobster. They went spear fishing. Did I tell you about the time I went spear fishing and ...'

I tuned him out, nodding every now and then to seem polite while he launched into yet another tale of spear-fishing derring-do. He didn't need much prompting from me to get enthused about his story, so I let him get on with his long-time-alone word-spewing.

Not long after Jean-Paul mentioned the other boat, a small old yacht came moseying round the corner and parked – with a bang – alongside the outermost jetty. Jean-Paul jumped out of our cockpit to go and help them with their ropes.

I could hear him from three pontoons over. 'Hey! How was the spear fishing? Did you get anything?'

The other sailors, when they came over a few minutes later, were cool, as Jean-Paul had said, and they were up for a party. The three of them had bought a cheap yacht in Florida, brought it down the Intracoastal Waterway and sailed across to Bimini with a modicum of shared boating knowledge between them and a copy of *Sailing for Dummies*. Two were blond Swedes: a lanky one, Emil, who reminded me of Paul Bettany, and a stockier chap, Sven, who looked like he had been brought up on a diet of raw meat and fish. The third member of their crew, who looked a little like Bruno Mars, was a Costa Rican friend who had swapped the tropical climate of his homeland for the dark and freezing mountains of Scandinavia. Eduardo's skin had been tanned a deep brown by the Bahamian sun and he made even Ben look pasty in comparison.

All three were a few years our junior and it was good to see younger people sailing. At thirty-four, I wasn't exactly a spring chicken, but in all the months I'd spent sailing around the world to this point, I'd met very few younger crew, outside of my own boat. Most were in their fifties or older and, while they had great stories to tell and I counted some of them as friends, conversation just flows more easily when you share more cultural reference points. It's a bit like if I hang out with friends who have children – we can have good chats, and I can sympathise with their conundrums about getting into the right school or finding a babysitter so that they can go to a wedding/get back to work/get drunk with the girls. I can understand their point, I can feel for them, I can offer ideas for a solution. But in a way there's a missed connection. It's just always easier if I'm chatting to someone on my level, like I don't have to think as hard. They get me and I get them. The connection works.

And the connection here, among this group of seven sailors from four very different countries, worked so well that within half an hour of meeting for the first time we were all agreeing to pool our resources and share a Christmas Day dinner together.

The Swedes had, to Jean-Paul's glee, been successful with their spear fishing and they had three large fish and two lobsters to bring to our pot-luck supper. Jean-Paul's contribution was his fish-filleting skills. He immediately took the catch off the boys, hosed down a stainless-steel table near the water's edge, and started slicing up the dead fish. Our offering – a little embarrassingly – was to be baked potatoes and coleslaw; I binned the turkey, as I was already dubious about it. Each boat brought its own little stash of alcohol.

I'd never seen lobster cooked from scratch before and Sven showed me how to cut lengthwise along the black shell of the tail and prise apart the two halves to pull out the meat. It was very chewy and sweet, with a slightly bitter aftertaste. I wasn't sure I understood what all the fuss was about. The fish, though, were delicious, steamed in their own juices in foil parcels until the flesh fell away from the bones.

When you are travelling, you make friends quickly. It doesn't really matter that you come from different countries, or don't speak the same first language. You find a common ground – usually the fact that you are both here, in this place, at this time – and roll with it. When else in our adult lives can we say this happens as easily as it did when we were children? When you start a new job, or move to a new town, making friends is almost like a courtship: you smile and say hello, which progresses to small talk, which might lead to a shy invitation to coffee or a tentative play date with each other's kids. Both of you are aware that this fragile new 'friendship' could fall apart at any minute, and you keep conversation light, clean and safe. When you get invited round to the other person's house with your partner on a Saturday night for a boozy dinner you know you're officially *in*.

When travelling, and particularly when sailing, when you might go for weeks without meeting anyone, it all happens in extreme fast forward. There are few barriers to conversational topics; you jump right in with toilet humour, sex jokes and mickey-taking. In the same way that small children pay no regard to polite social convention and say aloud what they are thinking, when you are removed from the ties of your 'normal' life you are freed from conventions, too. So you make buddies as quickly and easily as you did when you were six years old, when you'd wander up to a kid you didn't know in a doctor's surgery waiting room, or on a beach, or in the toy department, and smile and start hanging out together. Being out of the social norm takes you back to that, as an adult. The lubrication of alcohol helps, too.

After dinner, when we'd hosed down the dishes at the steel filleting table, we followed our ears and stumbled through the cooling sand to the End of the World Saloon, a wooden shack that served icy beers, strong rum and loud music. We drank and laughed, we danced and talked, and we scrawled our most sage sailorly advice on the wooden back wall in marker pen, adding to the spider's web of quotes that other travellers passing through had scribbled across the rough beams. We laughed and danced and drank some more until our throats were sore and our ears were numb and finally, in that darkest hour when everything goes still before the dawn, we slept.

Christmas Day, in the UK, is a sacred family day that takes months of planning, and saving, and anticipating. It's the one date in the calendar that even families who don't like each other very much wouldn't dream of spending apart. Traditions are hauled out of cupboards along with the dusty decorations and few would consider doing anything different from the obligatory presents-food-wine-food-TV-snooze-games-food-walk-more-

TV-just-one-last-chocolate routine of last year, and the year before that, and the one before that.

And yet here we were – Ben, Vicky and I, and also two Swedes, a Costa Rican and a French Canadian – a motley crew of rag-tag sailors who had only recently met on a small sandy island in the Bahamas where none of us lived, coming together on Christmas Day with food and drink and jokes and laughter, cooking (speared) fish on a barbecue, drinking strong icy rum, dancing in the sand inside a wooden shack until we were too dog tired to stay upright any longer. It was about as far away from a Coca-Cola-styled idea of Christmas as you can get – and it was also, precisely because of that, the best Christmas I've ever had.

17

Conch-ed out

'Fish! Fish! Fi-i-i-i-i-sh!' Ben yelled.

Excited, I looked to the back of the boat, where the plastic reel was tied to the strong metal rail. The thick line leading into the water was taut.

Ben was all over the place, leaping from one side of the cockpit to the other, lanky legs covering the width in just one stride, hand going in semi disbelief to his baseball cap and then stretching to the line again, to pluck it like a double-bass string. Vicky, caught at the helm, strained to look over her shoulder to watch what was going on.

'It's definitely a fish,' Ben said, pulling on the line a little bit, then releasing it when it dug too deeply into his fingers. 'We caught one!' We looked at each other in disbelief. We'd only left Bimini a quarter of an hour earlier and we'd already equalled our fish-catching record of the whole of the Andaman Sea and a fair chunk of the Indian Ocean.

We furled the sail to slow us down and Ben went below to get a pair of gardening gloves he'd picked up in Walmart in Texas that were far too large for him and made him look as though he had cartoon hands. He brought a small piece of rope and our bread knife, too.

He sat facing backwards in the back port quarter of the boat, his bare feet braced against the steel railing, and he hauled and hauled and hauled, hand over cartoon-gloved hand, until a silvery fish broke the surface and, free of the friction of the water, fairly flew up and into the boat.

I didn't watch as Ben slit its throat but kept peeking as he cut into it, crouched over in the narrow cockpit, and popped raw pieces into his mouth. Vicky did the same.

'Sushi!' she said.

She whipped it off down below and within minutes the smell of hot frying oil wafted up the companionway. My stomach growled. She followed soon afterwards with a pile of smoking-hot, lightly battered fish stacked on the chopping board and a bowl of wasabi mayonnaise, and then I did tuck in, hot juices running down my palm as I picked up the pieces with my fingers. Twenty minutes earlier that fish had been swimming in the Atlantic Ocean and now it was being digested in my stomach. You couldn't get fresher than that.

To get to Nassau, our next destination, on the island of New Providence, we had to pass over the Bahamas' grand bank, a huge shallow area of limestone that has led many a ship to wreck. As navigator, it was my job to make sure we passed over it safely, without running aground. On the electronic charts on the computer and tablet I could see a narrow 'gate' of sorts that would just allow *Papagayo*, with her 7-foot keel, to float through. As sod's law would have it, we reached the pass in the dead of night, when we couldn't see how deep the water was, and I woke Ben to be on the helm while I nervously watched the charts below, cross-referencing from computer to tablet to paper chart to hand-held GPS, all done in the red light of a head torch, double-, triple- and quadruple-checking that we were where we thought we were. With no buoys in the sea, and no landmarks or even land to orient ourselves by, we had to put all of our trust in the accuracy of the electronic navigation. If anything happened, we were a long way from anywhere and with limited means of summoning help. I was glad that Ben and Vicky had had the foresight to buy a liferaft – but I really didn't want to have to get in it.

I consulted the charts again and then dashed over to the steps to call up to Ben on the helm.

'Turn to port five degrees.' I ran back to my navigator's station. Twenty seconds later I was calling up again. 'Another ten degrees to port. Slow down a bit. Another five. Slow down a bit more.' The chart showed us we were slightly north of where we wanted to be. GPS is not pin-point accurate and in this case every foot counted. I stared at the charts until my eyes swam. I blinked to clear my vision and a sixth sense kicked in and told me we were going to hit the bank, even though I had no way of being sure. I ran over to the stairs again.

'Stop the boat!'

'What?'

'Stop! I'm not a hundred per cent sure of our position. Just stop and turn hard to starboard and I'll call up again in a second.'

I heard the engine rev as Ben gave it a blast of reverse to bring the boat to an almost stop, then he turned on to the course I called up to him and crept forward as slowly as he could.

Back at the chart table, I swiped at the sweat gathering on my forehead. We hadn't run aground, and I still couldn't be completely confident that this new path was the right one to take. But we hadn't hit anything yet, which was good. I took a deep breath, held it, and counted the seconds as Ben steered *Papagayo* on the new course. The electronic representation of a boat on the computer screen did a U-turn and was suddenly on the eastern side of the 'gate'. We were through. I exhaled noisily.

The rest of the journey to Nassau was a doddle and by the afternoon we were motoring past huge cruise liners that were tied up in a row, one after the other, like giant white National Express coaches in a bus station.

After the quietness of Bimini, Nassau was a shock. More 'marinas' of the same black rickety jetties lined the side of a channel that separated the main New Providence island from the small Paradise Island to the north. Boats were everywhere – sailing yachts, smaller passenger boats, fishing vessels, day-tripper catamarans overloaded with reclining sunbathers. It was like driving along a floating motorway. We passed marina after marina, all full to the brim, until we eventually struck lucky, spotted a space, radioed in and then circled in the channel, waiting for permission to go in and moor up. After struggling to get our mooring lines around their piles – thick posts driven into the seabed for this purpose – we switched off the engine and found we were in a completely different Caribbean.

This was the Caribbean ruled by the cruise ship – something I would become very familiar with over the coming weeks. We'd passed maybe seven or eight on the way in, each with thousands of passengers on board – passengers who had streamed off their liners like rats abandoning ship. Unlike rats, though, they'd be back long before sundown, scuttling back on board while it was still daylight and it was safe, as if they were warding off vampires.

I had read a few times in guide books and brochures about how Nassau was a dangerous place and you had to be on your guard against robbers, rapists and murderers at all times. The language in some of these tourists guides was hyperbolic and designed to strike fear into the heart of any homesick tourist. Obviously there was a grain of truth in it – it's never sensible to flash your relative wealth in a country that's poorer than the one you're from, and you need to keep an eye on your belongings and yourself at all times. That, to me, having lived in south London for many years, is just common sense. Be cool and you'll be fine.

The cruise-ship passengers I saw all over the Caribbean were anything but cool. And I'm not even talking about the brand-new sneakers worn with pulled-up socks, 'fanny packs' and hats. Their clothes made them stand out a mile but it was more than that – they were conspicuously white, middle-aged, usually overweight couples with blisteringly fair skin, sweating nervously if they strayed too far from the mother ship. They'd disembark, march a smart hundred or so metres from their ship and dive straight into the nearest (air-conditioned) shops. No matter what country we were in – the Bahamas or the US Virgin Islands, say – these shops were identical, selling coloured rum glasses, Hawaiian shirts, cigarettes, expensive watches and sunglasses and, for some reason, emerald jewellery. Why emeralds, I have no idea. In cruise-ship towns, white neo-classical shops lined the first two streets back from the port. This marked the point that was as far as the passengers dared venture. Any further than that and the buildings changed markedly into run-down, mouldering, concrete one- or two-storey block houses. It was all carefully constructed to allow the cruise-ship passengers a sip of the Caribbean that still looked remarkably like home. I've been to Cancún in Mexico and the spit lined with hotels there could just as easily be in Florida or California or any other new-build US city area with money. On the Caribbean islands I saw, every cruise-ship town looked the same.

I'm not against the idea of cruises per se. Obviously I love the sea and think it's a great way to travel, and I also think that if you've only got two weeks a year to spare for your holiday, it's a good way of getting to visit lots of different places without having to spend half your time unpacking and repacking to move to another hotel room in a different country. I've always liked the way that with boat travel your home goes with you – whether that's a 130,000-tonne ocean-going liner with 1,800 en-suite cabins or a 40-foot race yacht where three of you sleep in the saloon and you have a plastic bag for a shower.

On that level, we should have had more in common with the cruise-ship passengers. But travelling by water was the only link between us. I don't think they were really there to travel in the way that I understand 'to travel' as meaning: to experience a new country, a different culture and a new people as it really is. They wanted to be fed and watered (and boozed) – and when they got stir-crazy from being cooped up on ships the size of large villages, they burst on to land for an hour or two to drink iced Starbucks, parade along perfectly paved sidewalks, sweat through their logoed T-shirts and take photos to present to the folks back home, pictures blown up on the giant flat screen while bowls of popcorn and tortilla chips are passed round in large plastic bowls to guests seated on dining-room chairs lined up in the den.

I'm in danger of sounding awfully snobbish about the whole thing and that makes me sad – but it also made me sad to see these towns. No doubt they bring much-needed work and money to the islands; it's just a shame that that's at the price of lost culture. It's a bit of a chicken-and-egg situation: which came first – the passenger demanding overpriced souvenirs and familiar brands or the marketing people with their ideas of the perfect holiday resort? And which came next – real crime, caused when careless tourists flashed too much cash in front of poor and green-eyed locals, or the fearful perception of crime that drove passengers back to the safety of the bars and casinos on their ships, where a different kind of person parted them from their hard-earned dollars?

Because we were 'proper' travellers – and because we didn't have anything worth nicking, and looked like we didn't, in our holey clothes and with our dirty hair – we did venture out into Nassau after dark. There were noticeably few white people around, apart from in the monstrosity that was the Atlantis hotel on Paradise Island over the bridge, where they swarmed in all their linen-clad glory across the patterned carpets and flocked to the restaurants for chilli fries and a slushie before taking in a Hollywood blockbuster in an air-conditioned movie theatre. I felt as though I was observing a different culture and a new people when we went over there to have a peek about.

Back on the main island, we found a wooden shack under the main road bridge and drank super-strong rum cocktails from plastic cups while the cook fried us some conch balls. We sat at an outside table and watched rays gliding elegantly through the water below us, their diamond bodies cast into silhouette by the overhead orange streetlights. Conch is a staple food in the Bahamas and the creatures' large pink spiral shells are often built into front-garden walls. In some places, huge piles of shells, each the size of two men's fists stacked together, litter the beach or street. You'd recognise a conch shell – In *Dr No*, Ursula Andress emerges from the sea in her white bikini to seduce James Bond, a conch in each hand; in *Lord of the Flies* the boys blow into them like horns. What you might not know is how to pronounce the word – it's 'conk' – and what it tastes like, which is pretty hard, chewy, rubbery seafood. Mixed with a lot of batter and deep-fried, it's bearable and provides a good workout for your jaw muscles. It's the cheapest seafood there is in those parts and abundant in the Bahamas, two factors that explain its enduring popularity, rather than any culinary value it might offer.

The same can't be said for grouper. This floundering, sad-faced fish is also common in the Bahamas but it's not that cheap and it tastes absolutely, utterly divine. It's not a pretty fish to look at but it gives the sweetest, juiciest flesh of all. I ate it everywhere I could find it and, when my stomach started to protest in horrible ways about all the deep-fried batter I was consuming, I started to pull goujons apart with my fingers so that I could still eat the meat and to ask burger bars to give me the plain fish and salad in a bun. I got some funny looks requesting that, and I got the impression that there was a fair bit of head-scratching going on in kitchens (how do you cook a fish if you're not deep-frying it?), but it was worth the mess and embarrassment. You can keep your cod and even your sea bass and bream (although it pains me to say that): grouper beats them hands down any day.

That first night in Nassau, after we'd sunk a couple of very strong rum punches and masticated our way through a handful of conch balls, we wandered back along the main road towards our marina.

'One more drink?' Ben asked and Vicky and I shrugged. Why not?

We could hear music so we followed our ears up a side street until we came to what looked like a massive street party in a disused car park. There were trestle tables set up to one side, loaded with insulated plastic vats that had been full of food and drink but which were empty now. A few beer cans and plastic glasses rolled about on the floor under the tables. Just beyond, a massive crowd of people was gathered, all looking in the same direction, their backs to us. We drew closer and saw there was a stage set up, with a sound system pumping out the music. A man had a microphone and the sound was turned up so loud, and his accent was so strong, that I couldn't really tell what he was saying.

The man was smiling and he had his hand on the shoulder of a younger woman who was clutching a piece of paper in her hand. Judging by the whooping going on and all the excited, grinning faces, the man seemed to be some sort of local celebrity. Like a game-show host, he turned the woman round so her back was to the audience and the pair of them faced a towering pile of large cardboard boxes.

The man said something into his microphone again, which I couldn't catch, then the woman replied. He repeated her words back into the microphone, for the benefit of the audience, which must have been 200-strong, and a huge cheer went up.

'Did she just say "microwave"?' I asked Vicky.

'I don't know,' she mouthed, over the cheers.

I turned back to watch the crowd. Ben, Vicky and I stood on the outside of the audience, trying to make sense of what we were seeing. This certainly wasn't the street party we had initially thought it was, nor was it an outdoor church service, which had been my second guess, given the sense of euphoria and excitement in the air and the way everyone was jostling to get a good look at the stage.

A few more words reached my ears that I recognised but they seemed so out of place that I was still confused. Oven. Fridge-freezer.

The penny dropped for Ben first. 'It's a raffle.'

And so it was. It was a white-goods raffle. The large boxes behind the compere would have given Argos a run for its money – fridges, vacuum cleaners, TVs. The next woman up, who chose an oven, was almost on the verge of tears as she told the compère that she'd been waiting for one for years. For an *oven*. Every time a ticket number was called out, excited screams rang out across the car park. It wasn't that unlike religious fervour.

After fifteen minutes or so of watching, we grew bored and started to move away, in search again of that last drink. But the crowd were just as transfixed as ever. Imagine a life in which the fact there's been a shipment from Electrolux has made your year. I guess when you live on a small island, where you can't nip online to order a replacement washing machine and have a nice John Lewis man deliver it the next day, these kinds of things are a big deal. Imagine also a life in which you don't have an oven in your kitchen because you can't afford one and winning one in a raffle is among the best things to ever happen to you.

As the only white people there, and as obvious onlookers, not participants, we – had we believed the hype we'd read in the tourist guides – might have expected there to be a bit of tension. But all I felt from those people was jubilation and excitement at their good fortune and it was a lovely thing to witness. I just wished some of the cruise-ship passengers had been there to see it, too.

18

Bahamian rhapsody

Cerulean. Turquoise. Aquamarine. Cobalt. All types of blue, and all words that wouldn't be out of place in a hyperbolic travel brochure for the Exuma islands in the Bahamas.

But unless you've got a dictionary to hand, or have a job as a colour-matcher for Crown paint, there's a chance you won't know the exact shade of blue I was referring to if I described the waters of Compass Cay, where we were now anchored, as lapis lazuli or azure.

So I'll give it to you straight and you'll just have to use your imagination. Blue. Take the bluest blue you can imagine and then Photoshop it in your mind to make it bluer. Add a blue filter and take out any hints of yellow or green. And then add some more blue. Got it? Are you imagining the blueyest blue that you can? Good. And yet you're probably only halfway to picturing the sea around the Exuma islands as it really is.

If I thought Bimini was beautiful, it had nothing on the Exumas. These are a group of 365 nubby islands in the middle of the Bahamian chain, stretching like the vertebrae of a spinal column 130 miles south-east through the Atlantic

Ocean. They're low-lying, sandy, palm-treed, surrounded-by-water, perfect tropical islands.

Their northern sides are exposed to the wild winds and waves of the Atlantic Ocean, where the trade winds whip up the water to a white froth that never ends. That side of the islands is no place for a sailing boat to be. One bad judgement and you're easily being dashed on to the limestone rocks and shipwrecked.

On the southern side, however, it's a completely different story. It's calm. It's shallow. It's protected. There's nothing there – precious few houses; no roads. There are creamy beaches where the only footprints are the ones you've just left behind you, and you can have a whole cove to yourself if you want. It's the Caribbean idyll ramped up to the max – natural beauty, space and isolation. Several of the Exumas are private islands with their own airstrips, popular destinations for the super-rich because they are so remote. This is where Gwyneth Paltrow and Chris Martin came on a 'break-up vacation' not long after they'd 'consciously uncoupled', presumably to talk without fear of a paparazzo photographing them from across the street. In the Exumas, that's unthinkable – there are no streets.

Papagayo was headed to Compass Cay (you pronounce it 'key'), one of these little nubs, for two reasons. The first was that at some point we needed to pass through the island chain from the sheltered south-west Exuma Sound to the northern Atlantic side in order to continue our journey. The other was that, although we were technically 'delivering' the yacht from Texas to St Lucia, and were in a bit of a hurry having lost several weeks in the States, we were still a bunch of travellers, we'd heard great things about the place, and we wanted to experience legendary Caribbean beauty for ourselves.

Getting *Papagayo* through a narrow, rock-strewn pass and into the bay we wanted to anchor in was not easy and the water was so clear that several times, hunkered over the cockpit table, pencil in hand and eyes flicking from charts to computer screens, I worried we would run aground, because it looked so much shallower than it was.

As Ben inched her nose slowly ahead, steering according to the instructions I called from below, I looked up at last from the charts and realised that the stress had been worth it. This was, without doubt, the most beautiful place I had ever been in the world.

I don't mean to brag but by this point I had been to some particularly spectacular spots. Beach-wise, ones that stuck in my mind were the eastern side of Long Island in the Andamans, nearly 10,000 miles from where we were now, where sea-smoothed pebbles dappled the sand beneath sinewy overhanging trees; and the secret emerald cave hidden inside the Thai island of Koh Muk, which you could only reach by passing through an ink-black tunnel in the rock at low tide.

But Compass Cay was in a league of its own. There was a small island to the right of us, another ahead and a third to the left. Each had its own empty stretch of golden beach – one for each of us. In between was our perch for the night – a patch of sandy seabed covered with flat, calm, protected water so clear that it could have passed for a swimming pool. It was A-list perfect – apart from the two other boats already there.

'At least we know it's a good anchorage,' Ben said, trying to make light of our disappointment that we wouldn't have the place to ourselves. It's not like it wasn't large enough to easily accommodate all three boats, and it was always reassuring to see other yachts anchored somewhere we were about to drop the hook, because it meant it was a viable spot, but it was a little bit annoying.

Then came the familiar clatter of an anchor being raised – and both boats motored slowly out of the bay, easing away like fish disturbed in their sunbathing spot.

'Result!' said Vicky. 'Let's get the dinghy out.'

We'd had little chance to use the dinghy so far, as we'd been staying in marinas, and tended to do our exploring by foot. Ben and Vicky had bought the boat in Texas and it was the smallest I'd been in, chosen it for its compact size on purpose so that it could be rolled up when not in use and put away below decks. Dinghies, also known as tenders, are expensive pieces of kit that can cost, with an engine, thousands of dollars, and Ben and Vicky weren't planning on using it much once they got to St Lucia, so they hadn't gone for an all-singing, all-dancing version.

If you're a cruiser, your dinghy is basically your car, and those who live on their boats long-term usually have larger, more robust models so that they can easily transport cans of diesel, a week's worth of food or water and all of their crew in one go.

Back in Malaysia, *Incognito* had had a large, heavy rigid inflatable dinghy that weighed about 100kg on its own. Add the engine and you were looking at 150kg. It could easily fit six people so with just Guy and me in it, and with the 25hp outboard engine throttled up, we could get it on to the plane and shoot along the surface of the water like a mini sports boat, which was invaluable when we were anchored half a mile offshore in Langkawi.

'Tender' was a suitable adjective for *Papagayo*'s dove-grey dinghy. Fully inflated by foot pump, which took only a few minutes, she could just about accommodate four people, if they didn't mind sitting with hairy knees rubbing against each other. The floor wasn't rigid and was not dissimilar to a deflated armband. The designers provided plastic planks to slot into the base to make it firmer, but every time I got into it I worried I'd step straight through the floor and leave a foot-shaped hole behind.

The outboard was a tiny 2.5hp, which made it very easy to handle. I could lift the engine off its storage slot on *Papagayo*'s rear rail, on to the dock and then fasten it to the back of the dinghy by myself. At sea, it was a slightly trickier manoeuvre, and I'd pass it down over the yacht's side to Ben, who was waiting in the dinghy to receive it, but it was still a million times easier to deal with than Guy's outboard, which had caused cuts and bruises to the boat, to our arms and legs and to our relationship whenever we had tried to move it.

We weren't going a long way here in Compass Cay, though, so we didn't need a hefty boat or an overpowered engine. Ben yanked on the start cord a couple of times, adjusted the throttle, and finally it sputtered into life and we puttered off to explore our first real Bahamian anchorage.

The Bahamas, and their neighbouring country, the Turks and Caicos Islands, which was next on our itinerary, aren't technically part of the Caribbean. Historically, they share the same story as the other islands, with landings by Christopher Columbus, the slave trade, plantations and being passed from ownership by one European country to another. But I defy you to get off your yacht and into your dinghy, to go 'eeny-meeny-miney-mo' to pick which of the three deserted beaches to land on, to step into ankle-deep, gently lapping water and, pulling the boat safely up the beach, to dive into a warm, clear sea and, surfacing, to tread water and turn to look back on to the land, the beach framed with pretty green bushes and pink flowers, and to not feel that you are in the Caribbean. It's as near as dammit.

I left Ben and Vicky on their own, to give them a rare bit of privacy, and swam around a small spit to find a beach of my own. I waded out of the shallows, the water slipping past my thighs. No one had been there since the last high tide and it was as pristine as it was possible to be, with not one scrap of seaweed or piece of stray litter to be seen. The beach was 12 feet or so deep and then the vegetation began: dense, dark-green bushes that were too tough to push through with bare feet and legs. I edged as far in as I could, balancing on a tiny patch of sand, and craned my neck to see the island's interior. I half expected this to be a false front, similar to when I had followed a pygmy elephant through the jungle lining a Borneo river and had found the tropical rainforest was only metres deep, camouflaging a massive palm-oil plantation, but here all was virgin shrubbery, with not a house, a fence or an electricity pylon to be seen. There were no signs of people, either. It must have looked exactly like this for thousands of years.

I went back to my beach and walked its length, then swam back to the others. Vicky was sitting on the sand and Ben was lying back over one side of the dinghy, his cap draped over his face to protect it from the sun. He raised it slowly when he heard me approach and lazily opened one eye.

'Not bad, hey?'

'Not too shabby.'

Looking down on him, I was suddenly hit with a massive pang of envy. This trip was just an extended holiday for me – but it was Ben and Vicky's work and life. As divers, they had lived and worked in the Caribbean before – they had even spent time at a resort in Turks and Caicos, our next country to visit – and they were about to start a life and business in St Lucia. This – warm sunshine, stunning beaches, afternoon siestas – was the norm for them. They didn't have to put up with an hour-long commute to a drab, grey office to sit in front of a computer screen at someone else's behest for most of the day. They got to be outdoors, in nature – and particularly spectacular nature at that – in charge of their own lives. How had they ended up with this life while mine had ended up in a boring routine? I had a moment of pure jealousy that was so intense I couldn't speak for a minute or two.

I knew that their kind of life couldn't be as easy as it seemed, though. Seeing family and friends only once a year, struggling with language and culture barriers, never being able to own much apart from what you could carry in a couple of bags and the odd memento that friends or family would store for you. Travelling had helped me become less attached to things, and the belongings back in my flat in London were pretty sparse compared to what they had been a few years earlier, but I still liked familiarity – and variety.

As if he'd read my mind, that evening, back on *Papagayo*, after the sun had gone down and we'd eaten and settled on to our bunk/settees, Ben got out their laptop and showed me photos of the dive centre they'd built up from nothing in Mozambique.

I'd heard some of their stories from Mozambique before – the venomous insect that crawled into Ben's T-shirt during the night, the snakes that wound their way into the house, the swimming pool they'd built, the dog they'd had to leave behind. It had all sounded, to my less-experienced ears, so romantic, to arrive in a strange country, the two of you against the world, and to build a home, a business and a life with your bare hands.

And then they showed me their photos and I got a bit of a reality check. Here was the tent they lived in for months while their house was built. Next was the 'house' itself – little more than a hut, to my bricks-and-mortar English eyes, with pricks of daylight seeping through woven reed walls.

'And this is the road we built,' said Ben.

'What? You built a road?'

'Yeah. It was impossible to launch the boats off the beach, even with the four by fours, so we built a road across the sand.'

I looked at the tiny screen of the laptop. This road they'd built wasn't made from tarmac or even gravel but the slim trunks of young trees, stripped of their branches and lashed tightly together and laid down on to the beach like a fallen fence, to give the four-by-four tyres more purchase. He clicked through the photographs and I realised not only the work it had taken, to chop down small tree after small tree, strip them back to form crooked poles the diameter of a man's arm, cut them to even lengths, transport them (presumably carrying them on foot, since there was no other road), fit, bind and lay them for hundreds of metres, but also the time it had taken. Weeks and weeks, if not months, of hard, physical work so that they could get their boats into the water and their customers out on to the reef dive sites.

While I admired their guts and resourcefulness, and as much as I was still envious of them and their adventures, I knew then that that wasn't the life for me. I'm not a skinny-latte-and-Jimmy-Choos kind of person, and I am probably happier than most women would be at the prospect of having to use a bucket for a shower and living in the same pair of shorts and flip-flops for three months, but there's a limit to how hard I want my life to be – and living somewhere where you have to spend months building your own road was definitely over that limit for me.

'Howdy!' a man called and waved as he drove past us in his dinghy. *Papagayo* rocked slightly in his wake. A few seconds later, another tender zipped past, headed for George Town.

This anchorage off Stocking Island felt like being in the suburbs. George Town, a small town on Great Exuma with a supermarket, shops and services, bank and petrol station, was a quarter of a mile away, across a pass, close enough for us to nip into on a daily basis to pick up a paper or a pint of milk but far enough away for us to feel safe, in a pretty location surrounded by a hundred or so other boats, and people just like us. I didn't like it.

I grew up in the suburbs of Nottingham, on a large estate built in the 1980s. There was a long road that curved left and right, like a river, with little cul-de-sac tributaries coming off it. The houses were all alike but with tweaks to make them 'individual' (the contemporary adjective would be 'bespoke'). Some had integral garages; in others the garages were detached. Some had faux-Tudor gables; others (like ours) were plain. Some were dead-on to the road; others (ours) lay at jaunty angles, as if dropped there by Dorothy's whirlwind. There was a supermarket at one end of the snaking road and a pub at the other and, about a third of the way along and just by our house, was a play park. Dog-walkers waved, teenagers cycled and the postman often cheerfully put down his bag of mail to help my mother bump-start the Mini up the drive when we needed to get to school. There were sparrows and butterflies and fat ginger Tom cats sunning themselves on the pavement and the steady tick-tick-tick of sprinklers watering lawns in the summer highs. Once an hour a small bus rumbled along the road to take the more elderly residents to and from the hospital and everyone knew everyone else. It was like living in a sitcom.

I understand why my parents took us to live there. It was the perfect place in which to bring up children. On long 1980s' summer days we'd call on each other, adding one or two kids to our number at each house we stopped at, and conga-ing along to the next place to ask frazzled-looking stay-at-home mothers if Dean was in, Paul, Lauren. Then, a chattering mass of scabbed knees and bony elbows, we'd decamp to the playground, where we'd swing off the monkey bars while the smell of sun-heated bark, which was scattered all over the park's floor to cushion us if – when! – we fell, filled our nostrils.

We'd stay out all day, only breaking off in pairs or trios of siblings to dart home to eat when a mother, or older brother on a BMX, appeared at the park's entrance and yelled 'Dinner!'

When we grew older, it was still a great place for a teenager to be: only a 30-minute bus ride into the centre of the city, with its dual shopping malls, record shops and bars that turned a blind eye to badly faked NUS cards.

I had a great childhood, with no major traumas (in fact, I think the worst things that happened to me were getting a D in English once and being stung by a wasp that flew down the back of my shirt and couldn't find a way out again). But for some reason, suburbs give me the proper, full-on heebie-jeebies. It's something to do with the way they've been so meticulously planned out, rather than growing organically, and how all the buildings look so similar and are of the same age. The people who live in them, too, all seem to have very similar lives, following the same routines and varying only by generation. They feel quite soulless to me, the suburbs. Granted, they are generally very safe, clean, nice places to live. But with nice comes blah. Surely no one ever wrote a great album or amazing literature or made a fantastic scientific discovery while living in a three-bed, open-plan semi in a cul-de-sac with a rockery in the garden and gaily chiming doorbell?

And this anchorage felt, to me, just like that. All these boats, the majority of which were American, all choosing to drop the hook in the same spot, to surround themselves with similar people in a safe area, to establish a daily routine. It didn't feel like travelling or exploring to me; it felt like normal life, except with fibreglass walls to your house rather than brick ones. There was even a weekly folk-music-round-the-campfire social on Friday nights.

We'd barely been there an hour when people started coming over in their dinghies to welcome us and pass on tidbits of helpful information.

'Hey. Welcome to George Town. I'm Carole and that over there is my boat.' The woman, with short reddish hair and with unconstrained breasts moving under her T-shirt, pronounced it 'boot'; she was Canadian. 'Just wanted to introduce myself and let you know if there was anything you needed, you just have to ask.'

'Hi, Carole!' the three of us said, in unison. 'Thanks, Carole!'

'Hey there. I'm Pete. Y'all just arrived? Just wondered if you knew about the wonderful radio net that runs here in George Town every morning, 'bout eight?'

'Hi, Pete!'

'Good morning! How you doing? Just thought I'd swing on by and say hi. I'm Roger and this is Teresa. Have you heard about the Friday night sing-along?'

'Hi, Roger. Hi, Teresa.'

It was incessant. And it started to feel a little bit like we were being recruited into a cult.

We were always polite, and we plastered smiles on to our faces, but we never invited anyone on board. They wouldn't have come, anyway – they were busy whizzing about in their dinghies from George Town to Stocking Island, filling up every minute of the day with Important Boaty Tasks.

It became clear to us, very quickly, that these people weren't, in the main, travellers. They were on their annual, repeat holiday. It was January, and the Bahamas are not that far from the USA. The journey across for many of them wouldn't have been as tricky as the trip we'd made from Texas. They possibly even left their boats here during hurricane season in the summer and used them as week-long holiday homes during the winter. The sort of people who back home were probably sitting on the PTA and the town council, they'd kind of taken over the area and turned it into a project – it wouldn't have surprised me if there had been some kind of committee set up – so there was a special jetty to tie your dinghy to when we went into George Town, and there were signs pointing us in the right direction to throw away our rubbish. On Stocking Island, which was originally little more than a sandy cay, there were volleyball courts and an open-air church on Sundays. Someone had erected one of those signposts with fingers pointing in all directions telling you how far it is to various famous cities. This one was 10 feet tall and crammed full of names of American and Canadian towns I'd never heard of: Port Dover, Ontario, 1,175nM (nautical miles); New Burn, NC, 695nM. Some wag, amusingly, had also inserted Bognor Regis, UK, 3,775nM.

I don't mean to sound xenophobic or snobbish; it's just that these other sailors, with their volleyball matches, campfire sing-songs and 10am worship on the beach, were so different from us. They'd created a mini North America here, with little evidence of real Caribbean life, and to a boat of reserved Brits their forward friendliness and organised ways of having FUN! were a little alien, and made us even more stiff-backed, tight-lipped and English than normal. I might have even have given a sigh of relief as we pulled up the anchor and set off for our next stop, Long Island. *Maybe there we'll find more of the real Caribbean,* I thought, *not deserted private islands owned by Hollywood royalty or fake shopping towns built to appease cruise-ship passengers – and certainly not more weird little recreations of the Truman Show.*

19

Stranded

The turtle raised its wizened head above the choppy surface and took a gasp of air before diving down a few centimetres, using the water as a sunscreen to keep the rays off its shell back and leathery fins.

It had been a while – two years, I realised later with a shock – since I'd seen a turtle and it took me a few moments to recognise what I was seeing.

'Look!' I shouted at Ben and Vicky, with excitement, pointing ahead of the dinghy's bow as we reached shallow water just off the beach at Clarence Town, Long Island, our next stop. 'Turtle!' I have an astonishing gift for stating the obvious sometimes. 'Don't run over it.'

With a tight smile, like he was indulging a small child, Ben edged the tiller away from him, to divert our course a few inches. In this sea, though, we were going so slowly that there was little chance we'd be in danger of running over the turtle anyway. I watched the little fella take another gulp of breath. He didn't seem that fazed by us – probably he knew he was the stronger swimmer.

We'd arrived at Long Island the day before and had anchored for a few hours off an extraordinary beach called

Calabash Bay, which swept in an elegant, blinding curve up to the north-west tip of the island. We'd gone ashore to explore and even Vicky – who has seen so much of the world that she takes pretty much everything in her stride – was impressed.

'This has got to be one of the best beaches I've ever seen,' she said. Knowing how many hundreds she has visited, this was high praise indeed.

It was spectacular, floury and clean, and the sand was so pale that it bleached the tans right off our skins, so we looked English-pale in the broad daylight.

I was still a bit English-pale anyway, to be fair. I'd been living on a boat for two months and I'd have expected to be nut brown by this point but it hadn't really happened – mainly because the sailing conditions, into wind and waves, were so rough that we were still wearing full oilskins whenever we were moving.

I'd had an idea of what Caribbean sailing would be – glorious sunshine, blue seas and skies, perfect trade-wind conditions and never having to wear much more than the skimpiest of bikinis. And I'm sure, if we'd been going in the opposite direction, that's what Caribbean sailing would have been like. But not for us.

Because of where we were coming from and where we were going to, we were headed due east, or slightly south-east, most of the time. The trade winds – steady, reliable, medium-strong winds so named because they had pushed trade ships ahead of them from Europe to the Caribbean for hundreds of years – blew out of the east towards the west. Passing over the Atlantic for thousands of miles, they ruched up the ocean's surface into large waves.

Imagine smoothing a silk scarf over a table, then putting your hands on either edge and pushing them towards each other. The fabric would not stay flat but would rumple up into crests and troughs. The longer the wind crosses an expanse of water, the greater the rumpling effect and the bigger the waves grow. These trade winds had had thousands of miles of blowing from the east to build up waves and so by the time they reached *Papagayo*'s bow they were quite big. And a lot of the time they didn't stop at her bow – they hit her side, crashed upwards and were blown backwards to smack us in the face, time and time again. When you're wet you get cold and when it's windy you feel cold, too, so we were still wearing full ocean-going waterproofs while we sailed. When we stopped the boat, we'd feel the Caribbean warmth and quickly strip down to shorts and T-shirts. If we'd been sailing in the other direction, it would have felt completely different, and we'd have been in those skimpy bikinis, slapping on the sunscreen and calling down below for someone to bring us another cool drink (if the ice hadn't already melted). But heading directly into the wind and waves we got the full force of it, and, typically English, we dressed for the weather, although we did go barefoot as a concession.

Head-to-toe Gore-tex was a more effective sunscreen than SPF50, so I hadn't quite become the bronzed sea gypsy that I had been on previous travels on boats in tropical climes. My hair, however, told a different story. Alternating from wet to dry, as another wave walloped me across the head and then the wind whipped the moisture away again, and with the sun beating down on it constantly, it was rough to the touch and that peculiar shade of orangey-yellow often sported by brunette long-distance sailors. Out here, I didn't mind – I thought it made me look a bit cooler, like a more authentic traveller. Back in London in a month's time, though, I knew it'd be a different story.

For a while I'd been hoping that we might turn a corner in terms of the weather by the time we reached Long Island. It was January, so winter, but with the little bit of south we'd been putting in, we were inching ever so slightly closer to the equator. On Calabash Bay beach the previous afternoon, paddling ankle-deep through the shallows, I might have even broken into a sweat – possibly the first since Texas. It was another story when we reached our anchorage for the night a few hours later in what was, according to the guide books, a well-protected bay off Clarence Town. I looked at the chart and saw there was only a narrow entrance into the round bay, so I expected I could trust the book and find good shelter.

It was choppy when we dropped the hook, but nothing drastic, so this morning we had blown up the dinghy and loaded our dirty laundry into it in order to set off a third of a mile across the circular bay towards the marina in search of washing machines, bags of ice and cold drinks.

The dinghy bucked like a baby bronco as I climbed into it, holding on to two stanchions on the yacht's side and lowering myself down a metre from a sitting position, but I put the motion more down to my inelegant way of getting in than bad sea conditions. When all three of us were in, Ben started the engine and drove us away from *Papagayo* and out of the shelter that her hull had been giving us.

I don't know if you've ever seen the movie *The Perfect Storm*? It tells of what happened to a fishing boat that got caught in bad weather off the Grand Banks of North America. Towards the end of the film there is a climactic scene when skipper George Clooney, drenched to a shine with the amount of water the northern Atlantic Ocean is throwing at him, screams with machoism, determined to take on the mighty power of the elements and win the battle against the sea to get home safely. In a last gasp of daring courage, the fishing vessel *Andrea Gail* goes full throttle, the crew issue a battle cry and they try to drive directly up the front of the steepest, angriest, deadliest wave ever seen. It's a raw, emotive moment, when man recognises that he is but a tiny, powerless speck struggling against the enormous power of nature – but Clooney decides to have a go anyway.

Well, transpose that imagery to a small rubber inflatable boat, with a 2.5hp outboard engine, crewed by three skinny British people in shorts and T-shirts, trying to cross a pretty blue bay a third of a mile wide in the Bahamas. It might sound funny, and as the first wave swamped over the side of the dinghy and soaked us, we did laugh. When the next hit us two seconds later, our laughs got a bit quieter. As more and more came, relentlessly, we stopped pretending and gritted our teeth.

No matter what Ben did – tried to angle us differently to the waves, or slow us down, or speed us up (not really possible with three people and gear in a tiny buoyant boat), it made no difference. Within ten seconds of moving away from *Papagayo*, we were all completely drenched, through our shorts and T-shirts, and even our underwear. Our hair was wetter than if we'd just stepped out of the shower (at least in that situation I'd have been able to wring it out) and our eyes stung from the salt water. As a wave hit I'd instinctively blink, then have to blink again a couple of times to clear the water from my lashes and contact lenses before immediately being doused once more. The waves were probably no more than half a metre tall but in our tiny dinghy we were mere inches above the water, so they slapped us in the face and across the body and sloshed us around like a toddler with his toys in a bathtub.

'Well, that was fun,' Ben said, as we eventually reached the beach and waded into the water to pull the dinghy up the sand. It had taken us twenty minutes to travel what should, in flat water, have taken just five. Water was running off every part of us. Not dripping; running.

If we thought it was rough inside the cove, it was nothing compared to what was outside the bay. We could see the formidable sea state from where we stood on the beach. White horses, they call them – foaming spumes of white water galloping in off the tops of the waves. They were close together and angry and there was no way *Papagayo* would be able to pass through them. Even with the engine going full blast, it was likely that we'd try to run up the front of a wave, stall and be pushed back down again, like in *The Perfect Storm*, and with rocks behind us, we didn't have an option to even try it.

'Ten days,' the tanned white woman behind the counter of the sparsely stocked shop at the marina would tell us later. 'That's how long it's forecast for.' That meant we were trapped.

Not only were we to be storm-bound on Long Island for over a week, which took an enormous bite out of the time we had left to make it to St Lucia before my flight, but also the knock-on effect of the strong winds meant that the bay would remain just as choppy for the entire time. So every trip we made ashore was to be as difficult, uncomfortable and wet as that first one – both to and from the island. I tried going ashore dressed in my oilskins one morning, feeling absurd, but then I had to lug them around with me all day, because they were expensive and I was afraid to leave them in the dinghy. After that, I rolled up my clothes in a dry bag each time and rode in to shore in my bikini, shivering in the wind and wet and arriving at the marina peppered with goosebumps.

Now, at the end of our first taste of the world's most horrendous dinghy trip ashore, we took off our T-shirts, wrung them out and put them back on again, the wet cotton clinging uncomfortably to our skins. We were covered in salt, too, but there was nowhere to wash it off. Drying to a crust under the afternoon sun, we set off up the road.

'Hey, mon. How you doin' today?'

The man speaking to me appeared to be a living skeleton. A black skeleton on a bicycle with a small dog trotting alongside. He slowed down to match my walking pace, wobbling slightly as he pedalled backwards and forwards, the toes of his flip-flops scraping the road. He smiled and waited patiently for my answer. I told him I was fine. He smiled again and told me he lived here. I looked around – I couldn't see a house.

'Here?'

'Yeah. This is my grandfather's house.'

Ben and Vicky, who had walked on ahead, stopped and, seeing that I'd been trapped in conversation with a slightly crazy-looking Rastafarian, and knowing that I was nervous around dogs, came back to rescue me.

Ben introduced himself to the scarecrow, who had lain his bicycle down in some long grass. The scrappy little sandy-coloured dog, which I was warily watching out of the corner of one eye, scratched its ear with its hind leg, lips pulled taut in a rictus grin, tongue lolling.

'I am Bernard,' the man said, putting the stress on the 'ard' and extending a long, bony hand at the end of a long, bony arm in Ben's direction. He shook it and we went through a round of introductions.

Bernard was a man of indeterminate age, although his yellowed teeth gave a clue that he might be older than his unlined face, with its prominent cheekbones, suggested. He was a long person, tall and thin, all limbs and bones and angles, and his hair had grown to match the rest of his body and hung in dreadlocks down his back, oddly colourless, not grey, but as if some of the life had gone out of the black. His toes and toenails were gnarled and he wore a faded, short-sleeved shirt open over a greyish vest, and long, worn-out shorts, like a surfer who has fallen on hard times and started sleeping rough. His eyes looked in slightly different directions, the edges of the irises starting to break away and leach into the whites. The tips of his fingers were yellow but the rest of his skin was a mid-brown. He looked exactly like what he was – a slightly crazy Rastafarian.

Shaking his hand seemed to open the floodgates and words started pouring out of him. We were standing next to an overgrown field of sorts, a kind of garden crossed with a meadow, and he told us again that this was his home.

'Come! I'll show you,' he said, beckoning with his long skeleton's hand and high-stepping on his stick legs across the long grass. We had little else to do, so we followed him until we were standing underneath a dingy towel that had been strung out to dry on a piece of twine.

'This was my grandfather's house.' I looked around again but all I could see was the remnants of a ruined shed. Three stone walls remained, for the most part standing, but the fourth wall and the roof were long gone.

'Yeah, this house, it date back to 1800 something,' Bernard said proudly, slapping the bricks. I stared. This was a house?

It was absolutely tiny, nothing more than one small room. If Bernard had lain out at full stretch on a mattress on the floor, the flats of his pink-soled feet would have been braced against one of the remaining walls while his dreads squashed up against the other.

I looked around me at the meadow/field. Now I spotted the remains of a fire, a metal pan and a bowl. Over by the splintery pole that supported the twine from which the dingy towel was hanging were a couple of garden tools.

'Yeah, when Irene came, she tried to blow down my grandfather's house. But it's a good and strong house, still standing now.'

Ben asked Bernard how long he'd been living on the island for.

'For many years. I born here. But then I go to Nassau to work and I stay there eighteen years. Now I come back and

I find this –' he swept his twiggy arm in an arc – 'all blown down. But no matter. I start again and I clear the land – so tall the weeds grow! – and I plant my vegetables' – he pronounced every syllable of the word – 'and they are growing good again. My grandfather's house is still here and I know I have a good life. I have my house, my veg-ge-tar-bulls, my bicycle and my dog. It is a good life. What more can a man need?'

He had a point. As long as another hurricane didn't come barrelling through over the summer months, he'd probably have time to get his house in some kind of order.

'Well, there is one thing –' Bernard giggled, hopping from foot to foot – 'that a man needs but I can grow this also.' I looked at his yellowed hand and saw the stub of a joint tucked into his palm, pinched between his thumb and forefinger.

'You see all this land?' he asked, leaping to where we were standing and turning Ben by the shoulders to face the sea. That bony arm did another sweep to take in the view. 'This land all my family's land. The developers, they say to me, "Why don't you sell us your land? It will make you a rich man." But I don't need no riches, boss. I have everything I need here. Now, some other people, on the other side of the island, they sell their land to developers, and they take the money and they walk. But I say, "No, I want to stay here. This is my grandfather's house. He built it and now it is my house. One day it will be my son's house. What I want money for?"'

At this, he jumped away again and scratched his long but sparse stubble with the third finger of his left hand, while still holding the joint hooked into his palm.

'You know what I mean?'

We smiled and nodded yes, even though we didn't really know what he meant (I couldn't even understand everything he was saying, so I've filled in some of the gaps here), and because it's probably always better to agree with a slightly crazy, stoned Rastafarian man who has a scythe within hand's reach.

'You know, I like you boat people,' he said. 'I would like –' he pointed one finger straight up in the air, as if he had just been struck by a great idea sent down from above – 'I would like to invite you for dinner here at my house tonight. You come and I will cook you a good dinner of veg-ge-tar-bulls from my garden and we can talk some more. What you say?'

I was thrilled at the prospect. A home-grown, organic vegetarian dinner cooked up by a genuine Rasta man – how much more authentically Caribbean could you get?

But Ben was less keen and, given the scythe, probably sensibly so.

'We'd love to, man,' he said. 'But we're leaving. But maybe next time, hey?'

Bernard's smile dimmed a touch before he replied. 'OK, OK, boss. Whatever you say.' He spread his hands wide, and I could see every bone and knuckle of his fingers.

We smiled and backed away and he kept on talking, his words carried towards us on the wind as we followed the path over the hill.

'Yes, what more can a man need? As long as he's got his veg-ge-tar-bulls and his strong grandfather's house, and his garden...'

Because the journey ashore was such an ordeal, we decided as a crew that we would make only one run to the island and back each day and if anyone didn't want to go at that time, they'd have to remain on *Papagayo*. There were no quick trips, either – once we'd made the effort (and burnt through the petrol) to get over to land, we were there for several hours.

Clarence Town was a bit of a misnomer – there was no town. There might not have been a Clarence, either – I certainly didn't meet him.

We parked our dinghy each day at the marina, a small development that had just three yachts using its pontoons. Depending on the state of the tide, the clamber up from the dinghy on to the wooden pontoons was either a quick hop or a careful, full-body-stretched climb. The marina had a shed containing a top-loading washing machine – which they let us use – and a lovely, modern shower block – which they did not.

'Water shortages,' the woman in the dusty shop, which sold crisps and engine parts, told us. 'We have to save it for our customers.'

That was all well and good but they only had three boats in, and we were offering to pay for the showers. I thought it would have made business sense, but we were rebuffed. Our money was good enough, however, when we wanted to buy a small bag of ice for our cool-box. It was $6.

'Phew!' I whistled under my breath at Vicky. 'For that price we'd better hope it's super-charged ice that won't melt within a day.' If we were to be stranded for a week, that was going to be $40 on ice alone.

A path ran parallel to the small beach and then bent to the right, forking inland. If we followed our feet for a few minutes we ended up in the 'town' – consisting of only a shop that sold absolutely no fresh food whatsoever, only crumbling biscuits and tins of beans and veg, and a car-hire place. Another road off to the right – tarmacked this time – took us past a few houses and down to a small hotel restaurant called Rowdy Boys. A final right-hand hook completed the circuit and we were back at the marina, which had a small bar selling burgers and cocktails at certain times of the day. And that was the extent of our little world.

We spent a few afternoons at Rowdy Boys – which, being empty, was not rowdy in the least – carting all of our laptops, phones, tablets and cameras with us, plus their various plugs, leads and adapters, and eked out three Cokes and a bowl of fries for as long as we could, using their wifi and commandeering every single power outlet we could find to charge our equipment while we 'ate'. Thankfully the staff didn't seem to mind that the main thing we were eating was their data allowance and that we were running up their electricity bill; most of the time we were their only customers.

When you go and live on a sail boat, one of the big attractions is getting away from everyday life, including the constant demands and distractions of the internet, social media and text messages. When you do a long offshore passage, unless you've got a complicated SSB radio, or an expensive sat-phone system (and very deep pockets), you are forced to take a break from it all and you soon realise how much you don't miss it, that not being 'connected' doesn't really matter, that the world will still turn if you don't manage to update your Facebook status at least daily. I've always loved the feeling of freedom it gives me, to be unshackled from all that fuss and just to be myself, in the moment, without feeling the need to constantly be wired in, wondering, *What's So-and-so doing? Am I missing out? What's been happening in the world?* Yes, someone might have got a new job, or had a baby, or war might have broken out on the other side of the world, or some politician or celebrity been caught in the act of doing something they really shouldn't have. But if you don't hear about it and don't know about it, then it can't affect you. Not that it does affect you anyway, really, even if you do know about it. It's all just meaningless gossip we term 'news'.

It was strange for me at first, when I first went to live on boats, to be isolated from all that noise and chatter, especially since my job – my whole life, really, had been about listening to that noise, interpreting that chatter and passing on that gossip – aka news – for over a decade.

What was 'news' to us here, now, on Long Island, was only the very immediate stuff. What the sea state was like. How windy it was. Whether we were hungry. Where we were going to buy food from (certainly not from the town shop). What time sunset was, so we could make sure we were back on *Papagayo* before then. We really were living in today. It was all very Zen.

But at the same time we had to look to the immediate future, too, and that was why we needed the internet – to look at weather forecasts, and check routes and try to work out when we would be able to move on, so that we could plan to be ready.

Old habits die hard, though, and once we had electricity and wifi we were straight on to Facebook, email and Skype and even scrolling down the Mail Online's Sidebar of Shame. I hold my hand up – I was just as bad as the rest of them.

'From this Grib,' Ben said, studying the weather chart on his laptop, 'I reckon we might be able to leave on Sunday.'

I got out of my chair, the metal legs scraping loudly against the tiled floor, and went round to look over his shoulder. The wind strengths, shown by coloured arrows, were easing off slightly on Saturday. If we left the next day, we'd have twenty days to reach St Lucia, 1,000 nautical miles away as the crow flew. It would be a push, but it was just about doable.

I turned to look out of the restaurant's window, which had been smeared by salt spray from the ocean. The heads of the palms in the garden were bent over by the wind and the surface of the swimming pool was being whipped into waves by the gusts. The beautiful blue skies were incongruous. I looked beyond, to the open sea.

'Hope so. There's still plenty of white horses out there.'

Vicky piped up. 'That's three days from now. I think I might go mad if we have to sit around here for another three days, just waiting. Anyone want to hire a car and explore a bit?'

What a revelatory idea. I was so used to only seeing places we could reach on foot, which rather restricted our exploratory field.

Vicky pulled out a paper map of the island she'd got from the marina shop.

'There's a road that takes us north. Looks like there's a blue hole here,' her fingers traced the pale-grey line up the spinal column of the land, 'and a plantation up here. And there's what looks like another town along here. Maybe they'll have better food supplies than the Clarence Town shop. If we've got a car, it'd be easy to stock up.'

With nothing else to do for three days while we waited for our weather window, it was a no-brainer. We managed to fill the rest of the afternoon walking over to the car-hire shop, chatting to the assistant and filling in the form.

Working in a car-hire shop was evidently a glamorous occupation in the Bahamas. The office had air-conditioning, for a start, and pot plants and a little waiting area with low vinyl-padded seats.

The clerk, who welcomed us with a broad smile, wore a tight pencil skirt that skimmed over her rather ample but gravity-defying behind and a white sleeveless blouse and heels. Fanned out on a circular glass coffee table in the reception area was a selection of Caribbean women's magazines. I picked one up and flicked through it, becoming increasingly aware of how grubby I felt as the drying salt from the dinghy ride over prickled my skin. I tucked a crusty strand of hair behind an ear and studied my toenails. They were one part of me that weren't faring too badly in the sun – they'd turned a rosy shell-pink and gleamed against my tanned toes. No need for a pedicure here – well, the nail varnish part, anyway. It cheered me up a little bit, until I noticed a new hole in my shirt.

I handed over my driver's licence, aware of how different I looked in the photo, with my pale, greyish skin and dark, styled hair. The clerk didn't even bat a false eyelash.

The following morning the woman handed over a set of keys, clutched in jazzy bright acrylic talons, and we walked over to our little grey hatchback.

'Do you want to drive?' Ben asked me, jangling the keys in his palm.

I looked over at the car. It was right-hand drive but I always felt nervous about driving cars that weren't my own, and this one was an automatic, something I'd never driven before.

'It's OK. You can do it,' I said, thinking he was a man and they tended to like to be behind the wheel.

'Fine. We'll swap later.'

I climbed into the back, Vicky got in the passenger seat, the map stretched across her lap, and Ben set off, turning right out of the chain-link-fenced car park, up the hill and on to the one road that stretched up the island.

'What's to the left?' I asked Vicky, after five minutes of straight road, low scrubby bushes and little else.

'Not much. It looks like marsh land. I think there's some sort of quarry or something. But the blue hole is a bit further up and on the right.'

'What's a blue hole? I hope it's not like a black hole!'

Ben spoke. 'It's a really deep patch of water. They go down hundreds of metres. Freedivers like to use them.'

I leaned back in my seat and crossed my arms. Hundreds of metres deep? There was no chance I was going for a swim in that.

Despite being the major tourist attraction on the island, there was only one other car in the car park, and by car park

I mean a rough patch of land, when we pulled in. As I got out, I felt the wind whip around my limbs. Still no chance of leaving any time soon.

Across the way was a sign, red paint faded to pink in the sun. We went over to read it.

'Warning. Dean's Blue Hole is the deepest in the world,' I read out loud. 'It suddenly plunges to a depth of six hundred and sixty-three feet, two hundred and two metres deep. Blimey!'

I read the next part in silence. 'Caution. There is no lifeguard on duty. Swim at your own risk. Anyone who is not a competent swimmer should not attempt to swim in or near the blue hole.'

The sign had certainly done its job. I was both warned and cautioned – and now properly terrified of swimming in the blue hole – and I hadn't even seen it.

'Um … are you going to swim in it?' I asked the other two.

'Maybe,' Ben shrugged, and set off along the path.

I'm not a fan of deep water and, although I have swum in water that was deeper than 202 metres, in open ocean, to clean a boat's underside, I was fending off a rising panic the whole time. Ben and Vicky were both a lot braver than me and, more importantly, they were divers – so this was exactly up their street. I'd done my PADI open-water ticket but that had meant there was less than 18 metres of water above me and, oddly, I found it much less frightening to be near the seabed. The idea of there being 600 feet between me and the bottom was freaky. Who knew what would be lurking in there?

I swallowed hard and followed the others, trying not to let my overactive imagination run away with me.

They'd disappeared behind a rocky outcrop and, by the time I reached them, they'd stopped and were looking down at the blue hole.

Astrophysics-related jokes aside, black hole would have been a more appropriate term for it. It was a circular area of water, framed on one side by craggy cliffs and on the other by a shallow beach. The water on the beach was white at its furthest edges, gradually darkening to a pale aqua and through turquoise to blue, like a reverse chromatography experiment, and then it suddenly shifted to an inky blue-black in the centre, where the limestone must have dropped away, sheer, to that depth of 202 metres. It was as if an immense cylindrical plug had been drilled out of the earth. I had visions of paddling in the shallows and being sucked into the dark centre, like a giant natural bath drain.

Floating on the top was a strange white metal contraption, a little bit like the bottom half of a giant mousetrap.

'What's that?' I asked Ben, as we scrambled up the hill to the top of the cliffs to get a better view.

'It's a thing freedivers use to leave a record of how deep they've gone. They can wind a line down and they mark their depth before they come back up.'

It gave me chills to think about holding my breath and descending into the bowels of the planet like that.

'Why on earth would anyone want to do that?' I realised I was coming across as a big wuss and changed tack. 'I mean, is there anything to see somewhere like that, if it's that dark?'

'Well, the light goes down some of the way. And sometimes, when they're open on one side to the ocean, you get schools of sharks swimming in them, circling, waiting for fish to come up from the deep.'

My scalp crawled. Circling sharks and creatures from the deep?

We stood at the top for a few minutes, looking down on the hole. I had to admit it was quite pretty – or would have been, if the freediver mousetrap platform thingy wasn't slap bang in the middle of it. I just didn't want to go in it.

The idea of swimming across the bay from one side to the other and having to cross that void was starting to make me panic.

Thankfully, neither of the others was interested in taking a dip. We'd not long been dry from our boat ride to the island. As I followed them back down the way we'd come, I noticed three men sitting cross-legged on a flatish section of rock near the beach. The man facing me had his wetsuit peeled down to his waist, exposing an impressively wide chest. His eyes were closed and I watched his ribs slowly expand as he took an extremely long, slow breath in. Freedivers, I guessed, doing breathing practice before they went into the hole. *Rather you than me, any day*, I thought.

We tried next to get to a sugar plantation but the track marked on the map was so overgrown that we had to give up and reverse back a quarter of a mile to the road, crossing our fingers that the bangs and whipping noises we heard as 6-feet-tall dense grasses and shrubs reluctantly moved out of our way weren't the sound of permanent and expensive scratches being left in the hire car's paintwork.

Vicky directed Ben north again and we carried on, seeing hardly anyone or any other cars. Apparently there were 4,000 people on Long Island, but it certainly didn't feel like it. *Four thousand people*, I thought. *Where are they all? What do they do to fill the time? There's hardly anything here. And how do they make enough money to live? It's not exactly cheap to buy food here and, judging by the marina, water's scarce. I just don't get it. It was like this in Bimini. People living, somehow, but doing what with themselves?* I suspected that such a lifestyle would drive me crazy.

After half an hour we came to a small village, with a supermarket and a petrol station. Once we were through to the other side, it was just shrubs and nothingness again. We came to a fork in the road.

'Left goes back to Calabash Bay,' Vicky said. 'Right goes to the airport.'

'Anything else that looks like it's worth seeing?' I asked.

'Not really. We could go back to the village and have lunch?'

We had cold beers and deep-fried seafood overlooking the beach, then it was my turn to drive us, jerkily, my left foot through force of habit mistaking the brake for a clutch pedal, back to Clarence Town. My only saving grace was that there were so few other cars on the road.

A couple of nights later, sitting on the deck and looking out at white horses still galloping in, I thought about Long Island. This was to be our last stop in the Bahamas. We'd been here for three weeks and it was hard to believe we'd spent all of that time in one country. The islands were so varied: Long Island, with its few locals and bare amenities, had a lot in common with Bimini. I wondered how people found ways of carving out whole, complete lives in these places. They were little more than sleepy, dusty villages, wholly reliant on resources being brought in by ship from outside. If there was a sliding Bahamian scale, Bimini and Long Island would sit somewhere in the middle, Nassau, with its glitz and gleam and fake tourism-based culture, was at one extreme end, and the Exumas, with their A-list exclusivity and pure natural state, were the polar opposite. It was a wide variety, and yet none of these places felt real to me. I couldn't imagine myself being able to build a life in any of them. I sighed, stood, and tipped the dregs of my peppermint tea, rapidly blown cold by the wind, into the sea. Maybe at the next stop I'd find my Caribbean dream.

20

Beyond the pale

The beautiful woman leaned over the side of the catamaran steps and gracefully lowered her paddle board on to the water. It rocked ever so slightly in waves no bigger than those in a half-busy swimming pool. She sat on the edge of the steps, all slender brown limbs, bouncy brunette curls and white bikini, and lowered herself on to the board. One hand reached out to the catamaran's deck to retrieve the paddle, then she stretched to her full height and let the board glide away from the yacht. She dipped a blade into the water and pushed, her body ramrod straight and perfectly balanced, like a Victorian schoolgirl in a deportment class. Serenely, she did a lap of her boat, then headed towards the beach.

'I might take up paddle-boarding, if it gives me a body like that,' I said to Vicky, who was sitting next to me on the deck, looking out over Sapodilla Bay in the early morning sun and sipping her tea. She murmured her agreement.

We'd arrived in the Turks and Caicos Islands not long after dawn and had anchored off a yellowish crescent of a beach with a bracket of tasteful holiday villas just behind. There were only a couple of yachts in the bay, one of which was the very expensive-looking catamaran the woman had paddled away from. *Papagayo*, in contrast, looked small and tired.

'I think we can still make it in time, if we push hard,' I'd said to Ben and Vicky after dinner in the saloon on our last night in Long Island. They'd picked up the gauntlet and we'd started a ferocious journey, taking on everything the weather could throw at us, and pushing ourselves and the boat to the limit.

The sea had still been wild when we'd nosed out of Clarence Town bay but we'd put the engine ahead, leaning on the throttle a bit more, and hung on in the confused whirlpool waters, tugging the peaks of our fluorescent yellow waterproof hoods a little lower over our foreheads. The overnight passage to the Turks and Caicos Islands was broken up with a brief stop at Mayaguana, the final Bahamas' island, where we dropped the hook for a couple of hours and I dozed fitfully, not able to fully relax in the rolling motion of the boat.

I'd been through the navigation plan over and over again and had it down to pretty much precise military timings. There was little scope for sightseeing or relaxing – our mission was to get to St Lucia by the first of February, to give us a few days' leeway before my flight to the UK on the fourth, and, after a week's confinement on Long Island, I was up to the challenge. This Caribbean tour was now to be purely business.

Turks and Caicos ('kay-koss') is a small collection of coral islands east of the Bahamas and north of Hispaniola, which was to be the next point on my whistle-stop tour. I looked up the procedures for immigration in Providenciales, the largest island of the archipelago and our arrival point from the Bahamas, and decided that we could be in, across and out of the 100-mile-wide island series in three days, with two night breaks. After Provo, heading south, there was hardly any point in stopping anywhere because there were few facilities. Ben and Vicky had lived in Turks and Caicos before (was there anywhere they hadn't been?) and so were happy with my plan. The only thing preventing me from deciding to plough on, day and night, were the coral bommies that peppered the shallow water like landmines. We couldn't see them in the dark and if we hit one there was a chance we'd be scuppered. So I only had daylight hours to work with.

I was quite enjoying the challenge. It felt good to have something to focus on after all that time spent lolling about in Clarence Town and, before that, in Florida. I was feeling the need for speed. At 6 knots, a slow jogging pace, I wasn't really getting that, but I was getting motion, activity and purpose.

When it got to 08.45am, Ben passed the dinghy up from below and we inflated it on the foredeck, quickly and efficiently, used to the routine by now, each of us having our own role in the system. By 08.55am he was tugging on the start cord, sinews in his shoulders straining, and shortly after 09.00am we were round a small headland and driving, in flat sea, into an industrial dock. We pulled the dinghy up on to a short shingly beach littered with scrap metal and Vicky and I waited under the shade cast by a rotting ship's hull for Ben to come back from customs and immigration. He returned within an hour, slung his backpack into the dinghy and started to drag the boat down towards the beach.

'He let us check out as well,' he said. 'Says we've got forty-eight hours to leave.'

I nodded. That was one item ticked off the list. Next: fuel.

The petrol station was a half mile or so walk from Sapodilla Bay beach: easy enough when you're carrying empty jerry cans, not so much fun on the return when they weigh 25kg each, you've got four of them between three of you and the late-morning sun is beating down on your head.

The final job was cleaning. We'd been hit constantly by big breaking waves as we'd forced our way east the night before and the boat was full of water. While Vicky cleared out the forepeak, untying everything from the spider's web and pushing it up through the hatch and on to the deck to dry in the sun, I lifted up the heavy hardwood baseboards that made the yacht's floor and bailed out the gallons of salt water that had collected underneath, using a sponge to soak up the last drops caught in the awkward corners. It was backbreaking work, crouching while bent double, and a Sisyphean task; I knew it'd have to be done again in a couple of days. But I silenced the complaining voices in my head and got on with it.

That was pretty much all I saw on land of Turks and Caicos: a pretty bay, a dusty track, the inside of a petrol station (which looked the same as petrol stations all over the world), and the rusting, rounded whale belly of a boat carcass disintegrating on a beach.

Instead, I was to see an awful lot of the country's sea, and I got the impression that in Turks and Caicos that might be the draw. The islands, as far as I could gather from reading about the place and from little bits Ben and Vicky told me about it, were predominantly made up of wealthy holiday communes and wealthy expat communes, both presumably set up for advantageous tax reasons. Unless you were a rich person, or worked in a job designed to keep a rich person rich or happy on holiday, there wasn't much call to come here, pretty as it was. It was as if someone had taken part of the Bahamas, rubbed out any culture of any kind (I was willing to bet there were no Bernards here), and slapped a different name on it.

But the sea; that was something else. Turks and Caicos is not really a popular destination for keel-boat sailors – it's too shallow to feel comfortable – but it is stunning to look at. As we passed from Provo to Big Ambergris Cay and Big Sand

Cay, low and empty white-coral islands, it felt like we were gliding through another world. We had the engine on, to keep our manoeuvrability through the coral heads, but even the constant yarring noise of the engine couldn't spoil the experience. The water was iridescent and, even though it was windy, it was too shallow to be roughed up into substantial waves, so *Papagayo* slid through the sea easily and gracefully. I felt, looking down on this flat, bright-turquoise area, which stretched as far as I could see, like I was riding on the back of a giant ray, serenely half gliding, half skimming effortlessly for a hundred miles. After the uphill donkey ride from Bimini onwards, it felt like bliss.

The two days' journey wasn't without its stresses, however. It was so shallow that whoever was on the helm had to keep one eye on the depth meter all the time. We took turns doing bow watch, one of us standing right at the front of the yacht, polarised sunglasses on, looking out for upcoming coral bommies and relaying information about which way to turn to avoid them to the next person, standing at the mast, who relayed it again to the helm – who wouldn't have been able to hear the bowman over the engine – who adjusted course. It meant that all three of us were pretty much constantly on deck for ten or eleven hours a day, rotating position every hour or so.

With no spray coming over the bow in these flat seas, we'd abandoned the oilskins for the first time since leaving Texas, and ten hours in strong sunlight was hard work. Before I took up sailing, I was a sunbathing enthusiast. Holidays – and sunny summer Saturday afternoons – were all about getting a good tan to go home with. I knew the risks, and wore sunscreen, but would often 'accidentally' forget to reapply after swimming, or even to put any on at all on my last day, wanting to absorb as much of the sun's rays as I could before I had to get on the plane back to grey, overcast England. But even if you dedicate a whole day of holiday to sunbathing, reading and napping, it's unlikely you'd get as many as ten solid hours of sun exposure. When I'd travelled on boats in the tropics before they'd had sun shades – biminis – over the cockpit, but *Papagayo*, being an old racing boat and not designed for tropical cruising, had nothing to protect us from the elements. Most cruising yachts have spray hoods – plastic and canvas stretched on to steel frames that lift up, like a pram's hood, to protect the people in the cockpit from wind, spray and waves. *Papagayo* didn't have one of those, either; she was a naked boat. I liked the way it made her look – sleek and flat, and in the marinas she was a thoroughbred racehorse next to all the other fat, over-coddled ponies. But a spray hood would have been nice in all the head-to-wind, head-to-waves crossings we'd been doing, and a bimini would have been really useful now. We were bearing the brunt not only of the sun beating down on us, but also UV being reflected back off the pale water and the deck, so we had it three times over. By the end of both days I had a pounding headache and felt dried and shrivelled, the whites of my eyes blasted pink, scalding the insides of my eyelids when I blinked.

I also had a near-instant deep, dark tan. Gone was that feeling of English-paleness I'd had less than a fortnight ago at Calabash Bay. Just two days on the Turks and Caicos' water and I was as brown as an early retiree who spends six months of the year lying on a sun lounger on the Costa del Sol coated in baby oil. Except without the wrinkles.

I loved it. In a spare moment, I'd spread my fingers and marvel at the pinky-white valleys between them. I'd bring my hand up towards my shoulder, so the inside crease of my elbow turned into a dark-brown line. In the tiny shaving mirror Ben had glued on to the wooden cupboard door above the sink in the bathroom, I smiled to see how white my teeth looked in contrast to my face. Loose strands of hair that worked their way out of my ponytail looked white-blonde from the corner of my eye.

I'm not a particularly vain person. I make an effort with the odd bit of personal grooming, and I work out, as much for health reasons as I do to keep my weight stable, but I've never been one of those women who love shopping, and creating outfits, and accessorising, and spending hours tonging their hair. I am generally happiest in shorts and a T-shirt, and barefoot, with my hair tied back out of the way. But my vice is a suntan. I've always craved one, ever since I was nine years old. I remember one summer some girls from our street coming back from a camping holiday in the Lake District brown as walnuts, and I was absolutely fascinated by it. I'd look at their arms and legs and then look at mine, and feel an intense stab of jealousy. I don't know why – maybe a tan summed up summer to me, even then. At nine, I certainly didn't know of the other aesthetic benefits that being bronzed can bring; I wasn't aware that it made you look thinner and more toned, or that it helped disguise cellulite, thread veins and a multitude of other unsightly things. It was just beautiful to me.

Now, at thirty-four, I hadn't changed all that much. I was wiser, so I knew the risks involved, of sagging and wrinkles, of melanoma, but I couldn't shake the habit. Ben and Vicky were both always very brown. Ben's skin is naturally dark, even though he is white – 'Gandhi, they used to call me up in Hull,' he said. 'That, or Paki' – and the pair of them have lived a beach-side existence in hot countries almost constantly for nearly two decades. Contrary to the kinds of warnings you read in glossy women's magazines, neither of them looked wizened or had aged prematurely; in fact, with their slim, toned bodies sustained by an active lifestyle they looked ten years younger that their chubby, pasty contemporaries slobbing out on sofas back in the UK.

As well as being beautiful, dark skin is also interesting to me. I think it must be because it tells a story of difference, of abroad. Either of a heritage that is way more exotic than a bog-standard upbringing in a British Midlands' town, or of travels to far-flung places. I found it odd that in Malaysia the pharmacies, and even the wooden-shack village shops in the remotest of places, sold skin-whitening creams – bars of soap, lotions and even deodorants that falsely promised to lift skin tones a shade or two. And I had a boyfriend from Central America once who hated his brown skin. I loved it and tried to encourage him to show it off more, but he hid it away, out of the sun, and even wore a T-shirt by the pool when we went on holiday.

As well as making me look better, having a tan made me feel better, too – something that must have been due to more than just having elevated vitamin D3 levels. I felt different – braver, somehow, less repressed and suppressed, more able to do reckless things, to have a go. Tanned Emma was free-spirited Emma, an optimist who felt she could do anything she wanted to, who was away on an adventure and not in grey England. Being brown actually made me more comfortable in my own skin. Occasionally, after Turks and Caicos, I'd look at the back of my hand and it'd look like that of a stranger, kind of like when you lie on your arm when you're sleeping and, in the moments before the pins and needles come, it feels like someone else's arm. In that split second before I recognised myself I was free from whom I thought I was and that freedom was exciting. The woman who owned this brown hand was a traveller and an explorer. She was cool. She was me but not me.

Once we'd cleared the last of the bommies, and before we went into a night passage down to Hispaniola and the Dominican Republic, there was chance, in a rare, relatively calm sea, to do a bit more navel-gazing during a solo watch.

As I took the helm, I checked around to make sure there were no other boats or hazards to crash into – there was nothing as far as the horizon, which was melting with the twilight – and thought about this latest part of the trip.

I'd been feeling for a couple of weeks that we weren't really getting anywhere and now I was pleased with the progress we'd finally started to make. I thought back to the start of my trip, nearly two months ago. We had actually made a hell of a lot of headway, nearly 2,000 miles of it, from Texas to Florida, through the Bahamas and Turks and Caicos, but because it had come in fits and starts, with long, land-bound fits and short sailing starts, I had somehow got the impression that we had stalled.

I'd set off from England with the intention of getting to the Caribbean. Technically, while we were in the Bahamas and Turks and Caicos, we weren't actually in the Caribbean. Now, a few hours' sail from our stop of Luperón on the north coast of the Dominican Republic, we finally were.

I'm in the Caribbean, I thought now, and smiled as I held on to the steel wheel and guided the boat across the sea by myself. *I made it.*

The Caribbean had become a small obsession of mine since a daydream I'd had a couple of years earlier. It was clearer than a daydream – I called it an epiphany – and I saw a vision of myself living on a tropical island. When Ben and Vicky had got in touch to ask me to help them move *Papagayo* to St Lucia, I'd partly said yes because I loved sailing but a big draw was the destination and the chance to explore my way through the region. In my world, the Caribbean was somewhere where people went on holiday on honeymoon; I knew very few people who'd been there. It helped that my sailing friend Jon had some amazing pictures on his blog of his time spent cruising through the islands.

While I thought the Bahamas and Turks and Caicos were physically stunning places, they didn't quite manage to capture my imagination, or my heart. They both felt like holiday destinations, rather than real places where people lived real lives. It was a frustrating sensation, being in these beautiful locations but feeling a bit removed from them, like my dream was just out of reach. With the Dominican Republic I was hopeful that I might find that spark, like the jolt you feel when you first meet a new lover. I was pretty certain that when I reached the place I'd only briefly glimpsed once in my mind's eye, I'd know. *Dominican Republic*, I whispered into the night, under my breath, *you're just a few short hours away. And who knows? You may be the one.*

21

The Englishwoman's Guide
to Passages East

The dog, a rangy, mangy yellow thing with long legs and a lolling tongue, trotted after us down the street. It seemed like it knew its place – while we stuck to the pavement (where there was one), the dog stayed in the broken gutter. It watched us keenly, but with a reasonably friendly look on its face, and every now and then darted ahead of us before stopping, turning to check where we were and waiting for us to pass so it could follow on our heels.

There were a lot of dogs in Luperón, mostly lying in patches of shade, bitches with swollen teats snoozing through the airless afternoon while their pups piled on top of each other in a hot, hairy heap. The sleeping ones, because they were still and lazy, didn't bother me so much, but I kept a wary eye on our active yellow friend, wishing I knew the Spanish for 'go away'.

There were a few people in the street, paying us no attention, going about their business, and the air felt thick with pollution, although there were few cars driving around.

We'd arrived outside Luperón before dawn the night before, and were forced to slow to a halt, waiting with the engine idling for the sun to rise high enough for us to be able to see our way through the narrow mouth of a harbour and into the anchorage marked on our chart.

We entered through a straitened pass between two low hills and then did a sharp hook to the right. It felt a bit like turning into a supermarket car park, and as we straightened up the yacht we realised it looked like one, too, except instead of cars neatly lined up in white-lined tarmac bays, we found hundreds of yachts at anchor in a mud-brown bay, positioned carefully so that all of them could be fitted in while making an attempt at keeping a reasonable distance apart. We had to do a few circles, like a dog getting ready to sleep, before we found a suitable space in which to stop.

The anchor had only been down a couple of minutes when three local men came over in a wooden boat, one blank-faced young man steering, another crouching in the bow, and a jolly man in a brown shirt and moustache smiling broadly and waving as they drew up. The driver killed the engine and guided the launch next to *Papagayo*, not bothering to use fenders, so there was a loud crunch as their hulls collided. I looked to Ben. He hadn't let his fixed grin waiver but he muttered 'here we go' under his breath.

'Good morning, *Papagayo*!' said the smiling man, stepping up on to *Papagayo* to shake Ben's hand. His shirt, the same colour as both the water and his skin, was taut over his round belly. 'Welcome to Luperón! Welcome to the Dominican Republic!'

He introduced himself as Cal and promised to be able to get us 'anything you want. Anything at all. Water. Diesel. Laundry. Spares. Repairs. I get my boys to bring to you.'

I looked down at the 'boys', standing wide-legged in their boat for balance. They were young men, in their late teens or early twenties, strong-looking and fine-featured, with gleaming chocolatey skin and hair cropped close to their scalps. One flashed me a flirtatious smile.

While Ben tried to fend off Cal's offers of supplying everything under the sun to *Papagayo*, I found myself fending off advances of another kind.

'My name is Moses,' said the boat boy with the smile. 'Where you from?'

'London,' I told him, crouching down on the deck so I was closer to his level.

'London, England? I have girlfriend in England. She is called Helen.' He paused, and I wondered if he was about to do the American-style thing of asking if I knew her.

I picked up the small talk. 'You have a girlfriend in England?'

'Yes.'

'You are from here?'

'Yes. I am from Puerto Plata.' I knew from the guide book that this was the big resort town on the north coast, with large hotels offering all-inclusive packages that attracted a different crowd from the usual Sandals' brigade. The Dominican Republic was, to Brits at least, the place to come to for Caribbean-on-the-cheap. It was also, to a certain kind of lonely, older female tourist, the place to come to pick up local men. The Dominican Republic is one of the sex-tourism capitals of the world, but with the rich Western women doing the picking up, not the other way round.

Moses was standing in his wooden boat, holding on to *Papagayo*'s metal toe rail with one hand. The wake from a passing dinghy shifted his boat and he adjusted his grip on the yacht, steadying himself. The hulls clunked together again. I asked him how he met Helen.

'I used to work at a resort in Puerto Plata. I meet her there.'

'She was on holiday here?'

'Yes. She tell me that I can come live with her in England. First I have to save money, but last year the resort closed. So now I do this work with Cal.'

I looked over towards his boss, who was still trying to charm his way into Ben's wallet, gesticulating with his hands. Ben had folded his arms over his chest and Vicky, standing next to him to offer solidarity, had copied his pose.

I looked back at Moses. 'And when do you think you will go to London?'

His smile was a little dimmer than before.

'I don't know. I hope soon. My cousin, he also live in England. He marry English wife also.'

I knew the question was coming. I could almost have done a countdown to it. Three ... two ... one...

Moses: 'Are you married?'

I looked into his handsome face and I saw a flash of his life. I saw a uniform – white shirt tucked into black trousers – and I saw him carrying a tray of brightly coloured cocktails over to a high, round table, where two pale women giggled behind their hands. I saw an off-duty drink at the bar, a late-night dance with a woman – freckled skin, hair curling in the humidity. I heard the whispering of promises, a tearful goodbye, the click of buttons on his mobile phone as an album of photos was scrolled through again and again. I felt the silence, and his hope starting to evaporate slowly over the months.

I stood, and brushed my hands together, even though there was no dust to rub away.

'No, I'm not married,' I said, and stepped away.

We'd read a lot about Luperón in a guidebook we carried that had promised to teach us the tricks of the Caribbean and make our passage east from the Bahamas to the US Virgin Islands a doddle. When each of us had been doing our research ahead of the trip, we'd all heard from various people that Bruce Van Sant's *The Gentleman's Guide to Passages*

South was 'the bible' for the route we were to take. It was a tricky journey, heading, as it was, into the trade winds, but Gus, as we nicknamed him, promised to share with us the secrets he'd gleaned from heading east multiple times from his homeland to America's furthest reaches, the US Virgin Islands. He promised us that if we followed his advice, and 'sailed the night lees', we'd have a fairly easy time of it.

After 700 miles of absolutely not having a fairly easy time of it, Gus had become a vilified man among the tired, wet, seasick and salty crew of *Papagayo*. We didn't trust him as far as we could throw him – and the only thing that had stopped us from tossing his book into the ocean was the fear that on the next page there might be some gem of information that would prove vital to our journey.

Gus had made the Dominican Republic his second home after marrying a local woman, and waxed lyrical for pages about the area we were now in. According to him, it was the best place in the Caribbean for cruisers to stop; they could get anything they wanted here (I wondered after meeting Cal if the pair of them were in cahoots and the whole book was just an elaborate ploy – send a bunch of sailors on a long and arduous voyage, exhaust them and make them so thankful to find a place of refuge that they'll never pluck up the courage to leave).

Vicky picked up our tatty orange-covered copy of *Passages South* (we had two different editions on board).

'Let's see if Gus is any more believable on this country than he is on passage-making,' she said, sarcasm heavy in her voice.

As we motored through the anchored yachts in our dinghy, I realised that the place reminded me of Langkawi, where I'd spent months with Guy. They didn't look similar – Langkawi was a big bay, open to the sea, with cloudy but blueish water and sandy edges, while Luperón was a natural hurricane hole, a tight muddy inlet framed with mangrove, which knitted and knotted itself around the edges like cushioning – but both were clearly long-term hangouts for cruisers on a budget.

At the top of the inlet, where the water dried to a narrow creek, someone had built a long, low, wooden dock, perfect for yacht tenders and small local fishing boats. We tied up and followed the dirt road the only way it went: inland.

Customs and immigration were the most informal I'd come across yet: a series of sheds, each containing a solitary desk, with one man standing outside each, only a couple of them dressed in uniform – and those looked like they'd been picked up at a fancy-dress store. I felt a bit nervous as Ben handed over the relevant fees in cash US dollars, wondering if we were being ripped off.

I wasn't sure why I was feeling on edge. I think being in close proximity to hundreds of other cruisers had something to do with it. When you get a bunch of sailors all hanging out long-term in the same spot, things become cliquey very quickly. The ones who stay put aren't really travellers or interested in exploring or in local culture; they tend to want things their way – and cheaply, too. They'll spend money at local businesses but they strike a hard bargain and I think this can lead to some ill-will between the local community and the cruisers. All it takes is for a few miserly penny-pinchers to cause a row over a bill and all visiting sailboats get tarnished by the same brush. I've found the friendliest places to be ones where the odd yacht passes through every now and then – and the sailors you meet in those kinds of places are generally the nicest kind, too. Too often, a busy and permanent anchorage can turn into a dumping ground for a lot of washed-up, unhappy people.

After we'd been to the last of the port-authority buildings – the final one, at least, had a crest over the door, a map pasted up on the wall and seemed a bit more official – we followed the path a couple of hundred metres into Luperón town.

It was immediately apparent that we were in a poor country. The buildings we passed were little more than shacks and barefoot children scrabbled around in the dirt, playing between sleeping dogs. The road was about wide enough for two cars to pass and as we walked further along, the shack-like houses (that would after dark turn into impromptu bars) were replaced by cheap and crumbling concrete-block buildings with corrugated iron roofs. The first bar we came to, mentioned in Gus's book, was closed, shutters down around the courtyard wall and a thick padlock on the worn plank door. Pretty much everything was closed, which added to the impoverished feel of the place.

'Do they have siestas in the Caribbean?' I mused out loud.

The road carried on in a straight line for a mile or so, widening out about halfway along at what must have been the prosperous part of town. Buildings here, their use not immediately distinguishable by their shape or style, were painted different colours that had faded under the sun, turning reds to salmon pink and oranges to vanilla. Small trees dotted the left-hand side of the road and the air was a mix of drains, car fumes and blackened chicken. A dead puppy, probably no more than a couple of weeks old, lay on the pavement. I looked away.

At the main junction in the centre of Luperón high street, we passed a shop with glass windows and familiar plastic signage: Orange mobile. *How weird to find a British company in a place like this*, I thought.

We found a small supermarket, little bigger than a convenience store, where we stocked up on bits and pieces. We didn't want to dip into our store of US dollars any more than we needed to, so we totted up what our shop would cost and I nipped back into the street to withdraw as close to the right amount of Dominican Republic pesos as I could. At 44 to the dollar, it wasn't easy maths. I doubled-checked the figure before I pressed enter because we didn't want to get stuck with currency we'd have no use for after a few days.

That evening we came back into Luperón town after dark and found it a far livelier place. Small lanterns lit up the streets and hid the dirt and decay. People were out in force, sitting in white plastic chairs in their front yards, their children still scrabbling about in the dust by their feet. A man stood by half an empty oil drum turning chickens on a spit over a smoking wood fire. The smell made my mouth water. One of the small shack houses had thrown open its front windows and turned itself into a kiosk selling beer. Someone had hooked up a stereo system and loud, frenetic *dembow* music made the asphalt bounce beneath my flip-flops.

No one paid us any attention. There were no waves, no nods hello, no beckoning gestures to come on over, buy some beers, chat a little. I felt like a ghost drifting through a town that didn't want me.

It wasn't intimidating; it just wasn't welcoming. We walked until we found a restaurant, ate some deep-fried fish pulled out of a chest freezer in the middle of the room by an unconvincing transvestite, and headed back to *Papagayo*.

So is this the real Caribbean? I wondered as I sat on the deck the next morning. *If so, it is a bit of a let-down.* The water here was brown, sitting on muddy mangrove bed, and the skies an overcast grey. We'd heard on the VHF radio that morning that one of the yachts in the bay had been burgled the night before.

I wasn't naive enough to think that the whole of the area would be exactly like the front cover of a Kuoni travel brochure, but I will admit that I was disappointed. In a way, more than being disappointed in my surroundings, I was disappointed in myself for being such a travel snob.

I wasn't happy when I was in the Kuoni-brochure-worthy spots, thinking them too perfect to be 'authentic', but then

I wasn't happy when I came across honest real life, with its grubbiness and imperfections. *Authentic* grubbiness and imperfections.

As a longer-term traveller seeing the world on boats, I looked down on the kind of package-holiday tourists who believed their tour company's propaganda and resolutely stayed within the confines of their compound, drinking imported European drinks and dining on incongruous pizza and steak. I took pride in enjoying a local beer and some fried seafood I'd never even heard of before, in hanging out in bars and restaurants with plastic chairs and roughly hewn wooden benches, in taking local buses. Or I thought I did. Now I saw that there were boundaries to my open-mindedness and comfort zone. I was proud, in the way that proud means the same as haughty. And I found I didn't much like that about myself.

Knowing and acknowledging all that, I still found Luperón depressing enough to be unsettling. I didn't feel frightened or in danger here but there was an undercurrent of something that I couldn't quite work out. I was glad when, after two days, Ben yanked the anchor out of the mud and we motored back out into the Atlantic Ocean.

22

It's all fines

Mona had no smile for us.

Ever since leaving Texas, we'd been dreading this part of the trip. Mona is the name of a passage of water that separates Hispaniola and Puerto Rico. At about 180 miles wide, from Samaná in the Dominican Republic to Ponce in the south of Puerto Rico, it takes more than a day and a night to cross by sailboat and is famed for presenting yachts with ferocious weather conditions.

We were well used to 30–40-knot head winds and constant waves breaking over the bow and reaching us where we stood 30 feet back, but all the guidebooks and information we read warned us that the Mona Passage was dangerous territory. Once we jumped off, we'd be committed to the crossing, no matter how bad the conditions were. It had become our personal Cape Horn.

I kept an eye on the weather charts as we made our mad dash through Turks and Caicos and the Dominican Republic. I'd come to be mistrustful of the forecasts. Whatever they predicted, we seemed to get winds at least 10 knots higher. While the numbers were always off, however, the general pattern seemed to be reasonably accurate, so when we saw a relatively calm patch ahead for our Mona Passage crossing, we went with it.

Like anything you dread for ages before you get to it, it wasn't that bad when we left Samaná. I'd planned a 28-hour passage to Ponce, the country's second-largest city. Now I was on watch while Ben and Vicky were below, resting. The winds were 12–15 knots, which were among the lightest we'd experienced, and it was hot below with the engine running. Ben opened the small hatch above his bunk to let in some air.

This was a big mistake. While it wasn't windy, it was wavy. As I took yet another salty slap in the face from Poseidon, I heard a yelp from Vicky below, followed by muffled swearing. Moments later she appeared in the companionway. The same wave that smacked me had rushed down through the open hatch, dousing her and her bed and waking her in the rudest possible way from her sleep. After being yelled at, Ben sheepishly dragged her mattress into the cockpit to dry in the sun. I heard the hatch slam shut as he went back down.

I carried on with my watch. I scanned the horizon but we had left the Dominican Republic so far behind that there was absolutely nothing to see but blue water and the white tops of the waves. We were completely alone, with not even a bird to disturb us. This was one of my favourite parts of sailing, when you're far enough offshore that it seems like you're the only ones in the world. It's not only a feeling of freedom; it's also a sensation of release, release from all the pressures and stresses of everyday life that you aren't even aware are affecting you until they are taken away. When people say 'bliss', that's what bliss is to me – the chance to be myself, to just *exist* for a bit, nothing else. Now, happy, I zoned out, not even really listening to the instrumental music playing through one iPod earphone.

After an hour or so, Vicky came up to check on her mattress and crouched in the front part of the cockpit.

'Is it dry yet?' I asked, as she rubbed her palm over the rough blue surface. The mattresses also doubled as the settees' bottom cushions, and were upholstered in a textured royal-blue fabric.

'Not yet. I just hope another wave doesn't come shooting back from the bow and soak it again. I'd like to be able to get some sleep. Bloody Ben, opening the hatch.'

Suddenly, we heard an engine. Confused, I turned around sharply. There was an American Coast Guard gunship behind – and it was tracking us.

'What the—?' we said at the same time. I immediately felt a flush of embarrassment – I was supposed to be on watch, so how had I not noticed a 168-tonne, 110-foot ship emblazoned with a bright-red stripe steaming towards us until it was only a quarter of a mile away? As we watched, a troop of coast-guard officers climbed out of a door in the ship's side, down a ladder and into a black rib that broke away from the ship and started to come towards us. I looked at the back of the mother ship. On its flat back deck I could see the outline of a large mounted machine gun under canvas.

Vicky turned round and called down below. 'Ben! You'd better come up here.'

He staggered on to the deck in his underpants, hair sticking out at wild angles, rubbing sleep from his eyes with his knuckles. When he realised what was going on, he dashed back below to put on some clothes.

The rib pulled alongside us, about 5 metres off our starboard quarter, and the driver slowed his speed to match ours. Six officials, all in identical shorts, dark T-shirts, sunglasses and wide-brimmed hats tied firmly under their chins, a pale slick of sunblock on their lips and noses, stared at us with blank expressions, sitting in three rows of two and bobbing on the waves. All the men looked like they were exactly the same size and weight, like a pack of regulation-issue Action Men.

One at the front shouted over to me, 'Where's your captain?'

I turned to the companionway, trying to keep my voice steady. 'Ben!'

He flew back up the stairs, wearing shorts and a T-shirt this time.

'Sir – are you the captain of this vessel?'

'What?'

'Are you the captain of this vessel, sir?' The man was struggling to be heard over the noise of our engine and his rib's engine, and the wind snatched away portions of his words.

Ben confirmed that he was and the man produced a clipboard and began shouting questions at him about where we were from, the details of the boat, where we were going to. Both men had to repeat themselves two or three times to be heard.

'This is ridiculous,' Vicky muttered to me. 'Why doesn't he switch to VHF radio?'

We'd read, months ago, that the US authorities were twitchy. Puerto Rico is an American territory and they are worried about illegal immigrants, people-traffickers and drugs being sailed over the border. Their Coast Guard is also a Department of Homeland Security defence and patrol system – and anyone who has flown to the USA on holiday and faced a barrage of questions at the immigration desk that has left them feeling clammy and somehow guilty, even though they have nothing at all to be guilty about, will be familiar with the particular kind of stern-faced gravity that is these guys' stock-in-trade. I think if we'd been flying the Stars and Stripes off the back of *Papagayo*, we perhaps wouldn't have been given such a hard time. But the Mexican-sounding name, coupled with an incongruous Union flag, was a red rag to an officious representative of Uncle Sam.

The guy with the clipboard kept shouting questions at Ben for a good forty minutes or so, and scribbling down the answers on his papers. It must have been difficult trying to write while pitching up and down. His colleagues stared impassively ahead the whole time. They'd have made good guards at Buckingham Palace.

Incredulous that we didn't have a satellite phone – and suspicious that we claimed to have no cell phones, either (which was true: Ben's was at the bottom of the marina in St Petersburg and mine wouldn't work abroad), he eventually shouted over a number for us to call as soon as we arrived in Ponce.

'What do we tell them?' Ben asked. We hadn't been given a warning or reprimanded in any way by the coast guard; we'd just been answering their questions.

'Just say that you spoke to us,' the man replied. I wondered if a file was being prepared on us right now, on the cutter ship. *Suspicious aliens – keep watch.*

After he'd given us the phone number, clipboard man nodded to the man at the helm of the rib and they turned and roared away, then span round to face us again. I wondered if they were going to come back. But no – they stayed behind us, 30 metres or so back, bobbing in our wake, continuing to match our speed.

They were there from 3pm to 6pm, apart from a short break around 5pm (I suspected that was their dinner time).

It was creepy and I felt really self-conscious.

'What do they think we're going to do?' I asked Vicky. 'Start mixing up batches of drugs or let a load of illegal immigrants out of the lockers so they can stretch their legs on deck?'

I concentrated on ignoring them and getting back to the task of sailing to Ponce, pretending that the weirdness of being tailed by a rib and a coast guard patrol cutter across a stretch of open water wasn't happening.

Soon after 6pm, darkness fell and the rib went back to the ship. Not long after that, the green starboard navigation light faded away and I knew they'd gone for real.

I breathed a sigh of relief. The encounter had made me feel jumpy and, although I took the piss out of the experience with Ben and Vicky, it left me a bit on edge. And yet, compared to what was to come, it was a walk in the park.

Ben drove the dinghy alongside a low wooden dock and we all hopped ashore, carrying our rubbish with us. There had been no one around when we pulled into Ponce Yacht Club early in the morning, so we anchored with the other boats, got the dinghy out and motored the 100 metres or so to shore. The marina was deserted and looked a bit like a holiday park, with a large open-air bar and seating area, closed at this hour, and fingerposts pointing the directions to various amenities. I followed the sign for the women's bathroom and found myself walking through a 1980s-style gym that smelled of hot metal. A few older men, sweating through the fronts of their vests as they lifted free weights, ignored me as I passed through. The ladies was empty, and I dropped a bag of rubbish off in a cylindrical bin mounted on a lamppost as I went back to find the others, following the fingerpost pointing towards the yacht-club office.

When I got there, Vicky was hanging around in the reception area, enjoying the aircon.

'Where's Ben gone?' I asked.

'He's in the office, borrowing their phone to call customs and immigration and that number the Coast Guard gave us.'

She'd barely finished speaking when Ben dashed through the swing-top gap in the counter, ashen-faced.

'What's wrong?'

'We've got to get back on the boat. Immediately. We're in the wrong place.'

'OK.' I trotted behind him as he walked at almost a jogging pace. 'But why the panic?'

'Because we've apparently broken loads of immigration rules already. We've only been here five minutes. And we're looking at fines. Big fines. Thousands of dollars, the man said.' He reached the dinghy and jumped in, pulling the starting cord before Vicky and I had even got one foot in it.

Ben had been told by the officials on the phone, he said, that we weren't allowed to anchor until we had checked into the country. We were supposed to tie up alongside the fuel dock and not step foot on land but wait there until the immigration authorities came to us. We also weren't supposed to throw any rubbish into the bins anywhere – or we could be fined $1,000 a bag.

'Shit!' I said. 'We've chucked two!'

I offered to run back and retrieve them from the bins, but Ben said again that we weren't supposed to step on land. When we got back to the boat I grabbed an empty refuse sack and filled it with bits of food I knew we could spare, tipping out a carton of protein powder and slinging in a few damp teabags. Maybe, if I convinced them we'd done a rubbish run just before we left Samaná, the immigration officials would believe this was all the trash we'd accumulated in the past thirty-six hours. I tied a knot in the sack, trying not to inhale the vanilla-scented dust that flew out of it, and crossed my fingers. None of us had $2,000 to spare.

One of Ben's good qualities is that he is completely and utterly unable to lie. I'd witnessed this before, when he'd tried to avoid giving a straight answer to someone, or was attempting to bend the truth a little – he just couldn't do it. His hands and feet would start tapping nervously and he'd repeat the question back to the person quizzing him, stalling for time while the angel and devil on his shoulder had a fight over what to say. Lying produced an obvious physical tell in him. He'd have been hopeless at poker.

'And did you toss garbage since you arrived?' asked the official in dark-blue uniform, who'd turned up with a partner about an hour after we'd moved the boat to the fuel pontoon.

I looked at Ben, willing him to be able to lie. I'd shown him the fake bag I'd made and coached him in what to say, hoping that would help the fib come out a bit easier. *We've not got much rubbish,* I'd told him to reply. *This is what we've generated since Samaná.*

His foot started tapping on the ground, he rubbed his hair, his eyes roved around for something to fix on. *Come on, Ben!* I prayed. *Two thousands dollars. Say no. Say no!*

'Yes.'

Shit.

The man ticked something on a form.

'How many bags?'

One! I screamed silently. *ONE! ONE! SAY ONE!*

'Two.'

The man's eyebrows shot up. Scribble. Silence.

Oh god, I thought. *Please don't fine us two grand. I haven't got six hundred bucks to spare.*

'Can I see boat papers and passports please?'

Ben handed them over. The man flicked through the pages. 'Where are visas?'

'We don't have visas. We have ESTAs.'

The ESTA replaced the old US visa-waiver system. Certain nationalities can apply online before they travel and fill in an electronic form that allows them to enter the USA. The ESTA lets you stay for three months, and is valid for multiple trips to the States over two years. We'd all got them before we arrived in Houston, although Ben and Vicky had been there several weeks before I'd arrived at the beginning of November.

The official's eyebrows shot up again. 'You can't enter US territory without visa or ESTA.'

'But we have ESTA.'

'Not valid.'

'What? What do you mean not valid? Why not?'

'Not valid.'

'But we have them. I don't understand.'

We'd all flown to Texas and had been stamped in for a 90-day period. But we'd left the USA and had been checked into and out of three other countries since then. So this was a new arrival within our two years, and supposedly meant we'd get another 90-day period (although we only needed a few days in Puerto Rico and the US Virgin Islands). I'd sailed by yacht to countless countries by now, and mainly you applied for a visa when you arrived and paid the fees at the immigration desk. Some countries, such as India, required a visa to be sorted out in advance. America had the ESTA programme for Brits.

It took ages to work out, from the official's limited fluency in English and a frustratingly circular conversation, that ESTAs were only valid if you arrived in the States by commercial craft – usually a plane. So we had needed a visa in advance to come to Puerto Rico.

'But we went to immigration in St Petersburg before we left,' Ben said, his voice rising, 'and we asked them several times what the procedure was and they said we were fine.' He turned to Vicky and me. 'What was the name of the officer we spoke to?' My mind, in the heat of the moment, went blank.

'Sir, are you aware there is five hundred eighty-five dollar fine per person for entering United States territory without valid visa?'

Fuck! Five hundred and eighty-five times three, plus the two grand for the rubbish? I was incredulous. The whole situation felt completely unreal and the dock seemed to spin around me. Suddenly we were looking at $3,755. I hoped I could hold it together and not cry in front of the officials.

The man flicked through our passports again. He opened all three and compared them. 'Yours is OK, miss,' he said, extending one to me. 'You have five days left on ESTA.'

I had to stop myself from reminding him that he'd just said ESTAs were not valid. I pinched my lips together.

'I will keep these,' he said to Ben and Vicky. 'You must come to our offices and arrange for new visas. I let you off the fines for garbage, as you say you did not know the rules, but all trash from foreign must stay within vessel's railings.' We all nodded. I tried not to laugh at his phrase 'from foreign' – as if everything in the world was either American or not. I was still clutching the black sack of fake rubbish. I slung it from the dock into the boat's cockpit.

He handed Ben a faded photocopied sheet of paper. 'Here is address of the office. You come immediately.'

He nodded, turned smartly and went, taking their passports with him.

The whole thing made no sense. You couldn't arrive by ESTA and yet they'd let me do just that. You weren't allowed to throw your trash away, apart from rubbish generated in Puerto Rico, but how they could tell which empty tin of beans or apple core came from where, I don't know. There was no instruction to keep the sacks inside the boat, so I assumed any germs or spores could have been carried on the wind from the deck level, anyway. We weren't supposed to step on land until we'd been cleared in – but they'd left us to make our own way to the immigration office, which obviously meant travelling a few miles by land. They'd also technically left us free to run off into the centre of Puerto

Rico and start new lives as illegal immigrants. Well, I would be legit for five days. Then I'd be illegal.

It was all ridiculous. And it was about to get even worse, yet again – so bad, in fact, that I found myself being threatened with jail.

23

Tears for fears

I could barely keep my eyes open in the taxi across Ponce to the immigration department. I was utterly exhausted. Our sleep patterns were really disturbed – the odd night at sea, doing watches, and then a couple of normal days on land – so our body clocks weren't able to get into a rhythm. The other two seemed OK to me but I felt completely worn out: listless, disinterested and overly emotional. When I'd trapped the tip of my finger under one of the boat's floorboards when I was putting it back after cleaning the bilges, I'd sobbed uncontrollably like a toddler who'd grazed a knee coming off her bike.

I looked out of the side window of the taxi, watching Puerto Rico go by. It wasn't that dissimilar to Florida – flat, with American-style high kerbs, manicured lawns and big store complexes. Only the brands were slightly different.

The taxi pulled into a deserted dock area and turned right down a couple of side streets before coming to a stop outside an old, Spanish-style building with rough adobe walls. Grand, double-height, studded wooden doors towered above us. Ben pushed one open and we stepped inside.

A long reception desk barred our way. To the right of it was an airport-style metal detector. The four plastic chairs lined up against the wall behind us and a pot plant made the place feel like any office lobby area. A woman with teased reddish hair sitting behind the reception desk asked us to sign in. We did, then took a seat.

Chief Wiggum from *The Simpsons* came through a door to our right. I did a double-take. The man bearing down on us had an uncanny likeness to the yellow cartoon police officer, except he had a dark moustache. A badge displayed his name left of the Department of Homeland Security insignia: Officer Finga. I snorted, and tried to turn it into a cough.

I shouldn't have taken it so lightly. Officer Finga kept us on those hard plastic chairs for hours, with no food and nothing to drink. He kept disappearing into his office and coming out again with another sheaf of papers and more questions. We went over the same ground we'd covered with his colleague at the marina, over and over again, Officer Finga alternating between playing good cop and bad cop. He'd chat, all friendly, making it seem like the situation was out of his hands, not his fault, what a pickle we were all four of us in together, he'd see what he could do, and then – bam! – he'd come down hard on us, throwing his not inconsiderable physical weight around, showing us who was boss. He was clearly on a power trip.

Ben and Vicky, in the end, got Good Cop.

'I tell you what I'm gonna do. I'm gonna issue you new visas. Free of charge. Humanitarian parole.'

Their relief was palpable.

'And me?' I piped up.

He turned to me, and the mask of a smile vanished. He gave a small shrug.

'You have five days left in your ESTA. You must leave after this.'

'But I thought the ESTA wasn't valid if I arrived by yacht?'

Wrong move.

'You trying to tell me how to do my job?'

'No. It's just...' I paused; decided to try a different approach. 'It's just that I am helping my friends move their boat to St Lucia and we still have to be here in Puerto Rico a couple of days and then the US Virgin Islands. You see, I have a flight booked home from St Lucia on—'

He cut me off. 'Not my problem.' He disappeared into his office to create the visas for Ben and Vicky.

A nervous slick of sweat was breaking out on my forehead and my body ached from sitting on a hard plastic chair for so many hours. 'Shit. What are we going to do?' I asked the other two. I appealed to Ben. 'Could you have a word with him, tell him how I'm the navigator, how you need me?'

Ben said nothing. I knew he didn't want to risk being fined, or he or Vicky being blacklisted. I kind of couldn't blame him, but it was so frustrating. Finga had given them free visas – free. And valid for six months – so why couldn't he do the same for me? We were all from the same place, all going to the same place, after all.

Finga came back. 'I tell you what you can do,' he said to me. A flicker of hope that he was going to help, after all. 'You can take a flight out of Puerto Rico and then you can arrive back here by plane after five days, get a new 90-day period.'

My heart sank. This wasn't an option. Although I might have been able to scrape together the money to buy a flight out of Puerto Rico and back in again, there would be nothing left for accommodation in between. Also, doing that wouldn't leave us enough time to sail to St Lucia. We were already on the edge of our worst-case scenario, timings-wise.

My mind went into overdrive, searching for a solution. Tick, tick, tick, tick, tick. It found one.

'What about my journalist visa?'

Bad Cop scowled. 'You are a journalist?'

'Yes.

'You are here as a journalist?' Crap – what was the right answer to say to that? I began to feel a bit scared. I was well out of my depth.

'No, but—'

'Then you cannot use an I visa for journalists. Do not try to manipulate me.'

'I'm not trying to manipulate you. I do have one, in my old passport, from my old job. I have a new passport now, but I was told the visa lasted for ten yea—'

He cut me off again. 'I know very well who you are. I know very well you have an I visa. Are you trying to tell me how to do my job? I can throw you in jail, you know, you manipulate a Department of Homeland Security official. It's a very serious offence. You try to enter US territory under false pretences? I can throw you in jail for that, too.'

'I'm not trying to manipulate y—'

'Yes, you are.'

'No, I'm not, I'm just trying to find a solution.'

He spoke over the top of me. 'You are disrespecting me.'

A little bubble of spittle landed on his moustache. I shut up.

He marched off into his office again and I sat there, embarrassed, ashamed and frightened. I'd never been in a situation like this before. I couldn't believe he'd accused me of trying to manipulate him. Little old goody two-shoes me, who never broke a rule in her life? All I could think was how unfair it was. If anything, I was more 'legal' than the other two were, and yet I was the one being punished, the one being threatened with jail. I panicked again at the thought of what I was going to do, all alone in a hostile country, with hardly any money and a phone that didn't work. I also worried about Ben and Vicky, continuing that horrible journey with just the two of them. I'd done all of the navigation so far. It'd mean either Vicky having to get up to speed really quickly or Ben having to take on another task.

The thoughts and worries swirled round my head and my bottom lip started to wobble. Tears pricked my eyes and I tried to sniff them away.

'Why are you crying?' Vicky hissed at me.

'Because I'm stressed,' I said, trying frantically to stem the flow, realising that if Finga saw me he'd think they were manipulative crocodile tears, instead of what they really were – my body's way of handling the pressure.

I've always been a stress crier. I remember in the run-up to my A-levels, even though I was desperate to get three As, I procrastinated beyond belief when it came to revising. Two of my subjects – English and Maths – didn't need much revision, but Geography did: there were four box files of notes to go through, reduce down and commit to memory. I spent ages avoiding the task at hand. At first, it was over-confidence – I'd got an A in my mock exam six months earlier, so I took that as a sign I'd do well in this one. Then over-confidence turned to procrastination, which changed into anxious avoidance, which grew by the day, as the exam loomed ever nearer. Eventually, two days before the exam, as I sat staring at the four box files and the seemingly impossible task in front of me, it morphed into full-blown panic. My mother found me wailing loudly on my bed. She had no idea that I'd been digging this hole for myself.

'Right,' she said, ever practical. 'The rest of us are going out. You get on with it.' Once I'd finished snivelling, and got over that exhausted feeling that comes after a big bout of tears, I did knuckle down. Somehow I managed to cram through 8 inches of papers in two days, and I aced the exam.

Later, in my working life, I faced deadlines every day. In a way, this made them easier to deal with than one circled date on the calendar growing closer. In the same way that that impossible amount of revision somehow still got magically done in two days in 1996, in the newspaper offices, we always seemed to get the paper off within our given 12-hour timeframe. Sometimes it was by the skin of our teeth, re-writing reporters' copy at 8.50pm, while an anxious member of the production team kept calling every thirty seconds over the empty banks of desks, telling us things we were already well aware of: 'Are you done with it yet?' 'We're off stone in ten minutes.' 'We can't be late – we'll be fined.'

It wasn't just about being fined. There was no way a newspaper can be published with large blank spaces in it because a reporter hasn't managed to file on time or an editor hasn't managed to get legal clearance for an exclusive. There's no option – it has to be done. 'Just do it' must be one of the most frequently used phrases in a newsroom.

Obviously, what we're not trying to do in a newsroom is get six months' worth of work done in one afternoon, as I was trying to do with that A-level revision. But the pressure is constant. Every day it's the same. You get used to it, but it means your adrenaline levels are running really high most of the time. The hours are long, too, especially for a news editor. And there's no way that the pressure can be dealt with by having a weep and your mum popping in and telling everyone in the office to nip out for a bit, so you can pull yourself together and knuckle down to it. You just have to crack on. So I learned to repress my crying instinct and was, for the most part, barring the odd 'moment' locked in the loo, successful.

The red-haired receptionist offered me a pile of scratchy green hand towels from the bathroom and I pulled myself together. After more waiting, Ben and Vicky were handed their passports with six-month tourist visas in them. I didn't look at Finga as he gave me mine, open to the page where the Ponce entry stamp read 'Admitted January 24, 2013. Class WT until January 29, 2013.'

January 29. I had four and a half days to get out of Dodge – and no idea how I was going to do it.

24

Finding Shangri-La

I finally knew what they mean by the phrase 'Champagne sailing'. *Papagayo* was in her element, swooping through the bay, slicing through the deep blue water, heeled over at a sharp angle, loving her reins being freed so she could really run. It was the first time since the storm in the Gulf of Mexico that I thought of her as a proper sailboat and now, in perfect conditions, she was finally able to show off. She transformed from a plodding, working donkey to a sleek racehorse, galloping across the water. She was joyful – and so, clinging on as the deck tipped away beneath their feet at an unaccustomed angle, were her crew.

We were in the British Virgin Islands, we were on holiday and we were sailing. Finally, I understood all the fuss about the Caribbean.

After our narrow escape with Finga, we'd trooped back to Ponce marina in glum mood. Over a cup of tea in the cockpit, Ben had made a suggestion.

'I know we're all tired,' he said. 'And we're all a bit fed up with this never-ending slog to windward, and all the waves, and the engine noise, and the bouncing, and the slamming and never finding the bloody night lees.'

Vicky and I nodded.

'So I've got a suggestion. It doesn't look like we're going to make it to St Lucia in time for you to get your flight. So let's call it quits.'

I lifted my head. 'What do you mean? You want to dump me here?'

'No. Of course we're not going to do that. What I was thinking of was something a bit different. I was going to suggest we had a little holiday.'

I hadn't seen that coming. I'd been single-mindedly focused on the task at hand, on how to get the boat to St Lucia by that fourth of February flight, with the distance we still had to cover and the visa restrictions. My calculations put me somewhere just south of Martinique at the moment my British Airways plane took off from St Lucia Hewanorra.

'A holiday?'

'Yeah. Why don't we spend a few days enjoying ourselves in the BVIs? Explore the islands, drink some cocktails, do a bit of actual sailing for once. That kind of thing. You can fly from there to St Lucia to meet your international flight and Vic and I will take *Papagayo* the rest of the way by ourselves.'

I felt the sparkle come back into my eyes and a wide smile break across my face.

He went on: 'Course, it means a final push to get out of Puerto Rico and through the US Virgin Islands before your ESTA runs out. When is that again?'

'The twenty-ninth.'

'But if you can get a flight to St Lucia on the fourth of Feb to meet your plane, that'll give us about four days to have some fun in the BVIs.'

I squealed with excitement. A *holiday*. Although I couldn't argue we'd been to some splendid places, this trip had felt like work for quite a long time, pretty much since the storm in the middle of the Gulf of Mexico, two months ago. The constantly difficult conditions had started to wear at me mentally, as well as physically, and I was losing some enthusiasm for sailing. Living with two other people in a very small space was draining, too. When we were all down below, we were no more than a couple of metres away from each other. To dress, I'd either go to the front of the boat and drop the curtain or, if I was too tired, just turn my back. Sometimes it felt like the only time I was alone was when I closed my eyes at night, and then Ben would get up to make a midnight sandwich or Vicky would call out in her sleep and even that fragile sense of privacy would be broken.

'A holiday,' I said now, reaching across to slap Ben on the shoulder, 'sounds perfect.'

We'd rushed through Puerto Rico, taking just long enough in Ponce to buy some food and for me to drop into the near-empty bar at the marina to use the wifi to book a LIAT island-hopping plane trip from Tortola in the BVIs on the fourth of February that would get me to St Lucia a few hours before my transatlantic flight home. By the twenty-seventh of January we were out of Puerto Rico and anchoring in Escenada Harbour at Isla de Culebra, the most westerly of the US Virgin Islands. We didn't even bother to get the dinghy out and go ashore. On the twenty-eighth we paid a quick trip to the capital, Charlotte Amalie, to check out.

Charlotte Amalie, on the main US Virgin Island of St Thomas, is another cruise-ship town, like Nassau, but even more American, stuffed with surf shops and Rolex-toting jewellers along identically laid-out grids of neat, clean streets. Three ships sat, like floating blocks of flats, just outside the town, tenders ferrying the shopping-bag-laden passengers back for their evening meal on board.

We tied the dinghy to a low stone wall, using the lock and chain, and put our flip-flops back on. First stop was the immigration desk at the cruise port, where the guy didn't seem to care about the date in my passport.

Freed from bureaucracy, we now had an afternoon to kill before we'd be able to leave for the BVIs in the morning. Time had seemed to slow down, teasing us because we were impatient to start our holiday.

'How about a margarita?' Vicky asked, an impish grin on her face. I didn't need much persuading.

Ten minutes later we were sitting on a shady, cobbled terrace with wide-mouthed glasses of frozen margaritas in front of us, condensation pooling on the outside of the bowls and running down the stems on to the hardwood table. A waitress brought over a plate of nachos and we dug in greedily. The tomatoes, sour cream and guacamole tasted even more wonderful than usual; the margarita was extra-refreshing and tart. I was, I realised, enjoying myself, just sitting down, relaxing, chatting with my friends and watching the world go by. I was already on holiday.

Despite the past few days, which had involved more difficult motoring into head winds and choppy waves and, one morning, a 4am start, I felt the pressure was off. A tiny part of me was disappointed that we hadn't managed to make it to St Lucia in time but I knew that that was due to circumstances beyond my control – storms, broken engines, time-wasting officials – and wasn't anything to do with my navigational skills. I was immensely proud of the fact that I'd managed to get all three of us, and *Papagayo*, the 2,500 miles from Houston to here. Yes, there were a few bruises and injuries – Ben was desperate to get to the BVIs so he could have a rotten tooth pulled – but for the main part we were all fine. It was one of the biggest challenges I'd ever faced and, somehow, I'd managed to pull it off.

I wasn't, uncharacteristically, even that worried about money any longer, which was ironic, as I only had about £200 to my name. Knowing I had to earn some cash very quickly, after I'd booked my LIAT flight I'd immediately emailed the *Independent* and asked Chloe the assistant for reporting shifts the following week. I'd land back in the UK on a Monday. By Wednesday I'd be at work – she'd given me a night shift and put me down for three a week for the foreseeable future. So the pressure was off there, too. Part-time work would suffice while I settled back into London life. Until Monday, though, I wasn't going to give the world of work and the cold London winter another thought.

***

Boom! Like the gun fired to start a running race, the Norman Island cannon signalled the beginning of afternoon happy hour. Vicky was one of the first off the starting block to get to the bar. I found a spare table with a view of the bay and lowered myself into a rattan chair to wait.

If a travel agent had been able to look straight into my brain and see what my idea of the perfect holiday location was, Norman Island wouldn't have been far from what I was imagining. The British Virgin Islands as a whole had a glamour that I'd not come across anywhere before and Norman was a small island with a natural cove on its western side. Inland there was nothing but a hill and shrubs so the bay, called Pirate's Bight (a bight is a loop in sailing terminology), was the main attraction. Mooring buoys had been laid on the seabed to make it easier for yachts to stay over, and we'd picked one up and tied *Papagayo* to it earlier in the afternoon, Ben immensely relieved that he didn't have to manually lower and haul the anchor for a few days. The water beneath me was a lovely clear blue as I climbed down into the dinghy, and we made a gentle beeline for the white beach dead ahead, just diverting a little here and there to pass other moored yachts.

On the beach was a handsome and subtle bar-restaurant, with open sides and plenty of tables for enjoying the view out over the water. Everything was blond wood, clean and modern, and the sand brought in on people's feet made it look even prettier. It was the kind of place where everyone has a good tan and wears tasteful neutral-hued linen. No loud music, no screaming babies, no cars. Just the beach, the yachts nodding gently at their moorings, cushioned on either side of the bay by scrub-topped hills, and the first ice-cold drink of the day. Beach-chic bliss.

'Here,' Vicky said, putting two plastic cups on the table. She came back a second later with two more. 'I wasn't sure what to get and it was two-for-one so I got two piña coladas and two painkillers.'

'What's a painkiller?' I asked. 'Surely that's something you want in the morning? Or is it a hangover-free drink?'

'Not sure what's in it. But definitely lots of rum.'

I picked up the cup in my hand and my fingertips burned with cold. I took a sip through a thick black straw and an icy sweetness hit the back of my throat – rum, yes, but also pineapple, coconut, orange and nutmeg. The cold and the sweetness made my teeth ache. It was divine. I shuffled down a bit lower into my chair and put the straw to my lips again.

After a second drink, I was through tipsy and into mellowness. The light yellowed as the afternoon moved towards early evening and every now and then the tranquillity was broken by a dinghy buzzing slowly back to a yacht. A few people remained in the bar, chatting and laughing, but it was a large-enough space that it never got raucous or annoying. Island life here was slow, and so was the rate of drinking – this was not the kind of place where people sank pitcher after pitcher of beer.

The next morning, after a blissful full night's sleep, I went forward to the bow and untied one end of the line that held us to the mooring buoy. I watched as the end of the rope slid across the deck like a snake's tail and dropped into the water with a soft plop. Just like that, we were untethered and off for another sail: no shouted instructions back from the bow to the helm, no hauling of heavy anchor and chain. Because *Papagayo* didn't have the easiest-to-handle equipment for frequent anchoring, the chain, being dragged up hand over hand every day, had cut a wide scar into her side at the top. Ben wasn't the only one who was getting a respite by our using mooring buoys.

We headed off for another perfect day's sailing in the bay between the islands. The main island in the BVIs is Tortola, to the north-west, but we were playing in the smaller, unpopulated islands to the south-east, across a bay only 3 miles wide. We could see American territory, the US Virgin Islands, from where we were, just a couple of miles east of St John in the US Virgin Islands. The southern part of the BVIs consists of five small islands, all shaped like jagged bits of antler coral, in a line. Norman Island, with its peak, was the furthest to the south-west, followed by Peter, Salt, Cooper and Ginger. Their names spoke of their history – the spice trade, the East India Company, clipper ships, crewmen, pirates. In the same way that various places in the Bahamas claimed links with Ernest Hemingway, so some of the smaller islands here said they were the inspiration for Robert Louis Stevenson's *Treasure Island*. It was easy to imagine that little had changed here since the eighteenth century.

Our stop that afternoon was an island a little further east, Cooper, which was no more than a mile long from tip to tip. Here we found another well-planned bay with mooring buoys, a chic beach-side bar, soft white sand and clear waters. I hired a stand-up paddle board – before I'd had a drink – and paddled my way among the anchored yachts, gazing down at the corals and anemones beneath me. After a while, the act of using my core muscles and thighs to balance became automatic and I became so absorbed that I paddled out quite a way. Suddenly the seabed shelved steeply away and the water became a dark blue and I knew I was in deep water – and I wobbled, panicking slightly when I could no longer see the bottom. I turned around and headed straight in to shore after that.

In the beach bar's bathroom, I stared at myself in the mirror as I washed my hands. The face I was looking at looked both like me and not like me at all. This woman was tanned and the tan gave hollows to her cheeks, sculpted them. I'd never had cheekbones; I'd always had quite a round face with full cheeks. I peered more closely. The tan gave the woman's face a rosy glow, so she looked healthy; the sun had not only lightened her hair but also gave it a rougher texture, so it stood away from her face, instead of hanging down like a protective curtain.

I looked different from how I thought of myself. The face in the mirror was more assured, more grown up, more womanly. And yet at the same time I recognised myself in this face. I looked like the person I was always meant to be. I'd finally grown into her.

'Is that a BT phone box?' I said to Vicky, as we motored slowly through shallow turquoise water to our next stop.

'What? Where?'

'There.' I pointed, my arm outstretched. 'At the end of the fuel pontoon.'

The third day had been yet another perfect holiday day: a late start, a great, bracing sail, the salty wind blasting away any remaining hangover, lunch on the go and now, in the early afternoon, we were approaching Marina Cay, our home for the night.

Ahead of us was a fuel dock. I knew it was a fuel dock because the word *fuel* was writ large on a painted sign on the salmony roof of a pale-blue hut. To the left of the hut was some kind of bright-red rectangle. As we drew closer, I was able to make out glass panels in its side.

'It is!' I told Vicky now. 'It's a BT phone box. How did that get there?'

Later, after we'd hopped in the dinghy and pootled lazily over to the low wooden dock, I took a photo of the box, *Papagayo* the British yacht in the background.

Although called Marina Cay, there was no marina here at all. The island was tiny, barely 200 metres across, but despite its small size it had more facilities than Norman or Cooper. There was a small hotel complex, with a bar and restaurant that were open to the public, and a shop selling olde-sailing-worlde souvenirs – pre-faded caps and T-shirts and bottles of Pusser's rum. We went to the bar to ask whether visitors could book a table for dinner (thankfully we could) and a series of framed black-and-white photos on the wall caught my eye. I wandered over to take a closer look, idly following the series from left to right.

At first I thought it was the kind of paraphernalia interior designers seem to buy to decorate pubs and restaurants with – corn dolls, old lacrosse sticks, iron cart wheels, that kind of thing. But when I got to the far right I found some text, titled 'A Note on Marina Cay'. The text said that the island had been uninhabited until 1937, when Robb White and Rodie Mason, 'only four months married … decided to make it their own private Shangri-La'. They built a house of concrete, the note said, in the centre of the island. Literally built it themselves, Rodie included. Photos showed her labouring in the hot sun in trousers – surely not a very ladylike thing to be doing in the late 1930s. 'Their solidly built house gave them good shelter', I read. 'The sea gave them food. And a 13-foot sailboat was transportation.'

They lived there until the mid-1940s, I read, when Robb was called to war, but the island was then taken off them by the British government and they were forced to leave.

Later, on the beach, sitting on a sun lounger under the shade of a coconut tree, idly following my own thoughts while Ben and Vicky Skyped their families, I wondered about that couple. What an extraordinary woman Rodie must have been to have agreed, eighty years ago, to turn her back on civilisation and move with her husband to a barren rock, to spend arduous months transporting building materials to and from the rock on their sail boat, to have roughened her hands and probably jarred her back lifting sacks of sand and heavy tools, planks of wood and tiles and carried them from the beach up the small hill to the top of the island and to have helped her husband build their home, a home that stood there still – the hotel had turned it into a reading room and book-swap area, and I'd gone in search of it earlier, finding a cool, shady house with high ceilings, like a chapel, at the end of a climbing path.

The Whites' history chimed with me and I thought that, had I been around in the 1930s, Rodie and I could very well have been friends. I like the fact that she was brave enough to go against convention, that she was up for a challenge, that she was prepared to get her hands dirty, not just drift from tea party to tea party and only ever think about what outfit to wear.

Their story, I thought now, was not that different from Ben and Vicky's with their African dive centre and now their St Lucian sailing business, or even from mine with Guy – two people embarking on a project, them against the world. I'd put my faith in an adventure and a relationship and had stepped away from conventional life to do that. In the end, my spirit had proved weaker than Rodie's and I'd given up, but not until after I had had, in 1930s parlance, a jolly good go at it.

The difference between the Whites' story and mine and Guy's had boiled down to one simple thing – love. Rodie had done those things, followed those dreams, because she loved her husband. Although I'd thought, to begin with, that I was in love with Guy, what I felt for him, in the end, was not strong enough to see me through the physical hardship of our life on *Incognito*.

The last paragraph of the text on the wall of the Marina Cay restaurant had said this: 'Unlike stories of people desperately trying to escape from desert islands, Robb White and his wife Rodie very much wanted to remain on their island in the sun.' Ultimately, I hadn't been Robb and Rodie, wanting to remain; I'd been the other people, trying to escape from their desert islands – or, in my case, a boat.

And yet.

As my small propeller plane took off from Beef Island early the next morning and doubled back over the bay, I looked down out of the window at *Papagayo*. The dinghy was tied to her stern – Ben must have already gone back to bed after dropping me off in the pre-dawn hours near the airport. The three of us had said bleary-eyed goodbyes at 4am, our farewells far too short in comparison to what we'd been through together and how close we'd grown.

I felt a sharp pang as the plane moved higher, until I could no longer tell that the dark dot on the water was *Papagayo*, my home for all that time.

I'm not ready to leave, I realised. *I'm not ready to leave my island in the sun, either.* I didn't mean that Marina Cay, strangely magical though it had been, was *my* island in the sun. Mine was not a specific island but more a daydream that I didn't want to leave behind. I suddenly knew that my adventures weren't over. All I needed to do was find my Robb, the person who inspired me, supported me, who was my team mate, my partner, and work out where *my island* was, and then I would no longer be trying to escape. I would be, finally, just like Rodie.

25

Balancing act

London, March 2013

I eased my car into the country lane and had only gone a few metres when I was forced to come to a stop. Ahead, a herd of sheep, their fleeces finger-deep in the early spring, were skitting anxiously about, trying to avoid being forced into the back of a lorry. The writhing mass of animal bodies jerked first one way and then the other as a farmhand tried to coax them into the truck bed. Outliers sprang off and leapt over everything they could in their desperate attempts to get away: a rock, a farmer's boot, a fellow sheep's face. One managed to make a break for it and thought she was free and away, but then another farmhand cut her off a little further up the lane and soon she was swallowed up by the group as it clattered, reluctantly, up the ramp.

I sat behind the wheel of my car, the engine off, waiting patiently for the herd to be shepherded into the lorry. I was in no hurry.

My initial trip here, a few weeks earlier, had been the first time I'd been on a real working farm for years. I'd been to a children's petting farm in recent years with friends' kids – places with ticket offices and a million health-and-safety anti-bacterial hand-washing stations – but not somewhere like this since I was small, if ever. As a city-raised girl, farms were not in my blood, but as the farmhands jumped into the cab of the lorry and waved me a thanks for waiting, I felt a curious sense of homecoming as I continued up the stony track.

Spring had arrived early that year, and, despite all my travels to exotic and beautiful places, I still thought there could be few sights so lovely as the English countryside in the spring, particularly a Sussex farm in the spring, with tree blossom umbrella-ing out over hedgerows and garden birds darting about, busily collecting materials for their nests. In the few weeks since I'd returned to the UK, then in the middle of winter, everything in the countryside had turned light-green, bursting with fresh colour and life. It felt like a new start.

I pulled into a courtyard of tumbledown red-brick barns, their roofs crooked and mossy, and stopped. In the boot of the car were bags of supermarket shopping and I slid the handles of as many as I could manage into the crook of my left elbow, grabbed the rest with my hands, and staggered with the weight across the courtyard, boots sliding in the mud, jacket hood bouncing against the back of my neck, and into the sailing-school office.

About a fortnight after I'd landed back in the UK, into a dark February in which my suntan looked wrong, I'd had a call from Nigel, a friend who ran a sailing school on the south coast.

'I'm a bit swamped here,' he'd said. 'Fancy a bit of work?'

'What kind of work?'

'I could do with someone taking over the bookings for me – answering the phones, selling courses, taking details, that sort of thing. Bit of marketing, maybe.'

That 'sort of thing' had turned, very quickly, into dealing with customers, designing and sending out newsletters, overhauling the website and, now, getting all the food ready for the week-long courses on the boats and being down at the marina to greet the students as they arrived.

I loved it. The work I was doing for the newspapers was in the evenings, so I was at home during the days and Nigel diverted the office phone to my mobile. A few times a day people rang up to ask about a particular sailing course and, as I'd done them all myself, I was able to talk them through it. It was great speaking to like-minded people, and they were generally in a good mood because they were arranging to do something fun with their free time. It was a long drive for me from the flat in London to the marina on the south coast but it was only once a week and I was warm and cosy in my car with the heater turned up and the radio on.

I was having a great time. Three or four newspaper shifts a week, at only seven hours long, and in the evening, when the newsroom was run by a skeleton crew and it was quiet and peaceful and easy to concentrate; the sailing-school work, which kept me connected to the sea; and plenty of time in between to carry on writing my book. I got to be at home a lot, and the flat seemed enormous after three months living with two others on a yacht. Here, during the day, when my flatmate was at her office, I had five whole rooms to myself, a bed I could starfish in, a flushing toilet, a hot shower that never ran out of water. Sometimes I paced from room to room while I was on the phone, just because I could. What had previously seemed like a measly two-bed flat, when I had compared it to friends' whole houses, was now an acre of luxurious, stable space. The flat obviously hadn't grown – and in fact I was living in the smaller of the two bedrooms – it was just that my perspective had altered. Sometimes being forced to take a fresh look at things really can change how you feel about them.

The newspaper work and the rent from my flatmate were paying the bills, and the sailing-school job bought my food and petrol and took me into the countryside and to the seaside to put fresh air in my lungs a couple of times a week. Life was good. No – I'd go so far as to say life was great. I was in a happy place, still carrying a bit of sunshine with me from the Caribbean. I'd managed to find a balance in my life that let me do the things I loved. I was hopeful, for both the present and the future.

And then I fucked it all up.

The way to a girl's heart has always been through flattery. And Sean, the managing editor of the *Independent*, certainly knew how to stoke my ego.

'Hi, Emma, it's Sean,' a voice said when my mobile rang one morning in early April. 'Sean O'Grady. From the Indy.'

'Hello, Sean.' What was the managing editor ringing me for? Was he taking all my night shifts off me? Or had I got in legal trouble for a story I'd done the night before for the paper? Oh my god – was I being sued? Likely scenarios flashed through my brain. It had to be serious if he was ringing me, rather than waiting until I was next in the office or dropping me an email. *Shit.*

I kept my tone neutral. 'What can I do for you?'

He gave a nervous little laugh down the phone. 'It's nothing bad. Actually I was hoping you'd be able to help me out with something.'

'Oh?'

'You know Fran's obviously off on maternity leave soon?'

Fran was the news editor of the *i* paper. She hadn't worked there when I'd been at the *Independent* full-time, before I first went travelling, but had joined after I left. The company had launched the *i* paper, the cheaper little sister to the *Indy*, not long after my departure, and Fran was in charge of the news content. Now I was doing casual reporting shifts, she was kind of one of my bosses.

'Yes.'

'Well, do you fancy doing her maternity cover?'

This was a shock. I don't know why it hadn't occurred to me that the *Indy* might ask me to step up while she was away but it honestly hadn't. I thought I was just viewed as a casual reporter these days, not necessarily a candidate for an editor's role – even though I had more experience than a lot of the young news editors working on the paper now.

Before I'd left the *Independent* nearly three years earlier I'd been an assistant news editor. The three of us on the news desk at the time had rotated the role, so technically I had been in charge as news editor two out of the six days a week that we operated. But this would be a proper, five-days-a-week editor's role – technically a promotion. I'd have my own national newspaper news section to manage, with only a deputy editor and an editor above me. *I'm being offered the chance to be number three on a national paper,* I realised. I gulped, and felt my heart quicken.

'It'd be a full-time position, so no more night shifts,' Sean was saying.

I swallowed noisily, a little overwhelmed.

'So what do you think? I could really do with someone good.'

Good – he thought I was good at my job. Three years out of the game and I was still good. Coming from someone so senior, that was high praise indeed.

I was sold. I arranged with Sean a time to come into his office to sign the contract, and then hung up, smiling.

There's always a downside to most too-good-to-be-true offers — and the one that I was facing right now was that they wanted to pay me ten grand less to fulfil a role that was actually more senior.

'But that's loads less,' I said, frowning and pushing the contract away from me on Sean's desk.

'I know.' He sighed. 'But you've got to realise that it's a very different world now. That's really all I can do.'

'And it says five weeks' holiday. I used to get six.'

He spread his hands to signal it was beyond his control.

I was no good at negotiating – never have been, never will be. Put me in a room with someone I have to talk money with and I'd probably keep talking down my price, even if they didn't ask me to. My friend Aaron says I'm devaluing myself if I don't aim high – but aiming high seems like such an egotistical thing to do. It's an inherent female trait – we like to just be grateful that we've been asked to do something and so we go along with it, trying not to rock the boat or risk people thinking less of us for pushing for more. After a while, of course, after the happy feeling of being asked has worn off and reality has set in, we often end up kicking ourselves for not at least asking the question up front. But there we are – we've got ourselves into these situations so we only have ourselves to blame.

I sat back in my chair, chewed on the side of my thumbnail and stared at the carpet while I thought. Yes, it was effectively a pay cut, if I compared it to what I earned before. But I hadn't had a full-time salary for nearly three years, and it was a small fortune compared to what I'd been living off recently. In addition, the interest rate had gone down a lot and my mortgage payments were less than half what they had been last time I'd had a nine-to-five (or eight-to-eight). So if I looked at it that way, I was actually a lot better off.

Ever the optimist, I chose to look on the bright side. I picked up the pen and signed.

The *Independent*'s offices were in a glamorous building just behind an old art-deco department store where Kensington

High Street and Kensington Church Street meet, in rather a smart part of London.

The *Indy* rents space from Associated Newspapers, which owns the *Daily Mail,* so the *Mail, Mail on Sunday, Evening Standard* and *Metro* are all housed in the same building as the *Independent, Independent on Sunday* and *i* and all their associated magazines. That's a whole lot of Fleet Street hacks in one place.

On my first morning in my new role, I took the steps up the escalator two at a time, bouncing with energy, eager to start the job. The dress code at the *Indy* is relaxed, so I was wearing my standard work uniform of black skinny jeans and scruffy boots, the wooden soles of which made a loud noise as I strode across the marble floor to the glass entrance door. I buzzed myself in with my ID card, pulled open the door and marched through to my desk.

I didn't technically have a desk yet – it still belonged to Fran, who had a couple of days left before she started her maternity leave on May Day 2013. We were overlapping while she handed over to me. She was already there, dark circles under her eyes.

'You OK?' I asked her.

She pulled her eyes slowly away from the story she'd been reading on her screen.

'What? Yes, fine. Just tired.' She pulled off her glasses and rubbed her eyes. 'So tired.'

I logged on to the machine opposite her and started to open the various programmes: email, news websites, news wires. News editors are usually the first people into the office – apart, at the *Indy*, from the travel editor Simon Calder, who I swear either arrived at 6am every day or possibly even slept under his desk at night – and the quiet hours of 7.30–9am were when the real hard work of the day got done.

The *Indy* had its morning conference around 10am, when the editor Chris Blackhurst called all of the section heads into his office to present their stories and ideas. Our job as news editors was to put together a list of news stories to talk about and to present them in order of importance – what we thought was the most likely to develop into the biggest story was at the top of the list, for example, and would be the focus of our explanation. News conference was at 10am, but the paper wasn't printed until twelve hours later, so creating the list was often an informed guess at what would turn out to be important later in the day, using our news' judgement and years of experience to assign more or less value to the issues of the coming hours.

As well as a front-page story, or splash, we had to have a broad mix of articles – longer, in-depth reads as well as short news-in-briefs; light-hearted, human-interest pieces to counterbalance all the heavy politics; picture stories; concepts that could be explained graphically; pieces that lent themselves to outside expert commentary; and, most importantly, groundbreaking world exclusives that no other newspaper knew about, which would set the news agenda for the following day's TV, radio and newspapers.

To put together this list, we monitored all kinds of news sources. The reporters were tasked with ringing in or emailing over ideas of stories for the list each morning, with an explanation of what the piece was about. The most reliable ones for doing this were the specialist editors and correspondents, the ones who focused on Westminster, health, science, the environment, social affairs, defence and crime.

So the first job was to read through emails and ring reporters to get more of an explanation if there was something we weren't clear about. We were likely to face a barrage of questions from the editor and others in conference on any story, so we had to be prepared.

At the same time, we monitored rolling news. Not just the TVs bolted to the ceiling that ran BBC News 24 and Sky News constantly; we also trawled all the news websites and other online sources that we knew about – bloggers such as Guido Fawkes or the think tanks. Press releases came in constantly on email – I'd generally get at least a hundred external emails a day to my account, plus maybe twice as many internal ones, and more than a thousand would land in the generic inbox, which we used as a kind of filter to fob off time-wasters but that also needed checking in case any gems had been sent in. The phone rang constantly – often a chirpy PR calling to ask 'If you got the email I sent over?' You could tell from the sound of their voice that they were ringing from bed – something about the throatiness of a voice box not yet fully woken up.

They always got short shrift from us. Telephone the news desk of a national newspaper, and what you won't get is, 'Good morning, this is the *Independent* news desk. Emma speaking, how can I help you?'

If you're lucky enough to find the direct-dial number in the first place, what you'll get at most is a sharp bark of 'News', and the sound of furious typing going on, plus the distinct feeling that the person on the other end isn't really listening to a word you're saying.

And the reason for that is simple: they're not. They're too busy to give you their undivided attention. Even if you're a freelancer, and the news editor has emailed you, asking you to ring in, you still won't get all of their focus. There are too many things they are having to do at the same time.

Because while all this phone-answering, email-scanning, reporter-querying, TV-watching, radio-listening, Google-scouring, tab-opening, list-writing, reading, assessing, filleting and understanding is going on, they're also clicking through thousands of stories on the news wires – lists of stories filed by agencies such as Reuters, the Associated Press and PA – searching for gems, reading the words, understanding the basis of the article and making snap decisions after just a sentence or two about whether something makes it on to the list. A news editor is one of the fastest readers you will ever meet. These agencies pump out stories quick as you like. In the time that it has taken you to read the last page of this book, ten agency stories of twice that length will have appeared on the wire. There are thousands and thousands of stories a day – each of which probably took a reporter a whole day to file. And the news editor has to assess the validity of these at lighting speed, to read and judge and say yes, no, no, no, yes, no, yes at the same pace it takes to scroll down with the arrow key.

Oh, and they also have to have read all nine of that morning's other newspapers, have noticed what stories of theirs from yesterday have been copied, who had what different angles, which politician said what in response to this or that issue, which papers had exclusives that need to be followed up today.

They have to do all of this in the space of a couple of hours: speed-read through the equivalent of a couple of books, make a note of the pertinent points, understand complex issues that are probably beyond their field of knowledge, distil a lifetime's worth of information and then – ridiculously – crib it down into twelve to twenty bullet points in a Word document, making sure that the total explanation of each story is no longer than two lines.

And all by 10am, when most normal people have just finished flicking through their Facebook feed, have polished off their second cup of coffee and, round about now, are thinking about starting the day's work.

Today, as on many others, but it was particularly noticeable this day, the wires and news were full of child sex abuse.

The trial of Mark Bridger, the man accused of abducting and murdering 5-year-old April Jones in Wales, was about to begin. A report into abuse at children's homes in North Wales was also set to be published. Ed Miliband, not-long leader of the Labour party, was due to unveil his alternative Queen's speech. We'd already run a preview to what he was going to say in that morning's papers, but there'd be reaction and analysis to the live announcement to cover.

Steve Connor, the *Independent*'s science editor, had a story about gene therapy being used for the first time to treat heart failure. Three British men had been jailed in Dubai the day before for possession of a synthetic version of cannabis – and there was bound to be outrage and a campaign to get them freed. I fed Fran info on various other stories for the list.

At 10am on the dot, other section heads started to file into the editor Chris Blackhurst's office, a small glass box next to the newsroom. The *Indy*'s news desk was still frantically working away on their lists as the others wandered in and claimed a seat. I wasn't having to present in conference, so I grabbed my notebook and pen and dashed in to get a seat.

There were two black leather sofas in the office, pushed back against the glass wall, with a coffee table in between and a low filing cabinet to the side, the day's papers fanned out on top of it. In the left corner, under the window, was a round table, about the size of a dining table, with six chairs around it. To the right was Chris's desk. It being his office, he always got a seat. For the rest of us – and there could sometimes be more than twenty journalists crammed into this 4-metre by 4-metre room for an hour – it was first come, first served, then standing room only.

The two sofas were already full, and the round table was generally reserved for the deputy editors and section editors who were presenting their lists, so I perched on a sofa arm. One of the in-house lawyers, who was sitting on the sofa, smiled a morning greeting to me. A pile of stapled sheets was passed over and I took one, passing the stack on. As the room filled, so did my hands: I had printouts from the sports, website, arts, features, comment and foreign news desks. Last would come the *Independent*'s home news list.

'Right,' Chris said. 'Sport.'

The sports editor started to talk through his list of stories for the next edition, his words almost drowned out by the sound of twenty people shuffling through their piles of printouts to find the right one.

'Thanks. Web.'

More shuffling; more talking.

Chris Green, who had just started on the news desk when I first left to go travelling, was these days the *Indy*'s deputy news editor, and he came into the room with the home news list just as the sports editor was finishing. He plopped his lists on the round table. There was more disturbance as everyone pushed to grab a copy before they ran out. There was only one left by the time I made it across from the sofa arm and one of the arts staff was reaching out for it at the same time. I shot him a look that said 'I'm News. It's mine,' and whipped it out from under his nose.

'Foreign desk,' Chris Blackhurst said next. 'Comment.' 'Home news.' 'Features.'

On and on it went, each editor taking his or her turn to talk through their list of stories. Occasionally, Chris Blackhurst, or Dan Gledhill, his deputy, interrupted to ask for clarification.

On Bridger: 'When's the trial due to end?' On Miliband: 'What's Gricey's [Andrew Grice, the Political Editor] take on that?' On the gene therapy: 'How exactly does it work?'

Chris Green had to sum up complicated medical practices that had taken years to develop in a few words.

'Right. Get a comment piece on it.'

After the last list had been presented, the editors burst out of the office, scattering like schoolchildren released by their teacher from a classroom. They marched straight to their desks, to brief their writers on what exactly needed to be done before deadline, just a few hours away.

I sat back at my computer. A hundred more stories had happened in the hour I'd been in there and I needed to catch up before the backlog became too much to handle.

The *i* paper didn't have to present its list at the 10am conference; we were mainly there to listen to what the *Indy* had planned. *i* took most of its content from the *Independent* but ordered and presented it in a different way. What the *Indy* might run as a double-page spread, *i* might need to cut back to 300 words. Conversely, something the *Indy* considered only worthy of an 80-word nib, or news-in-brief, such as most crime stories, could need working up into a front-page story for *i*. We had one dedicated reporter for the paper but a lot of the job involved trying to persuade already overworked journalists to write a different version for us, and cutting back and rewriting material ourselves.

We had our own conference at lunchtime; consequently, we lost our lunch break. By the time we came out of our conference, which was much smaller, with just the editor Stefano Hatfield, deputy editor Rhodri Jones and Fran and I, we had just enough time to catch up on the news we'd missed again, draw up a plan of which stories were going on which page, give a harried briefing to our one reporter – Oscar, Liam or Oli, depending on who was on rota that day – and then we were straight into the *Independent*'s main afternoon conference, which was a repeat of the 10am meeting, but with lists updated to reflect what had developed or come in over the past five hours.

It was 5pm by the time we sat back down at our desks and started on the real work of filling the newspaper. Reporters had begun emailing their copy over to us and we had to read through it, making sure it fit any brief we'd been given from on-high and that we had pictures for case studies or words due in from appropriate talking heads when necessary. Read, cut, rewrite, check with reporter for clarification, read again, consult a lawyer if necessary, check the page plan and open the page where the story was due to go, paste it in, cut again to fit, rewrite after the cut, scan through, save and close for the sub-editor to take over, writing captions and headlines and doing a fine-tune. Cross it off the list and then on to the next.

When most people in office jobs are packing up their desks for the evening and heading off to the gym or the pub for a quick pint, we were gearing up for the second most frantic part of the day. From pretty much a standing start at 5pm, the sixty-four or so blank pages of the newspaper would have to be filled, fitted and checked by 8pm, headlines written, graphics and photos added in, puffs chosen and splashes designed for maximum impact. The only way to get through it was adrenaline – and a big dose of caffeine.

'Tea?' I asked Fran, Chris Green and Rob Hastings, one of the *Independent's* assistant home news editors, deciding I could afford to take three minutes to dash to the canteen and back. The newsroom was starting to empty out by now as writers and reporters filed their pieces and switched off their computers. One by one, the automatic ceiling lights flickered off as corners of the office emptied. In the hub, above the news and production desks, the fluorescent strips still burned brightly as the jigsaw moved on towards completion.

Seven o'clock and smells of food reached my nostrils as subs carted trays of chips, curry and pies back from the canteen to eat at their desks, simultaneously working a fork with one hand and a mouse with the other.

Seven-thirty and Fran said goodnight. 'You're only waiting for the splash and a couple of down-pagers and the news matrix, right?' she said. I looked up from my screen long enough to nod agreement, then got right back to it, frowning as I worked on cutting a complicated story to fit.

Eight o'clock and our production team was getting impatient.

'Any sign of the splash yet?'

'I'm working on it,' I promised. The reporter had filed only a couple of minutes earlier and I needed to get it past the lawyers, as well as getting it to fit the space on the page – and still make sense.

Eight fifteen and an email came through from the night lawyer. One word: 'Fine'. I pressed save and close and walked over to the production desk. Rhodri had already opened the page I'd just saved and was trying out headlines and sub-headings. I stood behind him and watched over his shoulder.

'What do you think about this?' he asked. I tilted my head to the side as I read the bullet points under the main photo on the front page. It was the care-home abuse story, and I knew the lawyers would be twitchy about hamming it up.

'Legal might be a bit concerned about that,' I said, pointing to the word *offences*. 'No one's been charged yet, so it's technically still an investigation and allegations.'

Rhodri clicked on to the word. 'OK, so how about we put inverted commas around it?' He added them in.

'Yes, could work. Maybe put them around "abusers" as well.'

He did it. We both re-read the front page again on his screen.

'Better,' I said. I pinched the bridge of my nose – now I knew my day was over, I suddenly felt exhausted. 'OK if I head off?'

He nodded. 'Have a good evening.'

It was coming up for half past eight when I pushed my way through the heavy glass door and started the walk down the escalator. If I hit the tube right at Kensington High Street I'd be home by 9.15pm. Just long enough to grab something quick to eat before logging on to the sailing-school's email and dealing with the booking enquiries that had come in during the day. I'd wanted to keep my hand in with the sailing school so I was still dealing with the admin and going to the coast one day a week, reducing my weekends to a single day.

As I stood on the tube platform, waiting for the Circle line train to arrive, my head was still buzzing with words and information and my body was fizzing with adrenaline. *It was a good day*, I thought. *A long one, at over twelve hours, but a standard day, nothing special. That's Monday done. More of the same tomorrow.*

26

Feint of heart

The pop of a champagne cork reverberated off the high, arched ceilings of the bar, the noise dimmed only slightly by the plush carpet and velvet upholstery. A minute later, a waiter, smart in black and white, brought a silver bucket over and lifted a linen cloth to show the bottle in it to me.

'This one, madame?'

I smiled and nodded. 'Six glasses, please.'

He went off to get the flutes and as I turned back to Sally, Dom and the girls I wobbled slightly on the low velvet pouffe I was sitting on.

We'd been drinking since seven – me since half eight, when I'd rushed into the restaurant that I'd booked, late after being held up at work. They'd seated us at a large round table with a lazy Susan in the middle, and the prosecco was in full flow as I took off my jacket and hung it round the back of my golden chair. I took a second to look around me as I sat to appraise the place, and tried to calm myself down after the working day and the quick dash from Kensington to Victoria to meet the others for our monthly girls' night out. I had been part of this ritual before I'd first gone travelling and during my post-Olympics stint in the capital, and I quickly slotted back in on my return from the Caribbean – it had even been my job to book a venue this time. Having been out of London for a more than two years, I didn't really know where was good to go these days, but had stumbled across a three-course online offer for this place, a Chinese restaurant within a hotel next to Victoria station. I'd done good – it was elegant, with vaulted ceilings and padded chairs, textured wallpaper and thick carpets that hushed the sound of your feet when you went to look for the ladies.

The food wasn't that great but it didn't matter. Everyone was giddy and in a happy mood and we moved upstairs to the bar afterwards by consensus, no one protesting that no, they really couldn't, they had to rush off to get a train.

More wine came, then cocktails. We talked about the kinds of things that women talk about when they get together, the kinds of things that result in loud cackling laughter frightening off everyone else within a 10-metre radius.

Drink after drink had been placed under my nose and drink after drink I had tipped down my throat. At what should have been my bedtime, inebriated into generosity, and feeling bloody well on top of the world, glad to be back in London, with friends who loved me, with a good job, in my own place, I slipped to the bar to quietly order champagne as a surprise.

'What's this in aid of?' Sally asked, as the waiter placed a flute on the low glass table in front of her. Five pairs of eyes turned to me.

'Ladies,' I said, slurring the s into three zzzs, 'today I got my first proper pay cheque in –' I broke off to count, frowning, on my fingers '– nearly three years. And so I feel like celebrating.'

They cheered.

'And also, I just wanted to say' – my eyeballs were hot – 'that I bloody love the lot of you.' A little bit of wine sloshed out as I gesticulated with my glass.

'Let's all make a toast,' Helen declared, her Leeds accent stronger after many drinks. 'I'd just like to say, ladies, that I think you're all effing amazing, and I think it's just great how everyone is so supportive and nice and, well, effing amazing!'

'Hear, hear!' someone shouted.

'To us!'

'To us!'

Six champagne glasses clanked noisily against each other – and the other hotel guests laughed quietly behind their hands.

Three hours later, we were still at it. Helen had shooed us into a taxi with a 'Come on, girls!' and we'd tumbled out in Mayfair and weaved our way through the reception area of Home House. Within minutes, Dom was ordering at a dark bar. The place was massive – a Georgian town house converted into a private members' club with gym, restaurant, multiple bars, meeting rooms – but we seemed to have it to ourselves. The lights were low, making everything an inky blue, as if we were in a nightclub. An empty nightclub.

'Dude,' I said to Dom, who was negotiating with a barman, 'I'll go and look for the others.'

After a couple of wrong turns in the hallway, I found them in an old-fashioned drawing room, which was also dimmed to navy, with Chesterfield sofas pushed back to clear the floor for dancing. In one corner a DJ stood at his decks – the only clue that we were in 2013. Otherwise we could quite easily have been excitedly milling about in an 1800s novel.

The dance music was loud and I could barely hear what anyone was saying. My vision was coming in static scenes, as if the room was being lit by slow-motion strobe flashes. It felt like a movie, not real life. Helen and Nat were dancing in the centre of what looked like a Lord's parlour and someone's cool fingers were grabbing my hand and pulling me to my feet. I tried to move to the music but I felt like my body was stuck in treacle. I stumbled, and went to sit back down.

In the next flash of vision, I saw Dom put a tray of tall glasses down on the low table.

'What's that?' I shouted.

'Sambucas.'

'They're massive.'

She grinned and her face, eyebrows up, was caught like a photograph.

'Doubles.'

She handed them out and I knocked mine back. Nat shook her head, hair falling about her face, and put up both hands. No.

There were two left.

Dom looked at me. 'Come on, Bammers.'

'I can't, Dom. I should really be at home. I've got to be on the south coast in the morning.'

'So?'

'So – it's –' I fumbled for my watch, pulling it close to my face so I could see its hands in the dark room. I closed one eye to cure the double vision. 'It's two am. I've got to drive at six.'

She didn't say anything, just looked at me. I looked back, then at the glass.

So what? I've earned this. I've worked bloody hard this week. Done sixty hours already, with a day still to go. I've got to be allowed some fun. Got to be able to blow off some steam. It'll be fine. I can handle it. Actually – I deserve it.

I reached out, grabbed the glass and knocked it back.

The next day was, obviously, horrendous. I didn't drive at 6am; I put it off till 9am, telling Nigel I'd do the shopping for the boat customers in London and drive it straight down. I knew I must have been massively over the limit but I felt fine in the morning – full of energy.

See? You can *handle this*, I told myself.

By 1pm, I was feeling sick as a dog, saliva pooling in my mouth. I slumped in the passenger seat of Nigel's car as we ran an errand, battling not to vomit into the car-door pocket. Next came tremors that wouldn't stop, not matter how many sugary drinks I sipped.

I didn't get home till 11pm, when I dragged myself, broken, into bed. I'd negotiated with the *Indy* that I'd work Sundays through to Thursdays for them, so that I could work for the sailing school on Fridays – its busiest day, when it was getting ready to accept new students on to the boats. Both jobs were long hours *but a change is as good as a rest*, I had told myself, and I loved getting the boats ready and greeting the students and instructors, so it didn't usually feel like hard work. Although facing the long drive back to London on a Friday evening wasn't the ideal way to end a week – even when I wasn't hungover.

Saturdays I had off, and these were my days for doing my chores – cleaning the flat, going to the supermarket and catching up on sleep.

Even on my day off I had to dedicate a few hours to *i*, to make sure I was ready to put together Monday's paper on Sunday. I read through all the Saturday papers on a Saturday morning so that I knew what was in them, and seated myself at my laptop just before midnight on Saturday night, waiting for the clock to tick over to 00.01, when I could access pdfs of the Sunday newspapers on the Clipshare website. Sunday papers are often full of exclusives and I'd need to know what was going on in time for my news list on Sunday morning.

When I'd worked for the *Daily Express*, years earlier, a taxi driver used to deliver the Sunday papers to my door at about 11pm on a Saturday night. I'd strip all the supplements out and leave them in a pile on the living-room floor – my flatmate was ecstatic that she'd never have to pay for the sports sections again – then flick through the news sections, ripping out pages of interest and circling stories to follow up with a red pen.

Times had moved on – and budgets shrunk – so the 2013 version of riffling through a couple of kilos of newsprint was to click through pdfs on a computer and make notes in a pad of editions, pages and headlines of interest. Think how long it takes you to read a Sunday paper – sometimes all week, right? Well, I had filleting the *Observer* down to a fine art; also the *Sunday Telegraph, Mail on Sunday, Sunday Times*... I'd give myself from midnight until 2am to speed-read through all the news sections, then I'd set an alarm for 7am, to be in the office just after 8am on a Sunday to start a twelve- to thirteen-hour day.

Even though I'd been back in the UK for over three months, among all this work there was little time for play and definitely no time for dating. I've always had a rule that I'll never go out with a journalist (they like to talk about work and politics too much and also don't tend to be the handsomest bunch out there), so I'd not been on a date for months. It was over a year since I'd left Guy and he had already joined the realm of 'what did I ever see in him?' ex-boyfriends. Then, one day in the office a colleague, Carl, lightly patted my cheek to add emphasis to a joke he was making and my skin burned like I'd been branded.

I jumped back in my chair. *That's weird*, I thought. As he walked away, I put my hand to my face. I could still feel it. He'd chucked me on the cheek, the kind of thing you might do to a chubby toddler. Nothing sexual to it at all. And my physical reaction hadn't been sexual – it'd been more like suffering a shock.

I thought about it on my way home that night, trying to make sense of it. Hours later I could still feel a faint impression, almost as if I was smarting after being socked on the cheekbone. *I don't fancy Carl. He's just a mate. So why does my cheek still feel like it's red hot?* I thought about it as the trunked wires of the London Underground system whizzed past the carriage windows as the train moved from Gloucester Road to South Kensington. I thought about it as I rode the escalator down even deeper to the Victoria line to Brixton. I probed my cheek with my fingertips, looking for clues, as I walked from Clapham South tube station home in the dark, past a brazen urban fox standing firm in the road, its eyes as yellow as the streetlights.

It was still on my mind as I brushed my teeth.

Only as I closed my eyes and started to drift off to sleep did the reason come to me: I'd been touched. A simple thing, but I realised no one had touched a bare patch of skin on my body – barring the odd brief handshake – in months. I was so busy, and mainly living in my head, that I had fairly little social contact with anyone, excepting the odd blow-out with the girls – and next to no physical contact. The nerve endings in my skin had gone into overdrive at such an unfamiliar feeling. Just a split second of skin-to-skin contact had produced a physical reaction in my body that was powerful enough to still be felt hours later. It was weird. It had never happened to me before. Just from a split-second touch.

You're going mad, I muttered to myself, before turning over and going to sleep.

'Are you all right?' the chief reporter Cahal Milmo asked me, as I sat down on the office floor right in the middle of the briefing he was giving me on his exclusive story for tomorrow's paper.

The day had started like any other – up early, check Twitter for the newspaper headlines, put on the rolling news while I dressed, scroll through newspaper apps on the tube, get into the office for 8am and start the information onslaught ahead of conference. It was late-May, Fran had been gone for over three weeks and I was managing *i*'s news section on my own.

I'd come out of morning conference, caught up on the news that had happened while I'd been away from my computer and had started my round of the reporters.

My newspaper's lunchtime conference was in forty-five minutes, and before that I needed to get a deeper understanding of some of the stories I wanted to put on my list. I started with Charlie Cooper, the health reporter.

'I've already gone through all this with Rob,' he pointed out, disgruntled that I was stopping him from getting on with his five pieces for the day by asking him to repeat his briefing on his main story.

I stood firm, biro poised over notebook. 'I know, Charlie, and I'm sorry, but we might splash on it in *i* and I'll be asked for more detail in conference. Please can you just go through it again?'

He sighed, made fleeting eye contact, then indulged me and started to explain the story. I scribbled furiously in my pad, firing questions at him every time I wasn't clear on something.

I moved next to Steve Connor. Steve and I knew each other from my previous *Indy* days. His reaction was pretty similar to Charlie's. So was mine.

I cajoled some detail out of him, then it was over to Mike McCarthy, the environment editor. I needed a whole different story out of him.

'Hello, top babe.' His greeting was warm – until I added to his workload.

'I've got to write a spread for the *Indy*, plus my column, plus the website want a version early doors,' he said, putting his palm on a different pile of printed-out press releases and background documents as he listed his tasks. 'I won't have time to write another version for *i* as well.'

'Please, Mike.' I put on my best persuading voice. 'It's just a short story – only three hundred words.'

He didn't reply. I stood my ground, in silence, waiting. I could feel the pulse in my temple.

He puffed. 'Oh, all right. Three hundred. But you'll have to wait until I've done everything else first.'

'Thanks, Mike. You're a star.' He waved me away with the back of his hand, his eyes already on his overburdened inbox.

In the period between my resigning from the *Independent* three years earlier and agreeing to come back to this *i* job, the editorial staff of the newspaper had shrunk considerably. There had been a round of voluntary redundancies and many of the older, more established writers, with books on the shelves and reputations they could leverage, had upped sticks and moved on. The pool of writers had shrunk but the workload had risen, from one paper to two, plus a website. The foreign desk, which previously had four members of full-time staff on it, had contracted to two. The picture desk was the same. The home news desk had one more person – me – than it used to, but we were putting out two newspapers. The hours were longer than I remembered them being before; Oly Duff, the home news editor, was in the office by 7am and never left before 8pm.

Even though the workload was greater, and there were fewer people to do it, it still had to be done. It's not like there was a lot of flab before – the *Independent*'s news section had always been a very lean machine, run on a shoestring. But a few years previously the special correspondents might have only had to write one story a day, which gave them time to work their contacts and dig out the world exclusives that the paper was proud of, and that helped it to punch above its weight.

Now there was still the same pressure on them to deliver top-quality goods but they had less time to do it in, because they had eighteen other things to do as well.

It was a world away from when I started in journalism, at the tail end of the golden age, a time when 'file by three; home for tea' was the catchphrase and when a lot of business was done in pubs during the afternoon and restaurants and members' clubs in the long evenings, all paid for by hefty expense accounts.

In September 1997, when I was nineteen, I did a week's work experience at the Press Association news agency and as part of that I spent a day at the Royal Courts of Justice, a fine old stone building on The Strand, shadowing their courts reporter. His job was to slip quietly into and out of courtroom after courtroom through the day, checking on proceedings in boring, drawn-out fraud cases and complicated suits for defamation, nodding deferentially at each judge as he entered and exited. I acted as a runner, taking his typed-out copy and walking out of the front door, round the corner, down a side street and through the low-lintelled door of the seventeenth-century Seven Stars pub. Inside it was small and dark, heavily panelled, with a flagstone floor, and I found the court reporters from the *Daily Mirror* and the *Star* sitting on hard wooden chairs with their backs to the bare wall, chatting and chain-smoking. I handed over a printout to the *Mirror* man, who untucked a pen from behind his ear and went through the precise Press Association copy, striking out bland words and adding his own drama and vocabulary – 'caged', 'fraudster', 'blonde stunner' – to the piece, between mouthfuls of beer. He picked up his mobile phone, extended the aerial and rang his office to dictate his story to a copytaker, 'point, par, close quote, spelling correct', and after hanging up he bought another round – including a lager for me. As the afternoon drew on and the reporters regaled me with tales of covering the Yorkshire Ripper trial or door-stepping Jeffrey Archer, my walks to and from the High Court meandered more and my face flushed. Three stories down and I was climbing up the Seven Stars' stone steps into their low loft to crouch over the ladies' loo – an experience akin to squatting over a chamber pot in a servant's cramped bedroom. It was the best day of work experience anyone could ever have hoped for.

Those days, of contacts and buddying up, of ringing through exclusives from smoky bars and buying kayaks for African rivers on expenses, were long gone and now it was all about producing ream after ream of copy, fast and cheap. Not even 'copy' any more – even that traditional term was on the wane as the digital era ushered in a demand for 'content'. Lots and lots of content, very very quickly.

Back in the *Indy, i* and independent.co.uk newsroom of May 2013, I continued to make my round of the reporters, getting them to round out the details of their stories. Next on my hit list was Cahal Milmo, the chief reporter, a mild-mannered man in glasses and V-neck jumpers who was fond of using six-syllable words. I made just enough small talk to not seem too bossy before I went in with my questions.

I was looking at my pad and writing when the room started to heel over. My pen jerked off the end of the page and I staggered a bit where I stood. I had a bad habit of standing with one ankle tucked behind the other, so I separated my feet to try to make myself feel more stable. Cahal was still talking, so I shook my head to try to clear the spinning feeling and attempted to focus on what he was saying.

His words turned into noise and I shook my head again. It was almost as if I had ringing in my ears – without the ringing. Something was getting in the way of his words. The room tilted and span some more. The world came at me in a rush.

Shit, I'm going to faint, I realised. *Don't faint. Not here, in the newsroom.* I had a split-second vision of keeling over and hitting my head on Cahal's collarbone on the way down. There were lots of papers on his desk. *It'll make a real mess*, I thought, my mind wandering. I tried to focus but found I couldn't. The spinning was getting worse, like my brain was rotating inside my skull. The need to do something to save myself grew urgent – but I didn't know what.

Subdued sounds, like I had my head underwater in a swimming pool. I concentrated. '– you all right?' Cahal was asking me.

I put my hand out to the back of his office chair. 'Think so. Just feeling a bit dizzy. I'm going to sit down.'

So I did. On the floor, next to the chief reporter's desk in the middle of the *Independent*'s newsroom. I knelt, sitting my bum on to my heels. I could feel the hard leather of my boots dig in.

'You sure you're OK?'

I nodded again. 'Yes – probably just need to eat. It'll pass. Go on.'

He stared at me for a second, then picked up where he'd left off. I made a massive effort to focus and make notes and, although it was like thinking through a thick fog, I managed to understand enough, I thought, to get me through conference.

I rocked back on to my heels and pushed against a pillar with one hand to get back up to standing. The dizziness was going, and the fog seemed to be easing, too.

'Thanks, Cahal,' I said, and went back to my desk. Within ten minutes, I was so busy I'd forgotten all about it.

The next day, it happened again – and the day after that. The dizziness would come on in a rush, like entering a windy tunnel, and I learned to sit on the floor as soon as it happened. Whichever reporter I was talking to would break off, mid-sentence, but I'd wave them off with an explanation – 'Stood up from my chair too quickly', 'Low blood sugar', 'Bit hungover' – and ask them to continue. By ignoring what was happening in my body, and focusing all of my attention on my mind, I found I could carry on with my work and the act of concentration seemed to make the dizziness go away. It never lasted more than a few minutes so I didn't worry much about it, or take it as a sign of anything serious. Sometimes I joked with others – and myself – that I was 'falling apart'. If only I'd known how ironic that was.

27

Stop press

Sitting on the edge of the sofa, I curled myself into an even tighter ball as the room swirled around me. The floorboards moved like the ocean and my brain span around inside my skull, over and over again. I squeezed my eyes shut and formed fists of my hands, trying to get the feeling to go away. It didn't.

Pins and needles shot up the right side of my body from my calf to my scalp and my skin crawled while my limbs started to tremble uncontrollably. The whole world was tipping, slowly, on an axis, rising diagonally upwards in front of me, while still continuing an interminable spin.

My mouth was dry; my jaw ached from being clenched so tightly. Sobs broke out from right in the centre of me. I felt them rush forwards and outwards, like mini explosions, one after the other, forcing their way up from a point underneath my belly and into my shoulders then out of my mouth like belches of vomit. I clenched my jaw harder to try to stop them, screwed my eyes ever smaller, but my body was more powerful than my will and I couldn't stem the flow. My body sobbed and fought and gripped and shook and all my shocked mind could do was sit in silence and ask, *What is happening to me?*

My mind felt completely detached from my body and from what was going on. It searched desperately for a rational explanation. It's 7.15am on a Tuesday morning. I'm not drunk, I haven't taken any drugs and I haven't fallen ill. All I've done is get up, get dressed, check the news online and then sit on the sofa with a cup of tea and a bowl of muesli.

It made no sense. It was a normal morning. BBC Breakfast news was on the TV. The fan of my laptop was whirring quietly across the living room on the table. I had used the remote to switch off the TV, went to stand up to go to work and then, suddenly, strangely, inexplicably, the earth had shifted and taken me with it.

My logical mind decided I could probably snap myself out of it, whatever 'it' was. I waited, in that little ball, for the rhythm of the sobs to subside a little, and until I was able to unfurl my fingers to swipe the tears off my chin. Somewhere in the back of my head, a tiny version of me, who for some reason wasn't being affected by this unremittingly vertiginous new world, said crossly, *What are you doing, just sitting there?* She put her hands on her hips. *What's the matter with you?* She tutted. *Why can't you just pull yourself together?*

I am a rational person, usually, so I attempted to do what she said. I braced both palms on my thighs and pushed myself slowly up to as close to vertical as I could manage. Everything was still spinning and I found it easier to cope if I held my head on a slight diagonal, too, and I passed hand over hand along the furniture, from sofa arm to door jamb to corridor wall. I reached my bedroom and picked up my bag and my keys. I walked gingerly, like a hospital patient taking her first steps after an operation, even though I wasn't in physical pain.

Outside the flats, I kept my gaze fixed on the floor, my breath sucking in and pushing out past clenched teeth. Like a superstitious old aunt, I counted my way forward according to what lay on the pavement in front of me. Blob of old chewing gum … half a sycamore leaf. A foot or so further on: an empty crisp packet. Tiny milestones helped me get 10 metres along. A double-decker bus screamed past me, pushing a noisy cough of air into the fragile space between my left ear and the side of the road. I flinched and looked up for the first time since I'd left the sofa. The bus stop was another 10 metres ahead. I looked back down again, before the woman waiting there with her shopping bags could make eye contact with me. *Just get to the bus stop*, I repeated to myself, in time with my steps. These words became my mantra; the bus stop my talisman. It wasn't even my final destination – the tube station a quarter of a mile further on was what I was ultimately aiming for, but I didn't let myself think about that. I just kept forcing myself on, bit by bit, as the world whirled around me. It took an age.

At the far end of the bus shelter, beyond the woman with the Tesco bags, past the plastic lean-against red seats and just level with the poster advertising some local authority service or other, I hit a wall. An invisible wall. Unlike its magical counterparts, it had no shimmering edge or rippling surface to give any clue to its presence. My torso and toes bounced off it and I stopped dead in the street. I tried again to move forward. Blocked.

I've run two half-marathons but I've never experienced the runner's wall. I'd been in physical pain and exhausted, things that slowed my mind and my legs and made my lungs feel full up, yet I'd always been able to carry on, albeit at a limping pace. Standing as a spectator at the sidelines of the London Marathon, though, I'd seen competitors hit the wall and stop dead on their feet, their shoulders, heads and arms drooping. And that's what was happening to me – I literally couldn't go on. Waves of sadness and fear rose up from my toes and the Lambeth council poster on the side of the bus stop blurred. I turned back and walked slowly home.

Back on the sofa, I sat, still in my coat and shoes, with my phone in my hand. The rational part of my brain that was still functioning knew I had to do something, get help somehow. My thumb scrolled through my contacts. I knew I ought to ring someone, tell them what was happening, ask them for help. But something stopped me. I'm quite a proud person, very independent, used to taking care of myself. Since I left home at eighteen to go to university, I've always worked through everything by myself, strived for everything by myself, achieved everything on my own terms. I was proud of being able to stand on my own two feet. Now, the funny thing (although it really, truly, wasn't in any way funny at all) was that I was physically incapable of doing that. I knew I needed help, I needed to lean on someone. Yet even though that was clear to me, it was still a massive struggle to do it, to make the call. I stared at the phone screen. It was eight o'clock in the morning – an unusual time to ring anyone. They'd know as soon as the phone rang that something was wrong. Who to ring?

Two names sprang to mind and I alternated between them, pulling up first one phone number and then the other on my screen. *You're being ridiculous,* the bossy part of me said as I hesitated. *Just ring and talk to them.* I took a deep breath, then another, and hit call.

'Hello,' my friend Karen said, instantly on alert. 'What's wrong?'

I cried down the phone to her.

'Oh, Emma.' Worry was clear in her voice. 'What's happened? Are you OK?'

'I don't know,' I managed to get out in a flat voice, my words thick with mucus. 'I can't stop crying and shaking. I think I'm going mad.'

I tried to explain that nothing had happened at all, that I had just woken up and then found myself like this.

'Ring your mum and dad,' she said, and I was relieved that someone was telling me what to do. 'And try to feel better.' I said I'd try.

My poor dad, bless him, has taken three of these phone calls from me in my lifetime. The first, at uni, was the fallout from witnessing a violent crime and, after spending all night dealing with the police, I was so overwrought and frightened that I'd needed to run to my parents.

The second, a couple of years ago, was when I was scared out of my wits over Somali pirates, who'd just murdered four people in a boat not far from where I was, on my sailing yacht, in the Indian Ocean.

Both times, Dad's immediate response had been to come to me – driving through the night across the country; wanting to jump on a plane to Arabia. He's a man of action in a crisis. It was the same this time.

'Me and Mum'll come and get you and bring you back up here. Just sit tight. We'll be there in about four hours.' I was grateful he was so firm about it. He gave me no option of trying to pretend everything was OK, of saying I'd be fine on my own, of not wanting to put them out. My dad – my hero.

He took control of the situation – told me to ring work, then the doctor, tell them it was an emergency, get seen straight away.

'But I'm not ill,' I said.

'You are. If you'd broken your leg you'd not be going in to work. And you'd go to a doctor right away. How is this any different from that?'

He had a point. And he was careful not to give a name to what was happening to me. He realised, before I did, I think, how serious it might be.

'Gibbering wreck', 'cracking up', 'hysterical', 'nervous breakdown' – they are all common terms, frequently bandied about. My loose knowledge of a nervous breakdown was something Paul Robinson suffered in *Neighbours* when he got his company into too much financial debt and slumped, sobbing, into a crouched ball in the Lassiters' office. Celebrities suffered them. Gibbering wrecks belonged to asylums and Victorian times, and hysteria was a term coined from the ancient Greek to cover a wailing banshee-type of woman, as far as I was concerned.

Nervous breakdowns did not happen to a normal person at 7.15am on a Tuesday morning when they were just clearing up after breakfast.

Yet I knew that that was what it was. I couldn't think what else it could be. If it was an embarrassing thing to admit to myself, a shaming confession that made me feel so small, pathetic and useless, it was even worse to say it out loud to others.

'Can I make an emergency appointment?' I asked after someone answered the phone at the doctor's surgery, my voice sounding flat.

'Is it a genuine emergency?' the receptionist barked. I recognised her voice and pictured her imperial stare.

I paused, pinching my lips together, willing myself not to cry again.

'I'm not sure – I mean – I don't know. I— I—' I took a breath. 'I think I'm having a nervous breakdown.' My voice wobbled as I said it. It seemed so completely and utterly surreal, ringing up to report it to a GP's receptionist, as if I was telling her I had a sore throat or an ear infection. I worried I was wasting her time.

Her voice softened as she spoke again. 'OK, darling, I've got an appointment at 9am. Is that all right?' My hand shook as I ended the call. I slumped sideways on the sofa and closed my eyes.

The locum doctor, when I sat before him a short while later, my eyes puffy and glazed, shredding a tissue in my hands, didn't call it a nervous breakdown.

'It sounds like an anxiety attack,' he said, kindness in his voice. He wasn't a doctor I'd seen before – they never were – but I noticed that he seemed calmer than most other GPs. Instead of looking at his PC screen, scrolling through my past medical history, he sat with his hands in his lap and looked at me. I found it hard to meet his eyes. I was worried I'd break down again if I glanced up and saw sympathy there.

An anxiety attack? I thought. The diagnosis surprised me. It didn't seem to make any sense. I'm not an anxious person; I'm quite a confident one. I don't regard myself as weak. In fact, friends often remark on how strong I am. I didn't think I'd been anxious about anything in particular that morning. I didn't have a test or exam. It was supposed to be a standard working day. And yet here I was, in the doctor's office, being told I was suffering from an anxiety attack.

He asked me about my life and I told him about the past couple of years, the travels, the move back to London, the new job, the 80-hour weeks, the hard partying.

'That's a fairly normal reaction,' he said, when I admitted the heavy drinking. 'It's a natural coping mechanism. But it doesn't help matters, in the long run.' I nodded, looking at my lap. 'You need to have a serious look at things,' he went on. 'These eighty-hour weeks are not a good idea. I've got to warn you – if you carry on like this, you'll run the risk of it turning into full-blown depression.'

Shocked, I looked him in the eye for the first time. He held my gaze steadily. Then he did that little half-shrug thing that people do when they are about to tell you something obvious. The diagnosis he gave me was so simple and yet utterly truthful that I felt his words ripple through my heart as he spoke them.

'It seems simple enough to me. You've fallen out of love with journalism.'

28

Like a whirlpool

The car's gentle rocking motions as it drove up the M1 were soothing and lulled me into a half-unconscious state. I lay on my left side on the back seat of my parents' new hatchback, curled into a foetal position. The seatbelt bit into my right collarbone but I didn't mind. I kind of liked the pain. It made me feel more alive.

It seemed just a few minutes between getting back from the doctor and the door bell buzzing. I have no memory of what I did in those four hours. Perhaps I fell asleep, worn out from the crying and physical struggling, on the sofa. Maybe I just sat there, staring into space.

In the same way, the journey back up to Derbyshire took no time at all. Mum and Dad seemed to understand that I didn't want to make small talk or have deep discussions about my problems, and for that I was grateful. Instead, I squashed myself sideways on to the back seat of their car – something I hadn't done since I was a child – and lay, knees and ankles stacked neatly on top of each other, in a daze until we pulled into their driveway 200 miles later.

We're not big talkers in my family. Feelings are expressed in actions, not in words. They came, they collected me, they took me home, they fed me, let me zone out in front of the TV. They put cups of tea by my elbow and turned down the bed. It helped.

In the morning, I was capable of conscious thought again. I lay in the bed in the front bedroom. I hadn't grown up in that house and it seemed very much 'their' place. My mind was clear enough to allow me to think about what had happened to me and what I was going to do.

I knew that I didn't want to sign off work sick for an extended period of time. I didn't even want to formally acknowledge with HR what had happened. So far, only a couple of my closest colleagues knew that I wasn't in the office because I was unwell. I'd hinted at the reason in a text but hadn't confirmed anything to them. They said it was fine, that they would cover my shifts for the next three days (I was due to be going to Spain for a wedding over a long weekend anyway from Thursday to Monday), but I knew that it wasn't really 'fine' their end. I imagined Chris turning to Rob and Matt with a 'Shit!' as he realised he had to stretch his already massively diluted team even further during my absence. I never want to let other people down or cause extra work or hassle for them, and I think that guilt played a part in getting me into the position I was now in. I knew I had to learn to say no to things, but it went completely against my nature – I am a people pleaser (or 'sheep', as former *Indy* editor Simon Kelner once labelled me). I forced myself to remember my dad's comment about how if I'd broken my leg I'd at least take a few days off and focus on how much sense that made. I decided I wanted to see how I was feeling in a few days' time before speaking to work again.

I stretched, then turned on to my side, towards the window and the sunlight filtering through the light curtains. The doctor's advice, that the 80-hour weeks were too much, that I needed to sort things out, kept echoing through my mind. As soon as he'd said it, I'd known it was true. I'd only been doing the *i* role full-time for a few weeks but I had gone into it straight off the back of three months of often seven-day weeks doing newspaper shifts and work for the sailing school. As a freelance, I had constantly worried that the work would dry up, so I'd even sometimes agreed to work double shifts, writing during the day at the *Indy* while still answering the phone to sailing-school customers, then jumping on the Circle line across town to the old City to do the 8pm–2am night-reporter slot at the *Express,* then getting up in the morning to drive to the coast. No wonder I was exhausted.

The doctor had also diagnosed me as having 'fallen out of love with journalism'. I couldn't remember most of what he'd said verbatim, but every single word of that short sentence kept coming back to me now. *What an odd thing for a doctor to say*, I'd thought as soon as he'd finished speaking, while simultaneously thinking, *Of course! That's it! That's the truth!* It's surprising how sometimes a stranger can get to the heart of a problem without really knowing anything about you when you've been floundering around, confused, for months. Sometimes one simple statement can speak straight to your heart, bypassing the tricks and games your mind plays on itself. In one of my hippier moments, I'd say it was as if it was a message from the universe; the doctor just a useful conduit.

I knew that I never, ever wanted to lose control in that way again, to feel so helpless and frightened for myself. Some energy had returned, so I sat up, staring at my knees, and started to plan to protect myself.

I've always been a planner, writer-of-lists. When I went away travelling, I tried to get past that, to learn to go with the flow more, and I succeeded, in a fashion. But old habits die hard and I think that by the time you reach your thirties some of those old habits are so deeply ingrained in who you are that it's not possible to rub them out entirely. If you get rid of all those little things that make up who you are, how can there be any 'you' left? It's all part of growing up and by your thirties you start to accept who you are, all the little foibles that make you *you*. You have to be careful, of course, that you don't cling to them too tightly and become one of those people who are too set in their ways. But I think it is possible to accept that there are certain things about you that won't change but also to be able to keep an open mind to new opportunities and experiences. That's what separates someone who is stuck in their ways from someone who is comfortable in their own skin.

Now, in crisis mode, I reverted to 'planner'. Heading on the mental list: Reduce Stress. Action number 1: Cut working hours. So, much as I loved it, the sailing school went on the 'things to cut' list. Working hours were reduced by 20 per cent to sixty to sixty-five a week. Then I drew a blank.

Being a news editor in Fleet Street is a full-on job. I didn't know anyone in my position on a national newspaper who worked fewer than sixty hours a week. Maybe they'd manage fifty-five, if they were a bit less senior. But that was just the way it was. I'd like to say that for this dedication to the job we were well rewarded, but we weren't. At least, I wasn't. I'd effectively accepted a 25 per cent pay cut when I'd taken on the *i* job. Money didn't really come into it, though – it wasn't lack of money that was the problem. I had a lodger, so I had enough cash. The problem was the hours.

Now the doctor's other words came to me again: 'You've fallen out of love with journalism.' There was so much truth in them. But what to do about that? I couldn't quit the newspaper and just work for the sailing school one day a week, and live off a tiny bit of commission (at some level, money always does have to come into it). I'd tried changing career, and had re-trained and worked for six months in the superyacht industry, but I'd hated the lack of freedom and I didn't want to go back there. When I tried to think of another line of work, I couldn't come up with anything.

So the newspaper was my only option at the moment. *I've just got to work out a way of not letting it get to me*, I thought. *Maybe the doctor is wrong. Maybe I've not fallen 'out of love' with journalism. Maybe it's just that I'm so stressed and worn out.*

It felt so alien to admit to myself that I was 'stressed'. I had always worked in a fast-paced environment and when I was younger I was fiercely ambitious. I wanted to be on a national, I wanted to be good at my job. It wasn't that I put in overtime; 12-hour days were just the norm. I never felt 'stressed'. I thrived on the adrenaline. It was what made my job exciting. It was what made it so much better than other people's. If a problem came up at work, my brain went into lightning mode to solve it. There was no option – it couldn't be left 'to sort out tomorrow'. There was always a workaround. *Always*. 'Just do it' wasn't only the slogan of Nike; it was the catchphrase of my entire industry. We worked at a pace that would have been punishing to someone not used to it but it was the baseline for us. It was normal. And so I paid it no heed.

There was a rumour when I first started in Fleet Street that one of the red tops had an account with The Priory, where it would send burnt-out news executives to recover. I remember laughing derisively when I heard that story for the first time. The tabloids were a completely kettle of fish from the *Express* and the *Indy*, and I had no doubt that their news editors were under the cosh even more than we were, so I half believed it, but it also seemed contemptible, to think that people would end up in a private rehab facility because they couldn't cope with their jobs.

Oh, I was a harsh 27-year-old. Partly it was the industry that made me that way. It is, by necessity, a very cynical place to be and it's only a matter of time before that cynicism rubs off on those who work there. Now I blushed to remember that. I hoped my 27-year-old self would have been kinder on my 34-year-old self, if she'd known of my plight. Yet I doubted it.

It seemed obvious now that I had been functioning with high levels of stress. I'd just been in denial. I googled 'stress and anxiety attack' on my phone (ever the journalist). Only some of it seemed to relate to me. I had no chest pains, nor did I feel that I was dying. Ironically, I was reading one site when my stomach flipped in recognition. I was reading my own words. Not just something that gelled with me but my actual, published words. I'd written a feature about phobias and hypnotherapy for the *Express* years earlier and a website about anxiety had mined my copy and used it to illustrate what anxiety felt like.

That's not right, I thought. *I was describing a phobia then. A phobia is completely different – I know full well what that feels like. And it's a rational reaction (well, an irrational reaction when it's caused by a five-pound Chihuahua), but it's a reaction that has an obvious reason for it. It's a reaction that's designed to get me away from the cause, the perceived danger, and once I'm away from that danger, the reaction, the fear, goes away. The thing I experienced yesterday had no cause like that.*

Of course, there was a cause. The doctor knew it, and over time I came to know it, too. I had a strong mind, a forceful personality, and for a long time my mind had been in control. That rational just-do-it part of me had kept on doing it.

At some point, just at the edge of that bus shelter, my body had decided that enough was enough and had stepped in and overruled my mind. It was my body that threw up that wall across the pavement. It knew that my will was very strong – it had been ignoring for weeks all the signs my body was giving it that I had to stop and slow down, that I wasn't well. It had made me feel utterly exhausted in a bid to make me lie down and rest. When that didn't work, it made the world spin, so that I would be compelled to stand still. But when I pushed on past that sign, too, it pulled out its winning hand and produced a breakdown. It was like how you get a stinking cold just after you've finished sitting your exams, or on the first day of holiday, except a more extreme version.

'You look like yourself again,' my dad said when I went down to breakfast. 'Your eyes are back to normal. They're not so glassy.' There was relief in his voice.

In my earlier in-bed googling, I'd read that relaxing and exercising were good ways of tackling stress and helping to prevent anxiety attacks. The three of us went for a brisk walk across Amber Valley farms and down twitchells between old mill workers' cottages into Belper to have fish and chips for lunch. Everything in London had been scorched yellow by now but in Derbyshire the land was still a vibrant, healthy green, and I sucked up the views just as I inhaled deep breaths of fresh spring country air, my feet sinking into tractor tyre ruts in the earth. I had bread and butter with my fish and chips and tucked in ravenously, not worrying for once about the saturated fat content, or protein levels, or hitting my five-a-day target. We got the bus back to the house and I sat in the living room in the evening, watching the sun stretch the shadows across the valley much as I had a year earlier, when I'd been living here on my own, not working, and writing *Casting Off*. Then, I'd been gloriously happy. Now I felt washed out, but the light and the view across the fields went a little way to making things better.

'Are you sure you want to go to this wedding?' Dad asked me, as he drove me to the train station the next morning.

I reassured him that it'd be fine, that some fun time with my friends and a few days in Spain in the sun was just what I needed.

'I'm not due back in the office until Tuesday, anyway,' I said. 'So it'll be a long break from work. It'll do me good.'

It didn't do me good. My friends were all lovely and understanding when I told them what had happened and, after a spot of sympathy, we changed the subject and got down to some partying – the 'relaxing' part of my anti-anxiety strategy. I stayed up until the early hours of Saturday morning drinking white wine. The next day, the wedding itself, I carried on. After the dinner, there was a free bar set up on a trestle table staffed by two young local men in white shirts and black ties. When I ordered a vodka, they poured it freehand, Spanish-style. With a dash of Fanta Limon, it tasted of little more than pop. It barely touched the sides. I ordered another. Then another. When the Fanta Limon ran out, I switch to gin and tonic. My friends were dancing but I didn't like the music, so I drank another drink and then another, to 'get me in the party mood'. I'd already had cava and white wine and red, too. I don't know how many glasses of vodka and gin I had. I stopped counting at eight.

I've never drunk myself into oblivion before, never turned to alcohol to relieve any kind of pain. I'm a social drinker; I don't really keep any in the kitchen and it's very rare that I'd have a glass of wine on my own at home. I drink in the pub and at parties, and I drink for fun. If I get too pissed, it's by mistake. It's not because I am sitting in the dark corner of a hotel lounge bar by myself, knocking back vodka after vodka. *What's the problem?* I told myself now as I did sit in the dark corner of the hotel lounge bar, vodka in hand. *I'm just having fun. And the doctor said it was natural.*

Except it wasn't fun. Or natural. It was just numbing. And a bit boring. And the next day I felt shocking. I lay in the bed, shivering and shaking, until 2pm. I didn't have the strength to stand upright. To go to the loo I had to hobble. Luckily I was so dehydrated I only had to go once in twelve hours.

It was a wake-up call. I was usually the grounded one, the one who held it together. When I told my friends later that afternoon how awful I felt, they laughed. Hangovers were funny; they'd all been there. I doubted they had. It wasn't the hangover that worried me so much as the night before, the unexplainable drinking. With that and the anxiety attack, I felt like my life was spinning out of control.

In London, I talked to my line manager Chris Green about why I'd been off sick. He offered to cut back my hours.

'How about you come in at ten, for conference, and make sure you leave by seven?' he said. That made it a 45-hour week. Because of the way the day and conferences were structured, I'd still have barely more than ten minutes for a lunch break, but it sounded like it would be a vast improvement on sixty-plus hours a week.

It wasn't. Arriving just minutes before morning conference meant I was behind on what was happening in the news that morning and I had no chance to get up to speed. Leaving at 7pm usually meant walking out before seeing and working on the splash, the front-page story, which hadn't yet been filed by the reporter. Yes, there was a colleague on night shift who could take over from me but he'd not been in all the conferences or heard the discussions about how we were going to treat the most important story of the day. It felt like I was doing half a job and the guilt was eating me up. The shaking and dizziness, the inability to concentrate and the embarrassing, shameful, sudden onsets of tears continued.

A friend who suffered from social anxiety tried to help me understand a bit more about what was happening to my body.

'Because you're stressed, you breathe shallowly,' she said, 'even though you don't realise it. You don't get enough oxygen, so you start to feel dizzy and faint.'

What she said made rational sense to me. I did more internet research and read about the stress hormone cortisol, the effect it has on the body and how alcohol and caffeine can make it worse. I hadn't touched a drink since the wedding in Spain and I decided to carry on being teetotal. I looked into what else I could do to try to take control of the situation. I cut caffeinated tea from my diet and stuck to herbal. I made sure I did an exercise DVD a few times a week, and I spent a few minutes of the extra time in the morning generated by my 10am start dancing to a 'happy song' in my living room or reading a book, trying to relax and taking care of myself. I made sure I ate proper meals.

Yet it wasn't working. I didn't have another early-morning invisible-wall moment. Instead, attacks would come on at random times, and always when I was in the office. The first sign was that my brain would feel foggy and I'd stare at my computer, unable to think, or even remember what I was meant to be doing. Next, the screen would swim before my eyes and my lips would start to quiver. I'd break out into uncontrollable crying fits all the time. Whenever I felt a 'moment' coming on I'd dash to the women's toilet, which inconveniently was right on the other side of the office, so I'd have to walk past all 150 other people, head down so I didn't catch anyone's eye, then lock myself in a cubicle, sit on the toilet lid and wait while my body heaved silently. I took to carrying a vial of Bach's Rescue Remedy in the back pocket of my jeans and sometimes, if I caught it quick enough, the bitter sting of the dark drops under my tongue would be enough to stave off an attack.

As well as the Rescue Remedy, the abstinence and the camomile tea, I tried to self-medicate with fast walks round the block whenever I got five minutes. *Fresh air will do me good,* I reasoned. *I'll do some deep-breathing exercises as I go. Multi-tasking and all that.* I was desperate to understand this 'condition', to master it. It was terrifying to lose control not only of my body but also of my mind in these attacks. But I didn't go back to the GP. I didn't want to go on medication (in fact, that locum doctor had told me he wasn't going to prescribe me antidepressants. I knew what I had to do to fix the problem, he'd said). Taking antidepressants would make me look like a failure, I thought. I already felt like enough of one, anyway.

There is such a stigma attached to mental-health issues. Admitting to suffering from anxiety, to having a nervous breakdown or to not being able to cope made me feel ashamed. Only a couple of people in the office knew what I was going through and I was desperate for no one else to find out. I didn't want to be labelled. That was the main reason I didn't go back to the doctor or take extended sick leave and file my reasons with HR. Every time I made a dash for the loos in the office, or squeezed the pipette of that herbal-remedy bottle, I felt a deep sense of shame. Shame that I'd failed. Shame that I wasn't able to manage what my colleagues could, cheerfully even, every single day.

The worst part of it was I'd failed at something I used to be able to easily do. It's not like I'd recently launched myself into journalism and was realising I'd bitten off more than I could chew; this was what I'd done, on a daily basis, for years – and done well. In a way, I was failing at being me, and that was what made it all the more confusing.

How can you admit to people that you're not able to be yourself any more?

29

Change of life

London had changed while I was away sailing the seven seas.

New skyscrapers were popping up, sharp as needles, all over the place, it seemed. I'd lived in the city for nearly a decade with a fairly low-level skyline, apart from at Canary Wharf, and now all this alien architecture was sprouting around the old City, like little shoots of Hong Kong or New York shoehorned in between the historic terraces and grand old art deco structures. Driving down the A3 towards Kennington, my eyes registered with shock a building shaped like an apple corer, with three curved clocks near its peak. If I leaned to the left, like Billy Connolly doing a sketch about Toblerone bars and the Alps, the vast, glimmering Shard shimmered into view, like a piece of gunmetal Kryptonite fired into the South Bank. All the development was a good sign – London was regenerating, people were spending money here, investing in its future – but it had a strange effect on me, like the opposite of catching a whiff of a familiar scent. It was a bit unsettling.

As I struggled on through normal life, still trying to pretend I was dancing with joy around my living room in the morning, still swapping PG Tips for camomile, still dashing off to the loos to force Rescue Remedy under my tongue, I found myself thinking more and more about Derbyshire.

I grew up in Nottingham, in a suburb too new to be described as 'leafy', but with areas fairly open to the sky and housing nowhere near as tightly crammed in as it was in London. By the time my parents sold up and moved to Derbyshire, I had long since flown the nest and was desperate to make my way in the Big Smoke. My university friends had all moved there straight after graduation and my boyfriend at the time had gone, too, and I'd visit them all at weekends as often as I could.

They lived in crappy shared flats, and we went to cheap chain pubs and restaurants – the kind you find in any British city – but I found it all really glamorous anyway. I paid no attention to the crowds on the Underground, the black grime covering the buildings, the rubbish and the crowds and homeless people on the streets. I ripped open the wrapper of my *Vogue* magazine as soon as it landed on my small-town doormat each month, and I read of Nobu and Momo, of boutiques in South Molton Street, of shagreen-covered notebooks from Bond Street that cost more than I earned in a month. I dreamed of London, I ached for London, I thought it was the only place in the entire world that I wanted to be. I planned for London. I moved to London.

And when I was there, it was great. There was no Nobu or South Molton Street for me – although I did live in a flat in Notting Hill for a while (Manolo Blahnik had lived in the same terrace thirty years before, I read breathlessly in *Vogue*) – and I hated the tube journey, and emerged pouring with nervous sweat every morning, but on the whole I enjoyed the city and accepted it for what it was, drinking in its energy and opportunity and aliveness.

When I bought my flat, I chose to look for somewhere to live near my friends, in Clapham, and so, constrained by my budget, I opted for a two-bedroom ex-council flat on the first floor of a large block of flats. The flat was fine, once I'd ripped out the kitchen and bathroom and painted everything white to make the most of the afternoon light that poured in through the large box bay window in the living room. Sometimes, especially on a sunny Saturday afternoon, I really missed not having a garden, but I was a practical person and I knew, for financial reasons, that I just had to live with it.

When I decided to go away travelling, seeing the world by boat, it wasn't because I was tired of London. I was bored with me, rather than with my city, and I wanted to see what was out there. I waved goodbye to London, full of hopes and dreams about the adventures that were about to start, and every few months I flew back to the grand old city and she was grey and squat and a bit ugly and grubby in comparison to the wild expanses of ocean I'd become used to, or the wild and brightly coloured tropical gardens I walked past as I explored new islands. She greeted me like an ancient pet, uncurling herself from her resting place and hobbling over to me, and I still loved her, even though my affections now lay elsewhere.

Now, though, I was starting to hate her. Everywhere I looked I saw stress and pain and hassle; dirt and grime; grit and ugliness. The people, pushing past each other on the pavement, shouting and shoving, were selfish and mean. The streets, clogged with both pedestrians and traffic, were hostile. The restaurants and bars, not so appealing without the softening effect of a drink, were worn and chipped and overpriced. Work, obviously, was eating away at me. Everywhere I turned in London, I saw horridness. The old friend had revealed herself to be a monster clad in hard stone.

I felt as if the monster had sucked all of the joy out of my life. When I wasn't having an anxiety attack I walked around in a permanent state of zoned-out flatness and found it hard to feel truly happy or excited about anything. If I laughed at a joke or got angry at some injustice the newspaper was reporting on, I wasn't really engaging with those emotions; it was more like going through the motions because I knew some kind of reaction was expected of me. One of the worst examples of this was when, out of the blue at work one day, I received an email from Liz, the Bloomsbury editor, telling me that she'd loved the rewrite I'd done and that Bloomsbury wanted to publish *Casting Off* – and I felt just *flat*. Obviously I was pleased, but I wasn't excited, I wasn't thrilled that my dream was coming true, I wasn't dropping everything to ring round everyone I knew and tell them the great news. At any other time in my life I would have screamed, jumped up out of my chair and hopped around with glee, clapping my hands (I revert to my 4-year-old self when I'm overjoyed). Now, I just pushed back from my desk, announced to the news desk, 'Oh, it looks like my book is going to be published,' accepted all congratulations with a quick half-smile and got back to frowning at the newswires. I wanted to be excited and thrilled and to be walking round with a smug 'I did it!' grin on my face but I couldn't. It was one more thing to add to the list, something else to take up my time, attention and fast-dwindling mental energy. Even now I hate London and the life I was living for doing that to me, for taking away what should have been one of the happiest moments of my life.

As I sat up in bed one morning about a week after my book had been accepted, waiting for my flatmate to get out of the shower, I stared out of the window. At this angle, half lying down, all I could see were the leaves of the large London plane tree that loomed over the car park. The branches made a light rustling sound as a breeze swirled between the two blocks of flats. I could hear car doors slamming and the trundle of the wheels of children's scooters on the tarmac of the car park but I tuned them out and listened only to the leaves. A squirrel, camouflaged when remaining still against the grey-brown bark, scuttled upwards, moving diagonally across the trunk to the next branch up. It lifted my spirits.

The mornings, before I set off for work, were the time when my mind was calmest and clearest, so this was when I had the chance to think about what I was going to do.

My tactics for tackling my anxiety attacks weren't working and I realised I needed a new plan. Dropping to forty-five hours a week hadn't helped me feel any better and not drinking when I was out with my friends made me feel like I was punishing myself further for being unhappy. Also, I was sick to the back teeth of camomile tea.

That morning, as I lay in bed, looking at the tree, a tiny bit of inspiration struck. *When were you last the happiest you've ever been in your life?* I asked myself. *Perhaps if you can return to that, this horrible, choking sadness will just melt away.*

There were two answers: first, when I was living on *Gillaroo*, sailing around Asia, visiting a new place every other day and a new country every month. As a permanent lifestyle, though, that wasn't really an option. You have to have some kind of income to live on a boat and travel around, and I hadn't won the lottery any time recently (it's kind of hard to when you never buy a ticket), and I'd tried working on charter boats and found it to not really be my cup of tea.

The second time I'd been the happiest was when I first came back from Malaysia and I'd stayed at my parents' house alone for a couple of months. Being in Derbyshire, in a village surrounded by stunning countryside, had been good for my soul. After effectively living outdoors for a couple of years – which is pretty much what you're doing when your home is a boat – it had felt natural to be living village life. When I looked out of the window in Heage I saw mile after mile of fields, woodland and cliffs. I always knew which direction the wind was coming from because the top of Heage windmill would turn to face the sails into the wind. During daylight hours, birds passed through the garden like commuters: robins, crows, sparrows, wood pigeons. One day, a pheasant landed on the fence and rocked precariously for a moment before deciding that the flimsy wood wasn't a stable-enough base for him, stretching his copper wings and flapping away. Great black birds of prey swooped over the valley, looking for creatures to pick off, silhouettes against the ever-changing clouds. Sometimes the farmer put horses out to graze in the paddock at the bottom of the garden; a frog lived in the hole in the lawn where the washing-line pole went; once, thrillingly, a dunnock hopped right up to the window to eyeball me through the glass.

It wasn't just the animals that captivated me, it was the country itself, the rolling hills and dales of this part of the centre of the county, whose names described what they looked like: Amber Valley, Derbyshire Dales. Sometimes I'd take my car off the main streets – if they could be considered 'main' – down an unfamiliar road, just to see where it led me, and after a few bends I'd pop out on a ridge and the view of the valley below me would still my heart for a moment.

Just as on a boat, I was attuned to the times of sunset and sunrise, to the phases of the moon, to the direction of the wind and the speed and even to whether rain was coming, because I could see great motorways of cloud rolling across the vast valley sky from where I sat on the sofa.

Now, trapped in a hulking city that I had started to demonise, I missed Derbyshire with an aching. I'd been happy when I was there because who could be sad and introspective when they were constantly being reminded of nature and the turning of the world?

There was another element to it, too. I'd not had a job for those couple of months that I'd stayed at my parents' house but I hadn't felt bored or frustrated like I had been on Guy's boat in Malaysia. Then, too much idleness had driven me near-crazy, yet living on my own in Derbyshire I'd had plenty to do, even without a job. I'd had the time and freedom to write, working on my book, and I'd treated that like a day job, sitting down to my computer at roughly the same time each day, losing myself in the task of writing, letting chunks of time fly past as I concentrated. I'd cooked two meals from scratch each day and made a clear delineation between writing time and relaxation time by working out in front of the big glass window, gazing out on to the fields as I stretched and strengthened my muscles. I had balance.

When, broke, I'd had to return to London to look for paid work sooner than I'd hoped, everyone had remarked on how well I looked – how healthy, relaxed, happy. I was thinner from the healthy eating and the exercise and still had the remains of a tan that lent me a glow but I think they were noticing something else, too: that I was content. The world seemed a friendly place – even London appeared full of opportunity – and I was excited about the future, then, optimistic about my writing, and strange and happy coincidences seemed to happen to me all the time – bumping into an old colleague by the train station in the middle of the day as I sat on a wall eating an ice cream; being approached out of the blue by a mortgage advisor from a decade earlier with an offer to ghostwrite a charity book; being invited by Ben and Vicky to go sailing, just as I was needing something exciting to look forward to. It seemed as if my planets had aligned, or the universe was doing its thing for me, or maybe just that I was open-minded enough to spot coincidences when they happened, and open-hearted enough to welcome the opportunities they presented.

So then, I thought, as I looked out of the window at the tree, ignoring the sound of Heathrow-bound planes overhead and traffic on the South Circular road, fooling myself that looking at a few branches of light-starved tree was still communing with nature, *that was it: Derbyshire was it.*

It was funny, because a couple of years earlier, when I was on a trip back to London in between bouts of travelling through tropical countries on boats, I'd had a similar feeling of homecoming. That, too, had been sparked by frustration at the ugliness of London, only then it wasn't only the capital I was railing against – it was the whole of England and the English way of life. I'd been sitting on an early-morning train from Stansted airport into London, freezing in December, exhausted after a cramped long-distance flight from Malaysia, and I'd suddenly had a vision of my future life. In this instantaneous daydream I'd seen myself living in the Caribbean, in a low yellow-painted house with a tropical garden, wearing shorts and T-shirts, working in some vague job based around the yachting industry. At the time I had this vision, parts of it had been so sharp that I could practically smell the wet Caribbean ground, taste the earthy spices in the food, feel the sun burning my forearm. Part of the reason I'd been so excited about the *Papagayo* trip was that I'd seen it as my chance to scout out possible locations, to find *my* island, where I wanted to live, to build my yellow house. It was serendipitous to say the least that I was being offered the chance to visit not one but a whole spread of Caribbean countries. It was one of those lucky coincidences again.

I didn't find *my* island. Each had its own charms or character – from the flat blue beauty of the Bahamas and Turks and Caicos to the down-at-heel authenticity of the Dominican Republic, the American mini-me that was Puerto Rico and the two very different sets of Virgin Islands – but none felt like home. They all seemed difficult places in which to live, and not just because of the constant battering from wind and sun that eventually bleached and tore things to shreds. They were harsh worlds where everything was a struggle. Even the basics had to be imported; little seemed to come naturally to these places. The people played by rules that I didn't have the first inkling about and towns, villages and even countryside areas always seemed alien, never homely. I only ever felt like a visitor.

But what if, I wondered now, doing a bit of pop psychology on myself, *the sentiment for that original vision was still correct; it was just the finer details that were wrong? Let's break it down. Your location is immaterial. The big points of that daydream are this: you have a home, in a rural location, with a garden. You have a job that's related to something that makes you happy, although in your daydream you don't specify what it is, so it can't be that important; it's the fact that it's in a field you enjoy that's the key thing. You fantasise that your wardrobe consists of shorts and T-shirts – that's partly because the weather is warm on this 'island' but also it could signify that you are relaxed and not in a formal environment. In other aspects of your daydream you imagine friends and family coming to stay – but would people regularly fly 3,000 miles to visit you?*

So let's rework it. Let's keep the simple home and the garden, the low-key job you enjoy, the casualness of the life, the closeness to family and friends. At the heart of all this is a really simple idea: balance. A balance between work and play, between time to yourself and time with people you love.

Nowhere in this is 60-hour or even 45-hour weeks doing a job you no longer like and living in a flat in a large, crowded but ultimately lonely city.

So what if you swap a Caribbean island for a Derbyshire village? A yellow-painted house for a granite-built one, a tropical garden for one filled with roses and apple trees and rolling views? Family and friends that visit all the time because they live fifteen minutes away? The natural beauty you love, a simpler, quieter life, time to yourself, writing and cooking and mucking about in jeans and woollies because no one cares what you look like, going for long walks through the Peaks and Dales, eating heartily because you've worked up a healthy appetite? Open skies, friendly faces, freelance writing work that doesn't consume you. Yoga, fresh air, seeing the moon rise every night. Balance again.

Quickly, the idea set itself in stone, until it was as if there'd never been any other option. Derbyshire was the answer; Derbyshire was the future; Derbyshire was balance and happiness. And sanity.

Now I just needed to make it happen.

30

Mistress of the universe

I found a small cream-coloured card inside an Easter egg one
year. Like a high-end version of a Chinese fortune cookie,
it was printed with words of wisdom from one Mr Booja
Booja (the manufacturer of the posh chocolates inside), and
was nestled in the indigo velvet lining of the wooden egg. *The
universe is not about you,* it said.

The message spoke to me (not only because it retained the
faint scent of rich cocoa for a while) and I kept the card for
years, tucked away in a jewellery box, coming across it with
surprise and a wry smile on the rare occasion I went hunting
for a pair of earrings.

Sometimes, though, the universe *is* about you. And now
was one of those times.

My friend Karen, the one I'd called when I'd suffered my
first big anxiety attack, had heard of a job in Derbyshire,
where she lived. It was part-time, doing communications
work for a local company, she said. It'd be just twenty hours
a week, and presumably not stressful at all. The best part?
The office was in the old stable block of a manor house right
in the middle of a private estate in south Derbyshire.

I was sold.

I had a telephone interview with Dave, the man who owned the company.

'I want to ask you something, and I want you to be honest with me,' he said, his Derbyshire accent coming across strongly down the line. 'You work for the *Independent* newspaper. In London. So why do you want to come and work for me?'

I paused. *I can't very well tell him I am cracking up. There's no way he'll hire me if I say that.* I thought quickly. I didn't want to lie, but I didn't want to over-dramatise things, either. I was pretty certain that once I got out of this city and into a slower way of life, the attacks would end.

I looked out of the window as I prepared to speak. I'd gone off to a corridor, to take the call as privately as I could manage in the office, and as I looked down to the street, all I could see were paving stones and the occasional top of the head of a besuited person rushing from appointment to appointment.

'You mentioned a minute ago that you were looking out of your window on to trees,' I said to Dave, praying that I was judging this right. 'Well, I'm looking out of a window, too, and all I can see is grey slabs.' I paused again. 'I'm tired of London. I've been here and done this. I've done this job for years. It's really stressful. I went travelling and I was outside most of the time and now I miss that. I miss the countryside. I don't want to work sixty-hour weeks and look out of a window on my coffee break and see grey paving stones.' I took a breath. 'I want more of a work–life balance.'

Shit! I scolded myself. *What did you say that for? Employers just want you to work; they don't give a toss about your free time, as long as you turn up to work and do a good job. They certainly don't care about scenery out of a window during a break, you buffoon. Oh god, you've totally blown it. Your chance to get away – and you've blown it.*

What I forgot to take into consideration was that Dave wasn't some ultra-competitive city-of-London corporate publishing boss. He was a Derbyshire man and they see things differently there. They take things in their stride. They're nice and kind and say 'Good morning' to strangers in the street and drop round paper bags of tomatoes and courgettes they've grown in their greenhouses. They have different frames of reference.

A view of trees was, apparently, just as important to Dave as it was to me.

I got the job.

The next coincidence came not long later. My brother rang me one evening.

'In the building I work in, there's these two guys and they're setting up a new business, running a show for graduate engineers, getting them to meet employers,' Tom started.

I said I had no idea what this had to do with me.

'Well, they asked me if I knew anyone who could put together a brochure for the show at short notice and I thought of you.'

I rang Tom's office neighbours and they explained what they were looking for. They had a designer already – they just needed someone with publishing experience to write the content and manage the project. They only needed me two mornings a week for a month.

Further offers of bits of work continued to fall into my lap. It was kind of spooky, in a way. Jung had a name for those weird coincidences that crop up every now and then and seem so specific to you that it's almost like black magic. He called it synchronicity, described, not that clearly, as the 'acausal connecting principle' or 'acausal parallelism', meaning that coincidental things that had no reason to happen still happened. My friend Aaron had another term for it: 'manifestation'. Mr Booja Booja, he of the Easter egg card, might have called it 'the universe being about you'. And me? 'Bloody brilliant', that's what I called it.

'I can't believe it,' my dad said, when I rang him to tell him. 'It's incredible how much you're in demand.'

'Yep,' I said, happily. 'Good things apparently do come to those who wait.'

Actually, good things come to those who plan – and those who keep their eyes and ears open.

The managing editor didn't think I was serious when I went in to resign. I held the letter in my hand, folded into three and tucked into a white envelope. I'd kept the letter extremely short and formal, with no thanks or other platitudes.

'You're just tired,' Sean said. 'Why don't you take a couple of weeks off?'

I laughed. 'A couple of weeks is not going to fix me, Sean.'

He laughed, too, exasperated, still thinking of it as a bit of a game. My leaving added to his workload – he'd have to find someone else capable of doing the job, and the other staff were already stretched to the limit.

His eyes lit up as he thought of an idea.

'How about we get you an iPhone 5?'

I looked at him, astonished. Presumably he was joking? *He thinks he can bribe me with a free phone?* I opened my mouth but couldn't think of a thing to say. I closed it again.

He persisted. 'Is that a good idea?'

I left.

A couple of days later, an iPhone 5 did appear on my desk, box fresh and already set up by the IT department so that the email account was configured with my work address. I snorted when I clicked on the envelope icon and saw hundreds of messages there waiting for me. If my work–life balance was so out-of-kilter in this place, how on earth would having 24/7 access to work help me? He was trying to be kind but I'd already made up my mind. I put the phone, still switched on, back in the box and into the bottom of my drawer. It stayed there until the battery ran out.

In my last couple of weeks at the *i* paper, ambitious young reporters started to come and interrupt me and ask if they could have a word. I would follow them out to the canteen, already knowing what it was they hoped to talk to me about – they all wanted the same thing.

'I hear you're leaving,' they'd say. I'd reply that yes, I was moving to Derbyshire, was going freelance. Practically before I'd finished speaking my sentence, they'd jump on me with eagerness. 'So it's true? They need a new news editor of *i*?' I'd nod. 'What's the job like? I mean, what do you actually do in a day? Do you think I could do it?'

I am an honest person, and I find it very difficult to lie when someone asks me a question outright, but I didn't want to open up completely to these young reporters (for they always were young – twenty-eight at most – and always men) or start telling them that it was a dreadful job, that it had made me ill, taken me to the edge of sanity, warn them off applying, tell them to find a different career before this one consumed them. I saw my inability to cope as very much my issue, rather than the job itself. Yes, there were elements to it that would be the same for anyone else coming in to replace me – the gruelling hours, the workload, the stress, the competition – but it didn't necessarily compute that anyone else would react to it in the same way I had.

In a way, these ambitious young journalists were me, a decade earlier, when I was so hungry to get on that I had had a full-time day job, been writing a novel, sold freelance articles to newspapers and had given up every Sunday to go into the *Daily Express* offices to do shifts as a reporter. At twenty-five I naturally had more energy than now but I was also greedy for success, and that bred energy, too. These youngsters (oh, how prematurely old, at thirty-five, it made me feel to think of them that way, but I did) hadn't, as my doctor had put it, 'fallen out of love with journalism'; they were absolutely, madly, head-over-heels for it, and their enthusiasm made them buoyant with optimism. I'd been a positive thinker and endlessly optimistic and persevering, once. Looking into the eyes of these young men now, as they handed me paper cups of tea in exchange for information, I caught a flash of that young woman who had never doubted that she could make editor – and who, more importantly, never doubted that she *wanted* to make editor.

I didn't want to take that innocent puppyishness from them, so I gave the boys a middle-of-the-road answer. 'It's really hard work,' I'd say. 'Long hours, and you're on your own a lot. But it'll teach you more about journalism, about how a newspaper works and is put together, and about how to write, than years of being a reporter will. You won't get many bylines and you'll feel that you're not writing but you will be – you'll be re-writing thousands and thousands of words a day, and editing other people's copy will make you a better writer, too. It's hard but I'm sure you could do it.'

'Thanks,' they'd say, their eyes gleaming, having tuned out words like 'long hours' and 'hard work', and seeing only the perceived glory of being an editor, of being in charge, of running a section of a national. 'I think I'll apply. Give it a shot.' And they'd smile and back away and rush off to their computers, to email their girlfriends to tell them the exciting news.

I plodded through the remaining days, getting the work done, sorting out personal admin in the evenings, like finding someone to move into my room in my flat, to cover the mortgage after I moved out. As always happens when you're busy, the time flew past, until suddenly it was Thursday, and my last day in the office.

It was A-level results day, and the statistics showed the widening of the gender gap between how boys and girls had done – but I didn't treat it as different from any other.

But when I pushed open the heavy glass door from the office into the atrium at 7pm, having left someone else to finish off the paper, and took the long escalator ride down to the ground floor, something did feel different. I knew that this was the last time I'd set foot in that grand 'Fleet Street' building. With every metre the escalator descended, I felt lighter and lighter, until I let go from the handrail and bounded down the last few steps and the rotating door dumped me on the street with a whirring whoosh. I took a big breath of fresh air and smiled. Freedom.

Postscript

The tricky part of writing a memoir is knowing when to begin and end your story. Life has one obvious conclusion but that, by its very nature, precludes writing about it. So, when to take fingertips off the keyboard and say goodbye to you, reader?

My time in Derbyshire was simply wonderful. It was everything I wanted it to be: restful, interesting, beautiful, full of time with friends and family. I rented a barn conversion on the edge of a village and had views across the fields on to flocks of sheep. In early spring, a pair of long-tailed tits tapped on my bedroom window every morning at 8.30am and watched me blow-dry my hair. I read. I took long naps on the days I wasn't working. I finally got excited about the upcoming publication of my first book and spent hours daydreaming about being a full-time author. I practised yoga again; went for long walks through the peaks and dales. I worked with a bunch of people who made me laugh till my cheeks ached. I dated. I had a normal life.

And a normal life does not an interesting read make. One day I might turn my pen to Derbyshire, to try to capture the essence of its undulating English beauty on paper, but not now.

A normal life does a balanced life make, though. The panic attacks stopped as soon as I changed my life. I still don't know for sure what caused them – whether it was the stress of the job in particular or if I was the reason: if I was, as my friend Dom says, 'doing my own head in'.

Every now and then on Facebook I see a meme that someone has pasted, which says that depression and anxiety are not signs of weakness, that they happen to one in three people at some point in their lives, that strong people are more likely to suffer from them. I have no idea if that's true, that 'stronger' people are more susceptible – what makes a person stronger, anyway, apart from a certain kind of stubbornness? And is that even real strength or actually cowardice? – but it no longer surprises that as many as a third of people go through some sort of crisis like I did, or worse.

The aim of these memes (if I take my cynical, ex-news editor hat off and don't say that they're all about data mining) is to try to get people to open up and talk more about their experiences with mental illness and things like anxiety and depression. There is still a huge stigma attached – a stigma that is often just in our minds. I'll never forget my dad telling me that if my leg was broken I'd go to the doctor, so why not if my mind was hurt? I'm sure that not everyone is as understanding as him but one of the positive things I took from my experience was how kind and supportive people were. No one turned away from me, stopped inviting me out or shunned me as a friend. The few colleagues that I confided in, or who witnessed the attacks for themselves, were really sympathetic, and helped make things a little bit easier for me.

As I began to open up about what I was going through, I found that people started to tell me the stories of their struggles, too. Sometimes it was something they'd experienced themselves – feeling unbearably sad after moving country and having to say goodbye to a close friend; finding it hard to cope with a demanding baby and all the life changes that brings; trying to set up a new business that turned into a money pit and took happiness with it down the plughole; delayed onset of grief after losing a parent. Other times friends told me of a family member or a friend of theirs who had gone through a tough time.

Each time I heard that someone else had struggled with their mental health, I felt a tiny bit less like a freak, a smidgeon less ashamed. Each time I spoke aloud about what I'd gone through, the embarrassment shrank a millimetre. The obvious conclusion to that was to write about it. I hope that, in the same way hearing of other people made me feel less alone, maybe someone will read my story and recognise themselves and it'll help them in some way.

I don't think I'll ever really know for certain what caused that first horrific anxiety attack. There's no doubt that overwork and stress in my job played a large part but I think I myself was just as blameworthy. My body, my nervous system, reacted so strongly because I wasn't listening to myself, to what my body and my mind needed, and in not being true to myself I came very close to making myself dangerously ill. Going travelling had changed me. Living on boats in remote places took away part of my independence – as a boat's crew you are part of a team and you learn that working together makes everything easier for all concerned – and as I lost some of my self-centredness I also lost some of my ambition to keep pushing on and on. I learned to relax and leave more things to chance – and to the universe. Going back and trying to be the same person in the same life was never going to work if the pieces of the jigsaw were a different shape.

It took me a while to realise how much I had changed, beyond the obvious fact that I had a whole gamut of 'This one time, in XXX,' anecdotes to hand. Once I'd fixed on moving to Derbyshire, and it felt so right, I stopped struggling against my stubbornness and ignored the part of me that thought that giving up on the newspaper job was failing. *It's not failure*, I told myself. *It's just change.*

In writing, you can be too close to the story to see the mistakes in what you've written. And in life, too, it can be hard to recognise the patterns of your behaviour that need changing. But just because you have been behaving one way doesn't mean you will always have to.

That doctor was only half right about my having fallen out of love with journalism. I still work as a journalist – I'm deputy editor of *Sailing Today* magazine (that ambitious 20-something me would no doubt be pleased as punch to hear that, since her aim was to make assistant ed by thirty-six) but I definitely fell out of love with newspaper news journalism. I stayed out of the profession for more than a year before I was drawn back into it and this time it was for all the right reasons and the right role, one that combines my love of sailing and my love of writing. I leave the office at 5.30pm every day – that is, if I'm not at sea. I finally found a way to make a living from the thing that I love most and with that naturally comes balance. And balance is the most important thing in life. Without it, we fall. You only get one life. Make it a balanced one.

END